Albert Sidney Bolles

Practical Banking

Albert Sidney Bolles
Practical Banking
ISBN/EAN: 9783337120627
Printed in Europe, USA, Canada, Australia, Japan
Cover: Foto ©Suzi / pixelio.de

More available books at **www.hansebooks.com**

PRACTICAL BANKING.

BY

ALBERT S. BOLLES,

EDITOR OF THE BANKER'S MAGAZINE, PROFESSOR OF MERCANTILE LAW AND PRACTICE IN THE WHARTON SCHOOL OF FINANCE AND ECONOMY, UNIVERSITY OF PENNSYLVANIA; AUTHOR OF "THE FINANCIAL HISTORY OF THE UNITED STATES," "INDUSTRIAL HISTORY OF THE UNITED STATES," "THE CONFLICT BETWEEN LABOR AND CAPITAL," ETC.

NEW YORK:
HOMANS PUBLISHING COMPANY, 251 BROADWAY.
1884.

TO

LYMAN J. GAGE,

PRESIDENT OF THE AMERICAN BANKERS' ASSOCIATION,

This Book is Dedicated

AS A TOKEN OF THE AUTHOR'S REGARD FOR HIS FRIENDSHIP,

AND ADMIRATION FOR HIS RARE UNION

OF A KNOWLEDGE OF

THE HISTORY AND THEORY OF BANKING AND FINANCE

WITH EMINENT SUCCESS AS A BANKER.

PREFACE.

An explanation is needful concerning the origin and composition of this work. For several years letters have been received by the publisher of the *Banker's Magazine* inquiring whether a work like this existed. Other letters of inquiry have been received concerning the *Banker's Common-Place Book*, which, after the issue of several editions, went out of print. For a long period I have been trying to find an opportunity to embody the more important matters contained in that work, with additional information in a new form, but the desire to complete other undertakings resulted in the postponement of this until after my connection with the School of Finance and Economy in the University of Pennsylvania, when the need of the book for the purpose of instruction was so great that the preparation of it was begun. The work, therefore, has been prepared to serve a double purpose; first, for those in banks, and elsewhere, who wish to learn how the business of banking is conducted; and, secondly, for use as a text book for the students whom it is my pleasure to instruct.

I have not aimed to produce an original work, but the best for the purposes mentioned. Accordingly, I have profited by the labor of others to a considerable extent, and it is fitting that I should acknowledge my indebtedness to them. In 1858 James S. Gibbons, Cashier of the Ocean Bank of New York, wrote a work on *The Banks of New York*, which ran through ten editions, and merited the favorable reception accorded to it. Changes, however, have occurred in banking methods since he wrote, while the style of Mr. Gibbons' work, though very lively and appropriate for the general reader, is not suitable for a class-room book. Nevertheless, I have drawn very largely from that source in the preparation of Part I. and with much pleasure I acknowledge my indebtedness to this pioneer in describing the methods of conducting the business of banking.

Aid has been derived from other sources. This has been acknowledged in various places, but additional mention may be properly made of several writers and sources of information. The more important sections of the *Banker's Common-Place Book* have been thoroughly revised and incorporated with other matter in Chapters VI. and VII.; and the essay entitled "Suggestions to Young Cashiers on the Duties of their Profession," is given in the Appendix. Another portion of Chapter VII., from pages 51 to 58, was written by George Walker, formerly Bank Commissioner of Massachusetts, and a banker of many years' experience, who has justly acquired the high reputation he enjoys as a financial writer on both sides of the Atlantic. Chapter XIV., on "The Bookkeeper," has been prepared by S. R. Hopkins, who has happily joined an exceptionally valuable experience as an accountant in all its forms, private, corporate and municipal, with excellent facility for description. He has also prepared the last part of the work relating to "Trust Companies." The chapter on "Private Banking" is from the pen of Eugene R. Leland, of New York, formerly a banker in Wisconsin.

Part I., relating to "Deposit and Discount Banking," with the exception of three chapters, has also been revised by Frederick B. Schenck, Cashier of the Mercantile National Bank of New York. For the interest he has taken in the subject, and for the valuable ideas and suggestions with which he has enriched this part of the work, I am profoundly grateful. To William E. Gould, Cashier of the First National Bank of Portland, Maine, I am indebted for the further examination and emendation of the proofs of Part I.; and to J. M. Dreisbach, Cashier of the Second National Bank of Mauch Chunk, Penn., for information relating to Country Banking and to the Balance Sheet in the Appendix; and also to Charles I. DeBaun, Assistant Cashier of the National Park Bank of New York, for his kindness in revising the chapter on Bookkeeping.

Part Second, relating to Savings Banks, with the exception of the first and last chapters, is the work of Charles E. Sprague, Secretary of the Union Dime Savings Bank of New York. A practical writer, and an experienced Savings bank officer, it is believed that no better description of the method of conducting the Savings-bank business could be presented to the reader.

The Third Part, relating to Clearing-Houses, has been prepared by Dudley P. Bailey, of Boston. For several years he has devoted much study to the subject, and some of his papers have attracted wide attention. I know of no one who could have given a better account of the method of conducting the business of these institutions. In this connection we would not omit to mention the names of Nathaniel G. Snelling, Manager of the Boston Clearing-house, and Wm. A. Camp, Manager of the Clearing-house in New York, for information and other assistance rendered by them in the preparation of this part of the work. Important assistance was rendered by W. D. Snow, Secretary of the American Loan and Trust Company, and by L. K. McKinney, Trust Clerk of the same Company, in preparing Part IV, relating to Loan and Trust Companies. Finally, it may be added that the entire work has been carefully read and revised by Benjamin Homans, a name familiar to the readers of the *Banker's Magazine*, who, from many years' experience as a banker, possesses a very complete knowledge of the details of the banking business, and who has been unwearied in his endeavors to render the work as accurate as possible.

I trust that the work will prove useful. That it may be improved in future editions, criticisms, facts and suggestions are solicited from every intelligent source.

ALBERT S. BOLLES.

PHILADELPHIA, *October 31st, 1884.*

CONTENTS.

PART I.
DEPOSIT AND DISCOUNT BANKING.

PAGE

CHAPTER I.
THE ORIGIN AND NATURE OF BANKING................................ 3

CHAPTER II.
THE UTILITY OF BANKING.. 6

CHAPTER III.
THE NATIONAL BANKING SYSTEM....................................... 9

CHAPTER IV.
STATE BANKS.. 14

CHAPTER V.
HOW BANKS ARE ORGANIZED AND ISSUE NOTES.......................... 16

CHAPTER VI.
THE PRESIDENT.. 24

CHAPTER VII.
DIRECTORS' MEETINGS AND DISCOUNTING.............................. 43

CHAPTER VIII.
THE CASHIER.. 72

CHAPTER IX.
THE PAYING TELLER.. 77

CHAPTER X.
THE RECEIVING TELLER... 88

CHAPTER XI.
THE NOTE TELLER.. 93

CHAPTER XII.
THE DISCOUNT CLERK... 97

CHAPTER XIII.
COLLECTIONS... 100

CHAPTER XIV.
THE BOOKKEEPER... 104

CHAPTER XV.
THE RUNNER AND PORTER.. 128

CHAPTER XVI.
DEALINGS IN EXCHANGE.. 130

CHAPTER XVII.
PRIVATE BANKS.. 139

CHAPTER XVIII.
COUNTRY BANKING.. 143

PART II.

SAVINGS BANKS.

CHAPTER I.
UTILITY OF SAVINGS BANKS.. 151

CHAPTER II.
JANITOR... 158

CHAPTER III.
THE DEPOSITOR 159

CHAPTER IV.
THE RECEIVING TELLER... 165

CHAPTER V.
THE PAYING TELLER... 170

CHAPTER VI.
THE BOOKKEEPER... 173

CHAPTER VII.
THE TREASURER... 177

CHAPTER VIII.
THE SECRETARY... 181

CHAPTER IX.
THE PRESIDENT.. 196

CHAPTER X.
THE BOARD OF TRUSTEES.. 197

CHAPTER XI.
THE ATTORNEY.. 200

CONTENTS. xi

CHAPTER XII.
STATE SUPERVISION AND REPORTS.................................. 203

CHAPTER XIII.
HOW INVESTMENTS SHOULD BE MADE................................ 208

PART III.

CLEARING-HOUSES.

CHAPTER I.
ORIGIN AND UTILITY OF THE CLEARING-HOUSE...................... 217

CHAPTER II.
ORGANIZATION AND MECHANICAL ARRANGEMENTS..................... 222

CHAPTER III.
PREPARATION OF THE EXCHANGE................................... 224

CHAPTER IV.
HOW CLEARINGS ARE MADE.. 229

CHAPTER V.
HOW OUTSIDE BANKS MAKE CLEARINGS.............................. 234

CHAPTER VI.
PAYMENT OF BALANCES... 236

CHAPTER VII.
CLEARING-HOUSE CERTIFICATES................................... 239

CHAPTER VIII.
THE RECORDS KEPT AND THEIR USES............................... 242

CHAPTER IX.
FINES... 246

CHAPTER X.
HISTORY OF THE NEW YORK CLEARING-HOUSE........................ 247

CHAPTER XI.
CLEARING-HOUSES OUTSIDE NEW YORK.............................. 250

CHAPTER XII.
FOREIGN CLEARING-HOUSES....................................... 263

CHAPTER XIII.
COUNTRY CLEARINGS... 274

CONTENTS.

PART IV.

LOAN AND TRUST COMPANIES.

CHAPTER I.
History and Scope of Loan and Trust Companies................. 281

CHAPTER II.
How Business is Conducted.. 283

APPENDIX.

Banking as a Profession for Young Men.......................... 293

Advice to Depositors.. 297

Suggestions to Young Cashiers on the Duties of Their Profession. 300

Daily Balance Sheet... 316

PART I.

DEPOSIT AND DISCOUNT BANKING.

PRACTICAL BANKING.

CHAPTER I.

THE ORIGIN AND NATURE OF BANKING.

The term bank is supposed to be derived from *banco*, the Italian word for bench, the Lombard Jews in Italy having benches in the market-place where they exchanged money and bills. When a banker failed, his bench was broken by the people, and he was called a bankrupt.

This derivation of the term, however, is probably wrong. "The true original meaning of *banco*," says MacLeod,* "is a heap, or mound, and this word was metaphorically applied to signify a common fund, or joint stock, formed by the contributions of a multitude of persons."

A brief account of the first banking operations in Venice will dispel the haze enveloping this subject. In 1171 the financial condition of Venice was strained in consequence of the wars in which the people were engaged. The great council of the republic finally determined to raise a forced loan. Every citizen was obliged to contribute the hundredth part of his possessions to the State, receiving therefor interest at the rate of five per cent. The public revenues were mortgaged to secure the interest, and commissioners were appointed to pay the interest to the fundholders and to transfer the stock. The loan had several names in Italian, *Compera*, *Mutuo*, but the most common was *Monte*, a joint stock fund. Afterward, two more loans were contracted, and in exchange for the money contributed by the citizens, the commissioners gave stock certificates bearing interest, and which could be sold and transferred.

* *Principles of Economic Philosophy*, vol. 1, p. 547.

At this period the Germans were masters of a great part of Italy, and the German word *Banck* came into use as well as its Italian equivalent *Monte*. The Italians ere long changed *Banck* into *Banco*, and the public loans or debts were called *Monti* or *Banchi*. Thus an English writer, Benbrigge, who wrote in 1646, mentioned the "three bankes" at Venice, by which he meant the three public loans, or *Monte*, that we have described. Likewise Count Cibrario, who wrote a work on *Political Economy in the Middle Age*, says, "it is known that the first Bank, or Public Debt, was erected at Venice in 1171." Other proof of the same nature might be added to show that *Banco* in Italian meant a fund formed by several contributions; and the Bank of Venice was really the first funding system, or system of public debts.

"A banker," says Gilbart, "is a dealer in capital, or, more properly, a dealer in money. He is an intermediate party between the borrower and the lender." The difference between the rate received by the banker, for the use of the money loaned by him, and the rate he has to pay for it, is his profit.

"By this means he draws into active operations those small sums of money which were previously unproductive in the hands of private individuals, and at the same time furnishes accommodation to those who have need of additional capital to carry on their business." In other words, a bank is a means for organizing capital whereby its full power may be utilized. The function of a bank in storing up capital, and thus increasing its power, has been likened to that of a dam put across a stream. Before the erection of the structure, the waters coursed their way through wood and meadow, contributing, it is true, to the diversity and beauty of the scene, beside satisfying a needful want of man and beast. To the poet, the stream gave forth an unregarded music, while a De Quincey would hearken with profound emotion and awe to the "sound-pealing anthems, as if streaming from the open portals of some illimitable cathedral." But by storing up the waters, a force is collected which can be used for running the largest factory, and thus ministering in a very potent way to advance the material prosperity of man.

There are several kinds of banks. They may be divided first into private and public banks. Private banks are conducted by individuals without incorporation. They are very numerous in our country. The number given in the *Banker's Almanac and Register*, not including brokers, for the year 1884, was 3,387. They exist in all the States and Territories. Some of them have flourished for a long period, and are regarded very sound, and worthy of the highest credit.

Chartered banks may be divided into two classes: those organized and existing under the laws of the United States; and State institutions. The latter may be again divided into Deposit and Discount banks, Savings banks and Trust companies. Each class will be described hereafter.

The business of banking consists (1) in receiving deposits of money on which interest may or may not be allowed; (2) in making advances of money, principally in the way of discounting notes; (3) in effecting the transmission of money from one place to another. This is true of the ordinary banks of deposit and discount, both State and National.

The disposable means of a bank consists (1) of the capital paid down by the shareholders; (2) the money deposited with it by its customers; (3) the notes it can circulate; (4) the money it receives in the course of transmission, and which, of course, it must repay at another place.

The expenses of a bank may be thus classified: rent, taxes and repairs of the banking-house, salaries of officers, stationery and postage. To this may be added interest upon deposits, if allowed.

The profits of a bank consist of that portion of its total receipts, including discount, interest, dividends and commissions, which exceed the total amount of expenses.

CHAPTER II.

THE UTILITY OF BANKING.*

1. Banks are useful as places of security for the deposit of money. Not long ago a Western farmer received nearly ten thousand dollars in specie from the Government in payment for bonds. Not regarding a bank as a safe place for depositing his gold, he put it in the bottom of a barrel in his wood-shed, filled it nearly full of ashes, and the remainder with straw; he then made a nest there, filled it with eggs, and put them in the custody of a setting hen. He thought that his sagacity was quite equal to the occasion. After waiting a couple of weeks he concluded, one Sunday, when having nothing else to do, that he would examine his highly original safe in the wood-shed. The old hen was decidedly cross, and did not enjoy his presence. Still she felt better than he did as soon as he had plunged his arm down the side of the barrel and found that some one had kindly relieved him of his gold. Probably he will think more highly of banks as places of deposit in the future.

The need of a safe place of deposit gave rise to the leaving of valuables with the goldsmiths of London. If money is deposited in a bank and lost, even though not negligent it is responsible. Robberies would rapidly multiply if much money were kept in houses. The depositing of it with banks spares many a house from the invasion of robbers.

2. A greater profit is acquired by the owners of money than would be if banks did not exist. The allowance of interest by "the new-fashioned bankers" has been considered the origin of modern banking. A large amount of money, in the aggregate, would remain idle and unproductive if these institutions did not exist. By offering to pay interest, persons having money are induced to deposit it with banks, and thus increase their gains.

3. Moreover, the payment of interest on deposits is a stimulant to accumulate money. Were there no Savings banks, a large por-

---

* On this subject Mr. George S. Coe, President of the American Exchange National Bank, delivered an admirable address before the American Bankers' Association, in 1882, answering the question, "What Important Function Do We, as Bankers, Perform?" See *Banker's Magazine*, vol. 37, p. 170.

tion of the savings deposited in them would never have been collected and saved. Probably the majority of these depositors have no thought of collecting enough to buy a bond or a few shares of stock. Such a process of saving is too elaborate for them. But when a way is provided for adding to their savings by simply depositing their money in a bank, thousands, nay millions, of persons in our country have availed themselves of the opportunity.

4. An important utility is that banks loan money to persons who wish to borrow it. Loans are made chiefly to persons engaged in manufactures, trade, commerce, and other business pursuits. Money is especially needful to them to conduct their enterprises. Indeed, if they could not obtain it, they could not maintain their place in the world of business. The credit that some mercantile houses have is worth more to them than the capital they actually possess.

5. Another utility is that banks save the transmission of money from one part of the world to another. Not only is the risk of loss from robbery and other accidents avoided, but the money is kept in more active circulation. Were it actually sent from place to place to effect all the payments that are daily made, a large amount must be locked up in the process of transportation, which otherwise would be more actively employed.

6. There is a saving of time in paying large sums by checks or bills of exchange. To count the money would be a long process in making the many heavy payments of our time.

7. There is less danger of error when checks are used than when money is paid. Of course there are some risks attending the use of checks. But in paying with money there is also the risk of getting counterfeits, light weight, or otherwise defective coin.

8. Besides, checks constitute a good record of one's expenditure. If an individual deposits all the money he receives with a bank, and draws it out by checks, his check-book contains the story of his income and expenditure. For persons who do not have strict business habits this mode of keeping their money and paying their bills is especially worth observing.

9. A bank account is very useful if a payment is disputed. Individuals do not always take receipts for the money they pay, and even if they do, sometimes lose them. If a bill be paid, but no proof can be furnished of paying it and payment be again demanded, too often it must be paid a second time. But if a check for the bill be given this is the best kind of evidence of payment.

10. If one has an account with a bank it is often a good channel for getting useful business information. If one has money to collect or to remit, a banker, when asked, will state the best way of proceeding. Not infrequently bank officials give valuable advice pertaining to investments and other matters.

11. An eminent English banker,* from whose work on *Banking* many of the ideas in this chapter have been obtained, has said that "banking also exercises a powerful influence upon the morals of society. It tends to produce honesty and punctuality in pecuniary engagements. Bankers, for their own interest, always have a regard to the moral character of the party with whom they deal; they inquire whether he be honest or tricky, industrious or idle, prudent or speculative, thrifty or prodigal, and they will more readily make advances to a man of moderate property and good morals than to a man of large property but of inferior reputation. Thus the establishment of a bank in any place immediately advances the pecuniary value of a good moral character. There are numerous instances of persons having risen from obscurity to wealth only by means of their moral character, and the confidence which that character produced in the mind of their banker. It is not merely by way of loan or discount that a banker serves such a person. He also speaks well of him to those persons who may make inquiries respecting him; and the banker's good opinion will be the means of procuring him a higher degree of credit with the parties with whom he trades. These effects are easily perceivable. It is thus that bankers perform the functions of public conservators of the commercial virtues. From motives of private interest they encourage the industrious, the prudent, the punctual, and the honest, while they discountenance the spendthrift and the gambler, the liar and the knave. They hold out inducements to uprightness, which are not disregarded by even the most abandoned. There is many a man who would be deterred from dishonesty by the frown of a banker, though he might care but little for the admonitions of a bishop."

* Gilbart.

CHAPTER III.

THE NATIONAL BANKING SYSTEM.

As we have seen, the business of banking consists in getting a common fund of money, and in lending a part of it. With this general conception is associated the discounting of bills of exchange, the collection of notes and drafts and the issuing of circulating notes. The business may be conducted by one person, who is called a banker; or by partners, as in any ordinary business, who also are called bankers. Again, a number of men may join their capital under a State law, and organize a State bank or association, the capital of which is divided into shares. Capitalists may also unite under the laws of the United States, and form a National banking association.

Under these varying forms a banking business is done. We may look at the reasons why men prefer one form to another. If a man has considerable means and enjoys the confidence of the community, he may prefer to engage in banking alone, unfettered by State or National laws. He may conduct his business in his own way; and if the people do not like it they need not patronize him. A firm may do the same thing. They may be a law unto themselves. But when men organize under a State law, they are bound by the law. They are subject to inspection. They must pay a tax on the amount of money used in their business. If they issue promises to pay, a coin reserve must be kept to pay them. By a National bank is meant not that the Government owns or runs it, but authorizes its creation and prescribes its mode of doing business. Every association under this law, whether in Maine or in Texas, is governed by the same principles, is subject to the same inspection, uses the same blanks in making returns to the Treasury Department at Washington, and is under the same penalties for the violation of any duty. All are treated alike. The advantage to the people, of this system over any other is, the existence of a power above the bank, to which they can appeal if injustice is done. Another advantage of this system is the general Government having seen fit to permit these associations to issue promises to pay, based on the security of

United States bonds held in Washington, for the absolute and prompt payment of every note issued on such security, the poorest and humblest citizen knows when he gets his pay on Saturday night in a National bank bill, that he has the faith of the Government behind his paper promise to pay. He need not see what bank issued it; for any bank must receive it for a debt due, and the Government must pay for it in coin if the local bank fail.*

The National banking system was based on the system of banking existing in the State of New York in 1862. That system had existed many years; it had furnished adequate protection to billholders; and in several respects was better than any system which had preceded it. The Rev. Dr. John McVicker, professor of Political Economy in Columbia College, was the author of the system, and set it forth in a letter to a member of the New York Legislature, entitled, *Hints relating to Banking*, written in 1827. As this is the principal banking system in the country, and the only one by which banks now issue notes of their own, the chief features are worth describing in this place.

By the National law, banking associations may be formed by five or more persons who must specify in their articles of association the general objects for thus uniting.

They must make "an organization certificate" specifying:

A.—The name assumed by the association.

B.—Its place of business.

C.—The amount of its capital stock and the number of shares into which it is divided.

D.—The names and residences of the shareholders and the number of shares held by each.

E.—A declaration that the certificate is made to enable them to avail themselves of the advantages of the act.

No association may be organized with a less capital than $100,000, except that banks with a capital of not less than $50,000, may, with the approval of the Secretary of the Treasury, be organized in any place with a population not exceeding 6,000 inhabitants. In cities with a population exceeding 50,000 persons, at least $200,000 capital is required. Any National banking association designated for the purpose by the Secretary of the Treasury, may become a depository of public money and be employed as financial agent of the Government.

Associations so designated must give satisfactory security by the deposit of United States bonds, or otherwise, for the faithful performance of their duties.

The association may sue and be sued, elect directors, who, in turn, may elect a president, vice-president, cashier and other of-

---

* See W. E. Gould's address before the American Bankers' Association, 1881.

ficers; discount and negotiate promissory notes, drafts, bills of exchange, and other evidences of debt; receive deposits, buy and sell exchange, coin and bullion; loan money on personal security, issue and circulate its own notes, and make all needful by-laws not inconsistent with the Banking Act.

There must be at least five directors. Each director must own at least ten shares of the stock; he holds his office until the election and qualification of his successor. Annual meetings are held in January. The capital stock is divided into shares of $100 each, and is transferable. The liability of a shareholder is limited to a sum equal to the par value of his stock.

Before beginning business, fifty per cent. of the capital stock of an association must be paid in, and ten per cent. of the remainder monthly, until it is all paid.

The next step is the transmission by the association of a certificate to the Comptroller of the Currency (who is the chief official of the Government in this particular department) stating that fifty per cent. of the capital has been paid, and that all the provisions of the law with reference to organizing a bank have been observed. He then makes such an examination as may be thought necessary, and if he finds that the law has been properly complied with, he gives to the association a certificate to that effect, and that it is authorized to begin business. This certificate must be published within sixty days from the time of issuing it.*

Formerly the entire amount of bank notes which the banks were permitted to issue was limited to $300,000,000, but in 1875 the law was changed, and they can now issue as many as they please, provided they have a certain amount of Government bonds deposited with the Treasurer.

As a necessary preliminary to furnishing notes for circulation, the Comptroller of the Currency under the direction of the Secretary of the Treasury, is entrusted with the important duty of engraving plates in the best manner, to guard against counterfeiting and fraudulent alterations, and to print therefrom and number so many circulating notes in blank as may be required to supply the associations entitled to receive the same.

After these notes have been signed by the president or vice-president and the cashier, they are issued, and circulate the same as money, and are received at par everywhere in payment of taxes excises, public lands, and all other dues to the Government, except for duties on imports; and also for all salaries and other debts owing

* The late Comptroller of the Currency, Mr. Knox, issued a very useful Government publication of forty pages, entitled *Instructions and Suggestions of the Comptroller of the Currency in regard to the Organization, Extension and Management of National Banks*. It contains, among other matters, many of the forms required by the National law, an excellent set of by-laws, and a summary of the principal restrictions and requirements of the National bank law.

by the United States, except interest on the public debt and in redemption of the legal-tender notes. They are also a legal tender for any debt or liability to every National banking association.

Every National banking association is required to keep on deposit in the Treasury of the United States a sum equal to five per centum of its circulation, which sum is counted as part of its lawful reserve. All notes of National banks worn, defaced, mutilated, or otherwise unfit for circulation, are forwarded to the Treasurer of the United States for redemption. Such redemptions are reimbursed from the five per cent. fund, and notes worn and unfit for circulation are then forwarded to the Comptroller of the Currency for destruction. After making a record of the notes thus received, the Comptroller directs their destruction in the presence of four persons.

National banks having a capital of $150,000 or less are required to keep on deposit with the Treasurer of the United States, United States bonds equal in amount to one-fourth of their capital stock. Other banks are required to keep on deposit not less than $50,000 in United States bonds. Upon a deposit of bonds the association making the same is entitled to receive from the Comptroller circulating notes equal in amount to ninety per centum of the par value of the United States bonds so deposited, but the total amount of such notes issued to any association may not exceed ninety per centum of the amount of its capital stock actually paid in.

Every bank annually examines or has examined the bonds deposited in the office of the United States Treasurer, comparing them with the books of the Comptroller, and with its own record of them, and if the bonds exist and the record of them is correct, executes a certificate to that effect to the Treasurer.

A National bank can hold real estate under the following conditions and no others:

A.—The building needful to transact its business.

B.—Land mortgaged to it in good faith to secure debts previously contracted.

C.—Land conveyed to it in satisfaction of debts previously contracted in the course of business.

D.—Land purchased under sales ordered by courts in order to secure debts due to the bank.

E.—In the last three cases the real estate cannot be held beyond five years.

The rate of interest which a bank may take on any note, bill of exchange, or other evidence of debt is the rate permitted by the laws of the State or Territory where the bank is located.

Every bank in sixteen of the principal cities of the United States must keep on hand always in lawful money as a reserve fund, twenty-five per cent. of the amount of its deposits; and the banks in other places must keep on hand fifteen per cent. of their deposits. The banks last mentioned, however, may keep three-fifths of their reserve on deposit with such of the National banks as may be selected by them, approved by the Comptroller of the Currency, and doing business in any of eighteen specified principal cities of the United States.

National banks in any of the sixteen cities excepting New York, may keep one-half of the required twenty-five per cent. reserve on deposit in the City of New York.

Whenever this reserve of twenty-five per cent. for one class of banks and fifteen per cent. for the other, falls below that amount, the bank can make no new loans, except by purchasing or discounting bills of exchange payable at sight, nor make any dividend until the requisite proportion of reserve to circulation and deposits has been restored.

They cannot make loans on the security of their own stock, except to prevent a loss on a debt previously contracted, nor can they pledge their own notes of circulation for the purpose of getting money to pay in their capital stock.

They are also subject to examination by officers appointed by the Government.

The banks must make reports to the Comptroller of the Currency according to the forms which he prescribes, exhibiting in detail the resources and liabilities of the associations at the close of business on any past day specified by him. The Comptroller is required to call for not less than five such reports during each year. These reports must be verified by the oath of the president or cashier and attested by the signatures of at least three of the directors.

In addition to the reports mentioned above, each association is required to make a sworn report within ten days after the declaration of any dividend, of the amount of such dividend, and the amount of the net earnings. In order to enable the Treasurer to assess the duties, each association is required to make a sworn return to the Treasurer of the United States of the average amount of its notes in circulation.

The Comptroller employs district agents to examine from time to time, usually once a year, the affairs and assets of the several banks. For this service a stipulated charge is assessed upon the bank.

The charters of many National banks expired in 1882. On the twenty-fifth of February, 1883, the charters of 297 more expired. On the twelfth of July, 1882, Congress provided for their renewal. Many of the National banks are now existing under this law. The same period of life is given to them as was given before—twenty years.

CHAPTER IV.

STATE BANKS.

Although 2,589 banks (April 24) are in the National system, nearly eleven hundred banks are flourishing under State regulations. These in most cases existed before the enactment of the National banking law. They declined to change, though they were obliged to retire their circulation. A larger number of these banks are located in Missouri than in any other State. At the beginning of the year, 1884, 153 State banks existed there; New York had the next largest number, 98, while Pennsylvania had only one bank less. In Iowa there were 78, in California 71, in Kentucky 66, and in Kansas 50 Michigan had 36, Ohio 35, Virginia 43, Wisconsin 38, Nebraska and Minnesota each 32. Other States had a much smaller number.

The Government imposed a tax of ten per cent. on the circulation of the State banks, which took effect on the first of July, 1866, under an amendment to the law creating the National banking system. This rate was too high to allow any profit on the State bank circulation, and consequently it was withdrawn. Indeed the object of the law was to expel it, in order to make room for the circulation of the National banks. In other respects, however, the State banks are conducted as they were before the creation of the National banking system. But the internal mechanism of a State and National bank is quite the same, and, therefore, in describing the methods of conducting a discount bank, no distinction need be kept in mind between a National and State bank. The former alone issues circulating notes, and the mode of doing this will be explained more fully hereafter. The main function of receiving deposits and of loaning them is performed in essentially the same way by all banks. Of course, there are minor differences; every bank has some ideas of doing business that are peculiar to it, but it may be truly said that the main features of the banking business are the same throughout the country. The greatest differences exist between banks in the large cities and the small places, and these will be explained in their proper place.

State banks possess some advantages, in the opinion of some bankers, that are worth mentioning:

1. They are not examined so critically; in some cases are not required to make returns to State officials, and in no case are such full returns required as the National law requires to be made. Yet the numerous requirements by the Government strengthen public confidence in the banks, and probably the majority of banking officials would not have them removed or lessened if they could. Not all think so, however; hence some banks remain under the shadow of the State instead of the Nation, because they are watched less closely and can do things which would not be permitted if they were National banking institutions.

2. There is another advantage which State banks claim to possess over their National rivals. They can certify checks in excess of the amount which the depositor may have at the moment of certifying. The National banks are expressly forbidden to do this. In several cases they disregarded the law, but the Comptroller of the Currency dealt with the offenders so severely that the banks which were the most desirous of continuing the practice withdrew and reorganized as State banks. The institutions that withdrew were located in New York City, and they maintained that whatever advantages they would gain if they continued to exist as National banks would not equal their losses if the practice of over-certifying could not be continued. Wishing to continue it and not infringe the law, they became State banks, and as such could continue this objectionable practice without legal hindrance.

3. Another advantage enjoyed by the State banks has been with respect to taxation. As the profits on bank-note circulation have declined in consequence of the advancing premium on the Government bonds which must be deposited with the United States Treasurer to secure the notes, and also in consequence of the diminishing rate of interest, the advantages of the National banking system are not so great as they were in the beginning.

The banking laws of the States possess many variations, and we have not space for even an abridgement of them. As no State banks issue circulating notes, all regulations pertaining to that subject are dormant. The main provisions of the banking law of New York are similar to those of the National Bank Act, which were described in the previous chapter.

CHAPTER V.

HOW BANKS ARE ORGANIZED AND ISSUE NOTES.

The subject of this chapter was so well handled by Mr. Wm. E. Gould, cashier of the First National Bank of Portland, Maine, at a meeting of the American Bankers' Association, that his paper may fitly be incorporated into our work.

Let us start a bank in a New England city. Some stormy winter afternoon a half dozen men are sitting around a stove in a counting-room on Commercial Street. They have discussed the weather and their neighbors, have whittled the chairs, have told a few stories, and have listened to the eloquence of a teamster who dropped in, as he cursed the banks and ventilated some new theory of finance. By the way, says Mr. A, it seems to me that if we had another bank here, we could have an easier money market, and could get better accommodation. Why, I took up a note the other day, to my bank, and they didn't discount it, though with my own eyes I saw the clerk put a discount on the little book for old Sykes, and I reckon my note is as good as *his*. The other members of the crowd, being well aware that Mr. A is a habitual growler, as well as a persistent borrower of $150 a day to make his checks good, and an inveterate swapper of checks, do not wonder at the obstinacy of the bank. In a few minutes Mr. A goes out, and in walks Mr. B, who is a well-known, honorable, retired merchant. The subject is renewed, and Mr. B remarks that he has had some talk of seeing some of the merchants and inquiring how they would feel about having a new bank. Some variety of opinion is expressed. But Mr. B at length says that he has determined to try it on, if he can find the right men to go with him. He wants a grocer and a lumber dealer, and a retired man, like himself, and one or two more good men, to make up a board of directors. He says that there is plenty of money seeking investment, and that with good management the stock will be worth $125 in three years.

In the course of a week or so Mr. B has selected five men who will sign a paper subscribing for at least ten shares each of a new bank, to be called the National Bank of Commerce, to be located in Portland, Maine. They write to Washington, to an officer of the Treasury Department, called the Comptroller of the Currency. He

HOW BANKS ARE ORGANIZED AND ISSUE NOTES.

makes inquiries about the needs of Portland and the character of the men, and at length sends some blanks for the signatures of the subscribers to the proposed capital stock of $250,000. He reminds the gentlemen that the law must be strictly followed, that the gentlemen who are to be directors must each own absolutely at least ten shares of the stock, and that at least one-half of the money must be paid in before he can grant them any rights. Mr. B takes his paper around among his friends, and in a few weeks he has the amount subscribed. Certain preliminary steps are now taken. A room is hired, a good vault built, and the subscribers are called together to choose five directors. A cashier is selected. There are many applicants for this office, but the directors choose Mr. Perkins, because he has been in another bank for several years, has borne a good reputation and knows his business.

The papers, duly signed and sworn to, have been sent to Washington for approval. They come back in a week, with a big seal, and a certificate that must be published in some local paper, showing that the bank is recognized by the powers that be. One of the stationers' houses has subscribed to the stock, and so they are making the new books. The cashier says they must hurry up first with a stock journal and stock ledger, as the money is to be paid in at once, and he must have these books. That old growler, Mr. A, comes round before the bank is fairly started, and wants to hire $500, on four months, with a poor indorser. When he is told that they can't lend any money till they get under way, he remarks that he thought *this* bank was going to help our merchants, and he would like to know what banks are for. The teamster, of whom we spoke a few moments ago, said, as Mr. A returned to his office, that he could tell what banks are for: " Yer see, they are jest to skin us poor fellows who haven't got nothing." Presently, however, our new bank has all of its $250,000 paid in. The directors are called upon to decide whether they will issue circulating notes or not. And for fear that some of you present to-night may think that banks are compelled to issue notes, and that their whole profit is derived from the profit upon the circulation, I will at this point explain a few things.

The business of banking does not, of necessity, include the function of issuing bank notes. The privilege of issuing notes is granted by the State or the Nation, as the case may be; but, for the privilege, certain taxes have to be paid to the party granting the permission. In addition to the tax, the expense of handling the notes, the expenses of the redemption of the same, the express charges, etc., make it a serious question with many banks whether it pays to issue notes. The fact is, though it is not often stated, that a very considerable number of large and well-managed banks long ago gave up their circulation, finding that it did not pay. In places like Portland, where the banking capital is not excessive, I think that a fair profit can be made if money is worth five and a half per cent. the year through. But the banks here would make a respectable living if they had no circulation.

Another mistake of the same kind is, the claim that the banks make large amounts out of the lost bills. I have heard it said that fully a quarter part of all that is issued never returns, and is consequently saved by the bank. Now, this is a great mistake, for, in the case of National banks the Government, and not the bank, gets all the benefit. Even in the case of the State banks the proportion of missing bills is very small. I was once connected with a State bank that had a circulation for several years of more than half a million of dollars. Its bills went all over New England and into the West and Canada. When our Maine soldiers went to the front they were paid in many cases in the notes of this bank. Those notes went thus into many Southern States, passed through many battles, were found in soldiers' pockets in the hospitals and on the field. Now, you would say that there must have been a large loss of money in this particular case. Well, the notes keep straggling back to Portland even to this day; they have always been paid, and they always will be. An old lady dies, and a crisp, clean bill is found tucked away in her pocketbook. Now and then one turns up from down south or the extreme west, but to-day there is only about $1,900 outstanding of all the many notes that were issued by this one bank that had so peculiar a circulation. Not long ago three clean five-dollar notes were presented for redemption. They had been hidden away in an old lady's wallet; perhaps she had kept them to pay her funeral bills. Eighteen years, at least, had passed since these bills were paid out. We occasionally read of some drunken swell who lights his pipe or cigar with a dollar bill; but I always think, when I read that story as it turns up periodically, that the bill in question was a poor counterfeit, laid by for an emergency of brag and show.

Having cleared up these errors let us go back to our new bank that we left with $250,000 paid in. After discussion, the directors decide in favor of issuing notes. What is the process? You understand, of course, that all National bank notes are based upon a security deposit made by the bank with the Treasury Department in Washington; that is to say, for every $1,000 United States bond deposited, the Government will grant $900 in new bills to the bank.* No bank, however, can have more bills than its capital, many do not have so much; and, as has been previously said, some banks prefer to have no circulation at all. Our new bank has $250,000 capital; and, taking up the newspaper, the managers are not consoled by the quotation of 113 for a four-per-cent. bond. But, to get their circu-

* See provisions of National Banking Law, Chapter III., page 12.

lation they must first deposit their bonds. So they easily can see that they cannot buy more than $220,000 of four-per-cent. bonds with their $250,000. In other words, $30,000 is sunk in premiums for which they have nothing to show. Or, to put it in another way, they have spent $30,000 for premiums before they have earned a dollar. An order is given to a broker in New York to buy $220,000 in United States bonds, drawing four per cent. interest. The broker telegraphs back that he has bought at 113. He has bought registered bonds—that is, bonds that have no coupons or semi-annual interest warrants, but are certificates of ownership of a certain quantity in the four-per-cent. loan of the United States. These certificates or bonds are in sizes of $10,000 in this case, and are payable to some party who indorses them over in blank, when they are sold. The interest on the bonds comes from the Treasury Department to the owners by check through the mails, in quarterly payments.

Now that the bonds are bought, and, of course paid for, they are sent to the Treasury Department at Washington to be lodged with the Treasurer of the United States to secure such an amount of circulating notes as, under the law, he is authorized to issue to the new bank. This officer issues a certificate that he has had $220,000 in United States four-per-cent. bonds converted into bonds bearing the name of the United States *in trust* for our new bank; that is, he holds the bonds as security for the payment of the notes that are to be issued by the joint act of the Government and the association. Whenever the bank surrenders the notes or an equivalent, then the shareholders can have their bonds transferred to them again. But, so long as the bank owes for its notes, so long must the bonds remain in the pigeon-holes of the big vault of the Treasurer of the United States, all done up nicely, and lettered and labeled, so that at any moment the agent of the bank can put his hand on them and see that they are safe. The Treasurer sends a document to the Comptroller of the Currency, stating that he holds the bonds, and the Comptroller issues an order for printing the amount of notes authorized by law, which is ninety per cent. of the deposit, the other ten per cent. being left as a margin in case of a depreciation of the bonds. So the bank has, in the first instance, sunk $30,000 in premium on its bonds, and now ties up ten per cent. more to make the public absolutely safe when they take the bills of that bank. Only $198,000 is allotted to our new bank. This amount is what is called the circulation of the bank.

The blanks come along in a few weeks, and though the officers may think it very pretty to see their names on a bank bill, yet before they have signed a quarter of the pile, their hands ache and they grow sick of their own names. But the bills must all be signed. Then they are chopped up, and finally make glad somebody's eyes. For the privilege of issuing these notes, the banks pay to the Government one per cent. a-year tax upon the average amount in circulation. Besides this tax, the banks pay the expenses of an office in Washington, where the notes of all of the banks are received, sorted, sent home for redemption, or, if too much defaced, burned and exchanged for clean notes. The expenses of this office for a bank of $250,000 capital would be, perhaps, $200 per annum. Added to this must be the express charges from Washington to the home of the bank. Every week or two a package of bills is sent home for redemption. The cost of this service may be $75 more. Then, again, the law provides that an amount equal to five per cent. of the circulation shall at all times be kept with the Treasurer of the United States, as a fund for paying these constant redemptions; so that the Treasurer gets his pay for the redeemed bills before they start from Washington, and this amount has to be kept constantly good by frequent remittances. You notice, therefore, that five per cent. of our $198,000, or $9,900, is tied up, dead and profitless, in Washington, all the time; so that really all the bank has to use of its $250,000 capital in this direction is $188,100.*

There is another side to this story, also. When a bank obtains circulation and loans the money derived from it in a community, the people in the region are helped. The wheels move round a little faster, and I do not know but that a bank is entitled to some share of the profit, if it takes all the risks of men's business, their tricks, their honesty, and their frequent failures. Very certain it is, that if the banks did not issue their notes the people could not issue their notes as they do at present. We will now leave this branch of banking, and see how our National Bank of Commerce makes money in another direction, and at the same time serves the people. I refer now to the loaning of money. What money has a bank to loan? 1. It has its capital. But, in the case we have supposed, instead of loaning its $250,000 paid-in capital, it will only have $188,100 to loan, which is the amount of circulating notes received from Washington, in exchange for its bonds bought with all of its capital. 2. The bank really loans its whole capital to the Government by its act of buying $250,000 bonds, drawing four per cent. interest, so that the bank receives four per cent.

---

* I mention these facts to show that the banks do their share in paying taxes, and in making the people absolutely secure in their funds, as well as to point out that there are some serious *outs* in what many people think is a huge monopoly. I shall not contend, however, that the banks do not make money out of their circulation. They do. But I think that they fully pay for their privilege. It is not possible for a new bank to start to-day and buy bonds at present prices, pay taxes and do an honest business, and make much money out of its circulation. I would myself to-day, as things are, run a bank—a new bank—as quickly without circulation as with it, if the institution were located in a city.

on this amount, as well as what it can make on its circulation.
3. It has its deposits to loan; that is to say, after reserving what is a prudent amount for the ordinary calls of its depositors, it can invest the balance in such a manner that it can be relied upon in case of need.

Experience teaches the bank manager how stable or how unreliable his balances may prove. In an old and well-established bank, perhaps two-thirds of the deposits may safely be loaned, on various lengths of time and various kinds of securities. In a new bank, or in a poor bank, the officer will not be surprised if his balances are as unstable as his own power to aid his dealer in an emergency. These three, then, are, in the main, the sources of means for a bank to loan and make money:

1. The capital. 2. The circulation. 3. The deposits.

Let us next see how the loans are made. What can our National Bank of Commerce loan upon? In walks Mr. H. He says he wants to hire $2,000, and will give as security his son Bill and his farm. He is told that the National Bank of Commerce cannot loan on real estate, as the law practically prohibits it. Whereupon Mr. H remarks that he would like to know of what earthly use banks are if a man can't raise money on a good farm and on his son Bill's backing. But he is reminded that farms won't pay debts, and that in loaning money belonging to other people care must be had that the money can be easily forthcoming when the debt is due. Mr. B presents a note by a man up in Baldwin, indorsed by the man's wife and by Mr. Jones of the same town. Inquiry fails to bring out the fact that Mr. Jones and the rest of the Baldwin family have any intention of paying the note when due; but shows that they want to hire the money to help build up a cheese factory. Now, while a cheese factory is a glorious institution, yet it is not the thing for a bank to loan its money on. In other words, banks are not established to make permanent loans, but to buy notes on short time, given for the actual purchase or sale of goods.

In country towns the practice differs. For instance, if there was a bank in Bethel, in this State, the drover would present a note signed by himself and three neighbors, and would want to hire for three months $2,000, so that he might go through the towns picking up cattle, and pay his note when he got through the operation. So, also, another man would hire money outright to buy hay and dried apples, and still another would want a thousand or two to fit out a winter logging crew. Back of all these transactions is the apparent ready ability of the hirers to pay their debts out of the commodities dealt in. The money is not tied up in a farm or a cheese factory as a permanent investment.

In cities the trader brings to the bank a batch of notes given for goods sold to country traders. There is a value received in every note. Flour, molasses, sugar, oil, pork, have passed out of the store in the city, and the note expresses the value. The dealer in the city wants to use his capital over again, and so sells his notes to the bank. The bank buys the notes, and gives the dealer a credit for the same upon his bank book.

In New York and some of the larger cities still another practice prevails. Merchants have a way of making their own notes and selling them outright at the price of money at the time. This can only be done by the strongest houses. Other houses go to the bank and say, you have for collection on our account a considerable number and amount of notes; now, hold these as security, and loan us a certain amount on our note. This is all legitimate, as you will see that the bank has abundant security on hand in a form that can easily pay a loan.

Still another method is that used largely in the Western States. I refer to the buying and selling of exchange on eastern cities. A man picks up a customer for 200 barrels of flour. The flour is ground in Minnesota, for instance. As soon as it is ready for delivery he puts it aboard the cars and gets a railroad receipt or bill of lading, showing that 200 barrels of flour have been put into such cars, shipped to Mr. Jackson, at Portland. The bank in Minnesota says that he can pin his bill of lading to the draft he is about to make on Mr. Jackson, and the bank will purchase the bill. The bank does not depend on Mr. Jackson's credit, for they instruct their correspondent in Portland not to give up the bill of lading until they get their money. This custom is confined to the West and South, and arises from their large sales of produce in the East.

The profit made by banks on their loans is the interest for the time that the note or draft has to run from the day it is bought by the bank till it matures. Who gets the profit? The stockholders, of course. The capital is divided up into shares, generally of $100 each. Twice a year the directors look at the balance sheet and say that, after paying the salaries and the taxes, they can pay a certain amount to the stockholders. But one old director remarks that they must first add to their surplus account an amount that the law prescribes before they can divide. The idea of the banking law is to make the public safe; so it is wisely provided that until the surplus of a bank is fully twenty per cent. of its capital no dividend shall be paid until at least one-tenth of its profits shall be added to the surplus.

There is another little trouble that sometimes prevents the stockholder from getting a dividend as he expects. A bank, like a merchant, loses money, sometimes, after exercising the greatest care and the best judgment, and saying "No, no, no," over and over again.

Sometimes a man dies, and everybody is surprised to learn that the estate cannot pay its debts. The bank holds his paper with only a fair indorser. This fair indorser can't respond to so much calamity, and so he fails. The bank settles off and loses fifty per cent. of its debt. Or, a fire burns a man's store and stock, and he is inadequately insured; the bank loses again. Or, what is worse, and what makes a bank man mad (and justly so, too!) is when a firm *lie*, telling all sorts of stories about their business and profits and expenses, and the community wake up some fine morning and find the bubble collapsed! ten cents on a dollar and nobody to blame.

The feeling of reciprocity between banks and their dealers ought to be encouraged. The banker is interested in the success of his dealer. He sees a great many accounts, and he can be of much aid to the merchants in exposing tricks and extended credits, and the peculiar ways of men who deal with the merchants. The merchant should feel that the banker is his friend, that if he criticises it is from good motives. For instance, here is a young man just starting in the wholesale grocery business. He is ambitious to do all the business that he can, and probably tries to do more than he ought to. In his anxiety he strikes out for new accounts, and sells some country traders very large bills. He takes their notes and carries them to his bank for discount, where he is kindly told that he is selling such a man too much for his good, and the bank declines his paper. Now, the banker notices that another concern is working hard to shove that customer off, and this ardent young man may get a big load before he is aware of it. I can recall very many cases where merchants would have saved many bad debts if they would but have taken a hint kindly given.

Young merchants especially ought not to attempt sharp practices on their banks. Fictitious balances, or balances arranged so as to look well the last day of a month, and exchanged checks, and a thousand and one little sneaking ways, only hurt a merchant and destroy his credit. The banker's ledger generally shows a continuous balance, varying with each transaction; averages, and not "put up jobs," show the value of an account. My judgment is, that there is now but very little "shaving" and "grinding" exercised by the bank towards the borrower. Nor is there any disposition of this kind in respectable quarters. Money is an article of merchandise; it has its price; its price varies like the price of sugar and flour. Firms of undoubted credit can hire money lower than can some others of lower credit, just as ready money and a sharp buyer can buy 100 barrels of flour cheaper than a man who purchases on four months and is slow pay. It is true that banks do not discount all the paper that is brought to them. Nor are they bound to. They have the right of choice as much as a merchant has whether he will trust out a bill of goods.

CHAPTER VI.

THE PRESIDENT.

The president is the chief executive officer of the bank, and presides at the meetings of the Board of Directors, but is not necessarily the business head or manager of the institution. Some banks have a vice-president. The vice-president in the absence of the president assumes the functions of the latter.

In legal matters the president must sign documents conveying real estate, and with the cashier must sign certificates of stock issued to shareholders, and the circulating notes. He, or the cashier, may verify the various reports required by the National Banking law to be made to the Comptroller, and must certify to that officer the payment of each installment of stock. He cannot act as proxy at meetings of the shareholders.

He is not required to give a bond to secure the bank in the event of not faithfully performing his duties, but all the officials below him give such security. It is supposed that his large pecuniary interest in his bank, and his well-known standing in the community where he resides, will prove an ample guaranty. Of course, bank presidents are sometimes recreant to their trusts, but happily not often. It is well to believe there are persons living in every community whose word is as good as their bond, and for them to give such an obligation, therefore, is superfluous.

The salary of a bank president varies from a very small sum to fifteen thousand dollars a year. When his duties are very few, and only a slight portion of his time is devoted to the affairs of the bank, no salary is paid. This is often the case.

We have mentioned that in some cases he is the real business head of a bank, and that in others he is not. The country banks, so called, by which is meant in this place, the banks outside the larger cities, are managed by the cashier. Here and there may be found an exception. In the large cities, however, the president is usually the chief business officer, going to the bank regularly, and spending his time there during banking hours. He is a hard-working officer, acquainted with all the details of the business, and interested in all matters pertaining to the prosperity of his enterprise. Occasionally the president of a city bank is a figure head, and then the vice-president or cashier is the chief business officer.

An author, from whom we shall frequently quote, has said: "It is considered desirable that the president should possess an independent income, and be free from the entanglements of trade. Engagement in other business would distract his attention from the bank, and might give rise to a conflict of interests. Under the pressure of personal embarrassment, with the means of relief in his official hands, even a rigid sense of duty might be overcome. The highest tone of sentiment on this point is, therefore, adverse to his connection with the hazards of commerce. Yet several of our most prosperous New York City banks have always been presided over by active, enterprising merchants.

"There are other reasons why a bank president should hold himself aloof from mercantile business. With large capital invested in a particular branch of trade, his views might insensibly become narrow and partial. An engrossing special interest would divert his mind from the close study of credits generally, and make his judgment less clear, as the condition of commerce becomes more critical. In a season of growing stringency in the money market, self-interest compels bank directors, in common with others, to withdraw their attention from all affairs but their own, and thus additional responsibility is thrown on the officers, particularly on the president. The discounting of paper is then less strictly confined to the sessions of the board. It is spread through every hour of the day, with specialities and importunities which can be dealt with only individually and privately."*

The truth of Gibbons' first remark has been illustrated in a startling manner on more than one occasion. A bank president ought not to be regarded morally as a very superior being. If he is engaged in outside interests of greater pecuniary or other importance to him than his bank, there is danger that he will neglect or use it for a personal end. This has happened again and again. Within a very short time several fresh illustrations have been added to those existing before.

It need hardly be said that a bank president should possess a very considerable knowledge, especially of men. It is true that many a successful bank president has had only a slight acquaintance with books, but he has understood men. To have this knowledge in a marked degree is a gift rather than an acquirement; yet the less fortunate should strive, nevertheless, to acquire by determined effort that knowledge of men which is so essential to business success.

A bank president should keep a keen watch on the movements of trade, on the strength and weakness of those to whom money is

* *Gibbons' Banks of New York*, p. 24.

loaned, or who are likely to ask for loans, for on the sagacious lending of the bank's resources mainly depends its prosperity. Some bank presidents read the trade newspapers with great care, and search in every quarter for information relating to the borrowers of money. If a considerable number of failures occur in a particular trade they are carefully noted. A bank president told the writer a few years ago that a great deal of tobacco had been injured in curing during that year, and that he should be especially careful about discounting "tobacco paper," because he expected that a good many failures would happen among tobacco manufacturers. This is the kind of vigilance required for a bank manager. Still, however wisely he may conduct the business of discounting, risks are unavoidable, and losses will accrue.

As correct sentiments beget correct conduct, a banker ought to apprehend correctly the objects of banking. They consist in making pecuniary gains for the stockholders, by legal operations. The business is eminently beneficial to society; but some bankers have deemed the good of society so much more worthy of regard than the private good of stockholders, that they have supposed all loans should be dispensed with direct reference to the beneficial effect of the loans on society, irrespective, in some degree, of the pecuniary interests of the dispensing bank. Such a banker will lend to builders, that houses or ships may be multiplied; to manufacturers, that useful fabrics may be increased; and to merchants, that goods may be seasonably replenished. He deems himself, ex-officio, the patron of all interests that concern his neighborhood, and regulates his loans to these interests by the urgency of their necessities, rather than by the pecuniary profits of the operations to the bank, or the ability of the bank to sustain such demands. When we perform well the direct duties of our station we need not curiously trouble ourselves to effect, indirectly, some remote duty. Results belong to Providence, and, by the natural catenation of events (a system admirably adapted to our restricted foresight), a man can usually in no way so efficiently promote the general welfare, as by vigilantly guarding the peculiar interests committed to his care. If, for instance, his bank is situated in a region dependent for its prosperity on the business of lumbering, the dealers in lumber will naturally constitute his most profitable customers: hence, in promoting his own interest out of their wants, he will, legitimately, benefit them as well as himself, and benefit them more permanently than by a vicious subordination of his interests to theirs. Men will not engage permanently in any business that is not pecuniarily beneficial to them personally; hence, a banker becomes recreant to even the manufacturing and other interests that he would protect, if he so manage his bank as to make its stockholders unwilling to continue the employment of their capital in banking. This principle, also, is illustrated by the late United States Bank, for the stupendous temporary injuries which its mismanagement inflicted on society are a smaller evil than the permanent barrier its mismanagement has probably produced against the creation of any similar institution.

The honor and pecuniary prosperity of his bank should constitute the paramount motive of every banking operation. A violation of this principle produced, in the year eighteen hundred and thirty-seven, a suspension of specie payments, which was visited on bank stockholders by a legislative prohibition of dividends, and visited on banks and bankers by a general obloquy. The banks suspended that the debtors of the bank might not suspend: or worse, the banks suspended that the debtors might be spared the pecuniary loss that would have resulted from paying their bank debts. A conduct so suicidal was probably fostered by the pernicious union, in one person, of bank director and bank debtor, a union from which our banks are never wholly exempt; nor are they always exempt from the same union, still more pernicious, in bank presidents and cashiers. With this inherent defect in the organization of our banks, we can the more readily understand why, in 1837, the banks assumed dishonor to shield their debtors, and why the dishonor was continued for some more than a year in our State, and longer in others; and would have continued longer in ours, but from a refusal of its further tolerance by the legislature.

Every suspension of specie payments might have been prevented, had the bankers performed their duty to their respective banks, by prudence in the quality of their loans, and vigor in the enforcement of payments. No proof of this can be more convincing than the successfully sustained refusal of the Union Bank of New York to unite in the specie suspension of the year eighteen hundred and thirteen. All the banks, also, of New England preserved specie payments. We admit that, had all the banks of the Union refused to suspend payments in 1813, 1819 and 1837, business would have severely suffered; but this is a consideration for the legislature, and not for the banks. They are creations of the law, and should obey their creator. In England, during its struggle with Napoleon, the Government prohibited specie payments by the Bank of England, when the suspension was deemed publicly useful. The suspension continued for twenty years, but the bank incurred thereby no disgrace, for it obeyed the law.

The subordination of the honor and interests of a bank to the avarice or necessities of its managers, or dealers of any description, is productive, not of suspensions only, but of every disaster which usually befalls banks; and unless such a subordination can be prevented by the officer who acts specially as a banker, no man who respects himself should continue in the position, when he discovers that such a subordination is in progress. The owner of a steam engine regulates his business by the capacity of his engine, but should he regulate it by the necessities of his customers, he would probably burst his boiler. A shipowner regulates his freight by the tonnage of his ship; a contrary course would sink it. So every bank possesses a definite capacity for expansion by which bank dealers can regulate their business; but, when a bank regulates its expansion by the wants of its dealers, or the persuasion of friendship, it will probably explode, or be otherwise unprofitable to its stockholders.

Banks charge for the use of money no more than the use is worth. Nothing is added for risk, and thereby money-lending differs from all other business that involves hazard. A great disproportion exists also between the amount hazarded by any loan, and the amount gained. The loan of a thousand dollars for sixty days involves the possible loss of a thousand dollars, without the possibility of a greater gain than some ten dollars. Banks, therefore, never regularly lend money, without receiving the security of more than one person who is deemed safe for the debt; and a good banker will err on the side of excessive security, rather than accept security whose sufficiency may reasonably be questioned. In the country, two endorsers are usually required on every note that is discounted; but in cities, where discounts are made for shorter periods than in the country, one endorser is more usual than two.

Independently of the wealth of the endorser, the banks derive from him a security founded on the natural desire of every borrower to protect his friends, should insolvency occur to the borrower during the pendency of the bank loan. An endorser, will, also, usually foresee earlier than the bank when mischances threaten the borrower, and when appeals for protection should be made. To derive these benefits from endorsers, they should be disconnected in business from the borrower, so as not to be involved in his calamities; hence, such disconnection is always one of the circumstances from which a banker judges of the sufficiency of any proffered endorser. Relationship of either consanguinity or affinity, between a debtor and his sureties, sharpens usually the desire of the debtor to protect his endorser; while again such relationship facilitates the concealment of a common pecuniary interest in enterprises, and facilitates collusions against the bank in times of disaster, that may more than counterbalance the benefits expected by the bank from the relationship.

The more lax the morality is of a borrower, the less will he probably feel the obligation to protect his endorsers; and the more lax the morality is of an endorser, the more will he struggle against the surrender of his property to pay an unprotected endorsement.

As a general result, however, debts are rarely collectable from the property of an endorser, unless his property very greatly over-balances the amount of his endorsement. Instances are continually occurring where an endorser who has become liable for a bad debt which his property could pay, and leave him a surplus, will ruin himself in successfully preventing the application of his property to the debt in question. Hence, when a debt is contracted wholly on the property of the endorser, the debt will not be safe unless it is small in comparison with the wealth of the endorser.

Men who are prone to extravagance in their domestic or personal expenditures rarely possess the amount of property they are reputed to possess. Men expend to be thought rich more frequently than they expend by reason of being rich. The rich are usually more inclined to parsimony than expenditure. Any way, persons who practice parsimony are in the way of becoming rich, whatever may be their present poverty; while persons who are profuse in expenditures are in the way of becoming poor, though they may possess a present opulence.

A man who transacts a regular business in a regular way is not liable to sudden fluctuations in his pecuniary solvency; but when a man's business is novel, and its results are untried, or when its results are frequently disastrous, the banker who grants him loans assumes some of the hazards and uncertainties of the business.

When money is to be invested in the purchase of merchandise, cattle, flour, or other property in the regular course of the borrower's business, the investment yields to the borrower a means of repayment; nothing is hazarded but ordinary integrity, and ordinary exemption from disasters; but when the borrowed money is to pay some pre-existing debt, none of the foregoing securities apply, and, possibly, you are merely taking a thorn out of another person's side, to place it in your own.

Notes which a man receives, on the sale of property in his ordinary business, are termed business notes. The owner, having received them as money, had satisfied himself of their safety; hence, when they are offered to a banker by a prudent man of business, they possess an inherent evidence of value. They were given also for property that will, in the ordinary course of business, furnish the means by which the notes may be paid; and thus they possess an additional ingredient of safety. Kindred to such notes are drafts, which a man draws on a consignee to whom property has been forwarded for sale. If the consignee be a prudent man (the consignor must deem him prudent or he would not trust to him the property) he will not accept unless the property forwarded is equivalent in value to the amount of the acceptance. The property, therefore, will pay the acceptance, and while the property remains unsold, it constitutes an equitable pledge for ultimate payment. A country banker, however, will usually be benefited, in a long course of business, by never loaning on city names without a reliable country endorser or maker, or both; for nothing is usually more unreliable than the reputed solvency of the merchants of large cities.

A factor will sometimes accept in confidence that the drawer will supply him with funds in time to pay the acceptance. This will not constitute a worse security than an ordinary accommodation endorsement; but the transaction lacks the reliability and security that are consequent to the acceptor's possession of consignments in advance of his acceptance, and so far as the nature of the acceptance is concealed, the ostensible character of the paper will give it a fictitious security.

Notes and acceptances are often assimilated to the foregoing character to facilitate the procurement of loans. Two merchants will exchange notes, and offer each other's notes at different banks, as business paper. Such notes are peculiarly hazardous by reason that the insolvency of either of the parties will usually produce the insolvency of the other. Acceptances are exchanged in the same way, and possess the same element of danger.

Sometimes a country merchant will draw on a merchant of New York, and obtain thereon a discount at some country bank. The draft will have some months to run before it will become payable; but when it is payable, the New York merchant will obtain the means of payment by drawing on the country merchant, payable some months thereafter, and getting a discount thereon in New York. Such transactions are termed "kiting." They are practiced on notes as well as on drafts; and by persons residing in the same place as well as at distant places. When practiced by persons who live at a distance from each other, the operation is usually very expensive, by incidental charges of exchange and collection. Bankers should suspect the solvency of parties who resort to expedients so commercially disreputable. The real character of the transactions is rarely avowed by the parties inculpated in the practices; but a vigilant banker will soon suspect the operations, and not touch them unless the security can be made very ample.

A country produce dealer, or manufacturer, will sometimes place in New York an agent on whom to draw; or he may connect his operations with some person there of no capital, whom he will use as an acceptor. Such acceptances are no better than the note of the country dealer. They constitute, moreover, a hazardous class of paper, as you may rely somewhat on an assumed capital in the acceptors. Such methods are rarely practiced except by persons who want to extend their operations beyond a limit to which a real consignee would restrict them. No prudential limit exists with the dummy acceptor, hence, the drawer is able to carry his operations to an extent unlimited, except by his own will, or his ability to find lenders; and men thus predisposed, and supplied with the requisite machinery, usually extend their speculations till they are overwhelmed in ruin.

Notes and drafts are often made to be sold at a usurious discount, by parties ostensibly solvent, but who are struggling to purchase a transient respite from bankruptcy, or to amend their fortunes by desperate enterprises. Banks are, therefore, usually reluctant to discount paper offered by brokers and other persons who are known to practice usury; for though usury laws have been greatly modified within a few years, yet no bank wishes to take paper which may form the subject of a lawsuit. In many places the defence of usury is said to be so discreditable that few men will avail themselves of it. In the country, people feel less fastidious in this respect, and any debt which can certainly be avoided by means of usury would be very apt to be uncollectable.

But the avoidance of loss is only a negation of evil. To make gains is the proper business of a banker, and, as the principal source of legitimate gain is lending money, the bank must lend to the extent of its ability—erring on the side of repletion, rather than of inanition; for a banker knows not how far his bank can bear extension till he tries; hence, if timidity, indolence, or apathy, limits his loans in advance of necessity, he may injure the community by unnecessarily withholding pecuniary assistance, and injure the stockholders by unnecessarily abridging the profits. A banker must not, however, extend his loans regardless of the future, but, like a skillful mariner, he should see an approaching storm while it is an incipient breeze, and meanwhile carry all the sail that will not jeopardize the safety of his charge: governing his discounts, at all times, more by the condition of his funds, and his own prospective resources, than by any reputed scarcity or abundance of money in other places and in other banks.

If a banker can make reasonably good profits on his capital without much expansion, he may keep more restricted in his loans than a banker should who is less favorably circumstanced. Every banker must, however, remember, that to be strong in funds and rich in profits are natural incompatibilities; hence, the more money a banker wishes to make, the poorer in funds he must consent to become. In banking operations, as in most other, wisdom lies in a medium between extremes; and if a banker can keep funds enough for practical safety, he had better forego excess of funds, and receive an equivalent in gains. Physicians say that the human body can bear excess of food better than deficiency. The excess can be discharged by cutaneous eruptions, as we see sometimes in over-fed infants; but deficiency of nourishment will not relieve itself; so in banking, a repletion of loans, if they are undoubtedly solvent, prompt and short, will soon of themselves work a relief to the bank; but a paucity of loans cannot, by any process of its own, cure the scant profits of the stockholders. Banks are rarely injured, therefore, by an excess of discounts. When banks fail, their disaster proceeds from the quality of their loans, not from the quantity.

No banker should keep his funds inactive when no better excuse exists therefor than that the business he can obtain is not so lucrative as the business of some other place, or as his own business was at some other period. The legal rate of interest is so high, that the voluntary forbearance of its reception for even a short period, is ordinarily a greater evil than the reception of any common description of solvent loans. Any way, a banker who keeps his funds inactive, to await the offer of loans more lucrative than simply the interest of money, should be well assured that the future loans will be sufficiently lucrative to compensate for the forbearance. But no disadvantages of position must be deemed a sufficient apology for the assumption of hazardous loans. When no safe business offers, no business should be transacted by a banker who entertains a proper respect for himself, or a proper feeling for his stockholders. Gains may be impossible, but losses are measurably avoidable. If any location presents the alternative of no business, or great hazards, a banker is accountable for the choice which he may make between the two alternatives; and he is accountable no further.

But ordinarily every banker is presented with more business than he can assume, and he is enabled to select the more profitable and reject the less profitable. In speaking of the profits of banking, we mean gains that proceed from some other source than the interest allowed by law for the use of the money. These gains are derived most largely from circulation and deposits; hence the loans are advantageous to a bank, in proportion as they increase the circulation or deposits of the bank. Money is sometimes borrowed to pay debts to a neighboring bank, or to a person who keeps his money deposited in a neighboring bank. Such loans yield no profit to the lender except the interest on the loan; hence they are not so profitable as loans to borrowers who will take bank notes of the lending bank, and circulate them over the country in the purchase of agricultural products. While the notes remain in circulation, the bank is receiving interest on them from the borrower—interest not for the loan of money, but for the loan by the bank of its promises to pay money when demanded. So, on a loan made by a bank to one of its depositing customers, the bank receives interest only on its promise to pay the borrowed money when the borrower shall from time to time draw for the same. And when a deposit is thus drawn from a bank, the draft is not necessarily paid in money, but in bank notes which may obtain a circulation. This advantage is a usual attendant of the deposits of some customers, and makes their accounts doubly beneficial to a bank. Whether a depositor asks for more loans than his deposit account entitles him to receive, is a question whose solution depends on whether the bank can lend all its money to better depositing customers, or more profitably use it in loans for circulation. A banker should, however, estimate liberally the merits which pertain to a steady customer; not deciding on any proposed loan by the amount of the proposer's deposit at the time of the proposal, but his antecedent deposits, which were doubtless made in reliance on the bank for a fair reciprocity of benefits. Competition for profitable customers exists among banks as eagerly as competition among borrowers for bank loans; hence liberality to customers by a banker is as much a dictate of interest as of justice.

Notes and time-drafts discounted by country banks, and payable in New York, Boston, Philadelphia, and other eastern places were payable in a currency whose value was enhanced by the rate of exchange, which existed in favor of the east and against the west. As country banks never allowed any premium in the reception of such paper, the benefit of the exchange was a strong inducement to a country banker for preferring loans thus payable to loans payable at his own counter. Borrowers would often take advantage of this predilection, and make notes payable artificially at New York, as a means of obtaining a loan of a country banker. Notes thus made were rarely paid at maturity; hence, so far as a banker relied on their payment, and founded his business calculations thereon, they were hurtful. To the extent that he colluded with the maker and supplied him with funds by which such note could be paid at New York, at a loss, to the maker, of the difference in the rate of exchange, the transaction was unlawful.

Banking is not exempt from the ordinary fatality which ever in a long course of business makes honesty the best policy. To gain unlawfully must also be a poor recommendation to a banker, with any thoughtful stockholder; for if a man will collude to make dishonest gains for his stockholders, what security can the stockholders possess that he will not collude against them, to make dishonest gains for himself? A country banker may properly discount a note payable in New York when the maker's business will make New York the most convenient place of payment, though the borrower's residence may be in the country: such is often the case with drovers, lumbermen, and some manufacturers. Transactions of this circuitous nature must, however, be spontaneous on the part of the borrower; for a note is usurious if, in addition to the receipt of legal interest, the banker superadds, as a condition of the loan, that it must be paid at a distant city, and consequently in a currency more valuable than that the lender received. But when such loans are legal, and possess the best commercial character for punctuality and security, they are not always so advantageous to the country bank as notes payable at the country bank, and connected with the circulation of bank notes or with deposits. The force of this remark can perhaps be better seen in what follows.

Banks can usually make as many loans as they desire to borrowers who will use the loan in purchasing from the bank a draft on New York or other eastern city, whereby the bank will obtain a premium on the sale of the draft, in addition to the interest on the loan. The operation becomes peculiarly advantageous to the bank when the loan is itself payable in New York, for while the borrower pays, in such a transaction, say an eighth of one per cent. to the bank for a bank draft on New York, he subsequently repays in New York the borrowed money without receiving any return premium from the bank. But howsoever profitable such a transaction seems, banks can rarely transact advantageously much of such business. Should the entire capital of a bank of three hundred thousand dollars be employed in discounting drafts on New York payable at three months from the time of discount, and should the bank pay therefor sight drafts on New York, charging for them a premium of a quarter of one per cent., the bank could not pay its stockholders above six per cent. the year in bank dividends.

As every loan is usually attended with some advantage to the bank, in the ways we have explained, beyond the interest paid by the borrower, the sooner the loan is to be repaid to the bank, the more frequently will the bank be able to reloan the money, and obtain a repetition of the incidental advantages.

Country banks being subject, at certain seasons, to a demand for currency, every judicious banker will endeavor to so select the loans which he makes during a year, that large amounts of them will become payable at the precise periods of the spring and fall when funds will be most needed. This is imitating the conduct of Pharaoh, who, during the years of plenty, accumulated provisions for the periods of apprehended famine. Many months of every year are months of plenty with every well-conducted bank. The paper which is selected for the future contingency will be useful in proportion to its reliability; and paper payable in New York, or other eastern cities, may be more useful than any other. No rule of banking is more practically valuable than the foregoing.

As banking is liable to panics and pressures which may arise without being preceded by any long premonitory symptoms, a banker must invest his funds in short loans, which measurably accomplish the feat that is proverbially impossible, "to have a cake and eat it at the same time:"—that is, by means of short loans, the bank keeps its funds always available within a short period, and yet keeps them always loaned out on interest. The banks of large cities are able to make loans payable on demand, or in a few days' notice; while country banks possess no such opportunities, but are able usually to deposit their spare funds in some bank in New York, subject to a repayment on demand, or on short notice; and in the mean time to receive interest on the deposit. Experience, however, has painfully demonstrated that the convenience of an interest-paying depository is not exempt from danger.

What is every person's business is proverbially nobody's; hence the safety of banks depends less on boards of directors than on some one person to whom the bank is specially confided. He is to be always present, and always responsible, in his feelings and in public estimation, for the prosperity of the bank; and for these services he ought to be well compensated, pecuniarily, so as to stimulate the faculties to their best efforts. We mistake human nature when we expect great efforts from any man, and supply no proper motive therefor.

In large cities, discounts are generally made to persons who are known personally or by reputation to some of the directors, but in country banking, the borrowers and their endorsers in many cases are residents of remote places, and unknown, personally, in the locality of the bank. A country banker, who should insist on a personal acquaintance with the makers and endorsers of all the paper he desired to buy, might find his business restricted to a circle too small for the employment of his capital. In vain will such a banker insist that he ought not to make loans to persons of whom he possesses no knowledge; the answer will be that he should acquire the knowledge. It is indispensable to his bank. He is bound to know a sufficient number of persons to enable his bank to employ its capital advantageously. Every note, therefore, that he rejects for want of knowledge, is ostensibly a slight reproach on him, in cases where he has not a sufficiency of known borrowers;'while every note that he rejects or accepts by means of his knowledge of the parties is a tribute to his industry and vigilance.

The preceding remarks will show why country banks are specially liable to loss from forgeries. Moreover, many of the makers and endorsers who deal with country banks write poorly, and their signatures bear but little internal evidence of genuineness, even when you are partially acquainted with the parties; for the same person will write differently at different times, and especially with different pens and different qualities of ink; and he varies these continually. Still, the greater the danger, the greater is the caution which the banker must exercise. He must bring to the difficulty all the scrutiny of which the case is susceptible, or he will not stand excused for consequent losses. A comparison of any proffered signature with one that is genuine, though encumbered with difficulties as above explained, is a guide that should not be neglected; and it is often the best that can be resorted to. Banks, therefore, keep a book in which every person who deals with the bank inserts his name. The signatures should be placed alphabetically, to facilitate a future reference to them. The endorsers may never visit the bank; but, when a note is paid, the names of the endorsers may, with the consent of the maker, be cut from the note, and pasted into the book, in their proper order. In no very long time, a mass of autographs may be thus collected. Some names on notes may not be deserving of such preservation; and in this particular, as in all others, the banker must exercise his judgment.

The law in relation to endorsers renders them liable only on due notice of the non-payment of the endorsed note. This avenue of loss is felt but seldom in large cities, but in the country it produces constant danger. A country banker, therefore, must know where endorsers reside, and usually the information can be obtained most readily when each note is discounted, and from the person who brings it for discount. The information can be written on the note under the name of the endorser, and it will serve as a direction to the notary public, should the note be protested for non-payment. The laws of New York required, formerly, that the notice of non-payment should be forwarded by mail to the post-office nearest to the residence of the endorser. This imposed on the banker a knowledge of postal locations that added much to the difficulty of his position. The law has since meliorated the difficulty by rendering a notice sufficient if directed to the town in which an endorser resides.

As a banker will lend to the extent of his ability, that he may make for his bank all the gains in his power, he must be well acquainted with the pecuniary means and abilities of his bank. He can keep on his table a summary showing the precise amount of his funds and where they are situated, and of what they are composed; also an aggregate of his various liabilities. Such a summary, when corrected daily, or more frequently if necessary, will constitute a chart by which he will be able to judge whether he can lend, or whether he must retrench existing loans. The funds that will be adequate to any given amount of liability a banker must learn by experience, embarrassed as he will be by a want of uniformity in the results of his experience, at different periods. Every bank must be liable, momentarily, to demands for payment of its deposits (and bank notes, if it issues any) beyond its present funds. Practically, however, if a banker has funds enough, day by day, to meet the requirements of the day, he has funds enough.

"Sufficient for the day is the evil thereof," is a proverb peculiarly applicable in banking.

But a banker must not be satisfied by knowing that his funds of to-day will be sufficient for the wants of the day. He must possess a reasonable assurance that the same will be his position "to-morrow, and to-morrow, to the end of time." To gain this assurance, he ought to keep also before him one or more lists in detail of his prospective resources, showing what notes and acceptances will be payable to the bank daily for some weeks or months ahead, and where they are payable. With such lists, and a knowledge of the reality of the paper thus going onward to maturity, he will be able to judge whether his prospective resources will need the aid of his existing unemployed funds; or whether he may loan them, and even extend his liabilities in anticipation of a prospective surplusage of resources.

By means of such lists as we have just described, should a banker discover that his existing resources will be small during, say, the month of June, he can aid the defect by discounting in the preceding May, April or March, paper that will mature in June. By thus regulating, prospectively, his future resources, he can be always provided with funds. And that a banker may, at all times, be master of his resources, he should never promise prospective loans, or make loans with any promise of their renewal. The more he keeps uncommitted, the better will he be able to accommodate himself to future exigencies. Banking is subject to sufficient uncertainties, without unnecessarily aggravating them by prospective agreements. A banker may be unable to fulfill such pledges, and be thus compelled to falsify his promises; or, he may be able to fulfill them only at a sacrifice of the interests of his bank, and thus be placed in the unwholesome dilemma of injuring his personal character, or of preventing the injury only by a sacrifice of the interests of his bank.

A banker is compelled to employ officers to whom he intrusts his vaults and their contents. Robberies are often committed by persons thus intrusted, and some such robberies have remained long concealed. The banker cannot be responsible for all such occurrences; still, vigilance can accomplish much in the way of security against mischances, and the banker is responsible for the exercise of all practicable vigilance. Robberies and frauds possess usually some discoverable concomitants. No man plunders to accumulate property that is not to be used. Its use, therefore, which can rarely be wholly concealed, is a clue which a vigilant eye can trace to the plunderer. Nearly every plunderer is a prodigal, and may thereby be detected; nearly every plunderer is needy, and should therefore be suspected. The banker should know human nature, and be able to trace effects to their causes, and to deduce effects from causes. To this extent he is answerable for the safety of his bank. The sentinel whose post happens to be surprised by an enemy may escape punishment as a criminal, but he can rarely gain commendation for vigilance, or escape censure for carelessness.

To permit overdrafts is to make loans without endorsers, and without the payment of interest. It is, moreover, to empower a dealer to control your resources. No mode of lending money can be more inconsistent with all safe banking, and it should never be permitted. Still, every man who keeps a bank account can draw checks for an amount exceeding his balance in bank; nor can the banker personally supervise the payment of checks. A vigilant banker will, however, provide vigilant subordinate officers: "The eye of the master maketh diligent," say the Scriptures. An intelligent and careful teller will soon learn whom he must watch; but, after all precautions, an overdraft may be perpetrated, and, whether by accident or design, the bookkeeper should forthwith report to the banker the occurrence, and he must act thereon as his judgment shall deem proper.

No system of banking can escape the casualty of doubtful debts. Usually the most favorable time to coerce payments is when they first become payable. Then the debtor has expected to pay, and if he is then in default no certain dependence can be made on his subsequent promises. He is also usually less offended by a legal enforcement of payments when they are promptly enforced, and when he knows the creditor is disappointed by the default, than he is after the default has been tacitly acquiesced in by a long forbearance of coercive measures. Additional security, when necessary, can also be more readily obtained at the time of the default, than it can after the debtor has become reconciled by time to his dishonorable position. His credit is better now than it will be subsequently, and he can more readily now than subsequently obtain responsible endorsers. In relation to the extension of time on receiving additional security on a weak debt, any extension that is productive of security is a less banking evil than insecurity; just as any protraction of disease that results in health is a less physical evil than death.

A banker will be often subjected to importunity by persons who will desire a deviation from the usual modes of banking. They will propose a relaxation of good rules, and allege therefor some pressing emergency; but if the relaxation involves any insecurity, any violation of law or of official duty, the banker should never submit, even when the result may promise unusual lucrativeness to his bank. While a banker adheres with regularity to known forms of business and settled principles, Providence is a guarantee for his success; but when he deviates from these Providence is almost equally a guarantee of disaster, both personal and official.

Banking is a business, and should be reciprocally beneficial to the borrower and the lender. When a borrower's business cannot yield the requisite reciprocity of benefit, he will often attempt to mend the defect by pertinacity of application, and by persuasions addressed to the directors of a bank personally, as well as to the banker; and by servility and sycophancy. Such conduct is a strong symptom of some latent defect in the applicant's pecuniary position, and the appliances should strengthen a banker in his refusal of loans rather than facilitate their application. Loans thus obtained rarely result favorably to the lender.

No man is safe when engaged in a speculation, especially when the price of the article that he purchases is above the usual cost of its production. The speculator's intellect soon loses its control over him and he will be controlled by his feelings, and they are unnaturally excited. He becomes a monomaniac in the particular concern with which he is engaged. He will increase his purchases beyond all moderation, and at prices which he himself, when he commenced his purchases, would have deemed ruinous. Many banks are destroyed by such speculators. A bank will loan to them till its safety seems to require that the speculation must be upheld against a falling market; and the effort is made till the continued decline in prices ruins both speculators and sustaining bank.

When a debtor arrives at a certain magnitude of indebtedness he becomes the master of his creditor, who is somewhat in the position of Jonah when swallowed by the whale. The debtor can say to a bank thus circumstanced that to stop discounting for him will ruin him, and that his ruin will involve a loss of the existing debt. No prudent banker will be placed in such a position, but should any banker lapse into so sad an error, he will rarely mend his position by yielding to the proposed necessity for further loans. He had better brave the existing evil than yield to an argument which, if already too potent to be disregarded, will acquire additional strength by every further discount, and render his inevitable fall more disastrous to his stockholders and more disreputable to himself.

With respect to his contingent expenses, the more a banker can reduce their amount, the more easily will he make reasonable dividends of profit among his stockholders, without an undue expansion of loans and consequent anxiety to himself. The income of a bank is only an aggregate of petty accumulations. Every unnecessary expenditure of one hundred dollars by the bank will nullify the interest on four ninety-day loans of fifteen hundred dollars each— loans often withheld from meritorious claimants. The economy of which we speak is not any unjust abridgement of properly remunerative salaries to faithful officers and servants, who should, however, labor diligently and perseveringly in their vocations, as men labor in other employments, so that the bank may economize in the number of its agents, instead of economizing in the magnitude of their salaries. A hundred dollars, or a thousand, when contrasted with the capital of a bank, may seem a small matter, and probably bank expenditures are often incurred under such a contrast; but the true contrast lies between the expenditure and the net percentage of a bank's gains. A bank whose net income will not exceed the legal rate of interest possesses no fund from which to squander. And banks often expend an unduly large part of their capital in architecture to ornament the city of their location, or to rival some neighboring institution, whose extravagance ought to be shunned, not followed. No person has yet shown why banks should be built like palaces, while the owners of the banks are to a good extent poor, and live humbly. The custom is perhaps founded on the delusion of deeming a great capital identical with great wealth. When several men, for any purposes of gain, unite their several small capitals, they may well need a larger building and more agents than each man would require were he unassociated; but that the association can afford an organization increased in splendor as much as in magnitude, is a fallacy somewhat analogous to the blunder of the Irishman, who, hearing that his friend intended to walk forty miles during a day, said that he would walk with him, and then they could walk eighty miles.

When solicited by a neighbor or a friend, few men possess vigor enough, or conscientiousness enough, to refuse a recommendation, or to state therein all they suspect or apprehend. They will studiously endeavor not to make themselves pecuniarily responsible by any palpable misrepresentation; hence they will so qualify the recommendation that it will admit of a construction consistent with truth; but the qualification will be so enigmatical or subtle that the banker will not interpret it as the recommender will show subsequently it ought to have been interpreted. Besides, the man who merely recommends a loan acts under circumstances that are much less favorable to caution than the man who is to lend. When we are in the act of making a loan, our organization presents the danger with a vividness that is not excited by the act of recommending. To believe speculatively that we will suffer the extraction of a tooth, is a wholly different matter from sitting down and submitting to the operation. Suicide would be far more common than it is, if a man could feel, when the act was to be performed, as he feels when he only prospectively resolves on performing it. This preservative process of nature no banker should disregard by substituting any man's recommendation for the scrutiny of his own feelings and judgment at the time when the loan is to be consummated; though he may well give to recommendations all the respect which his knowledge of the recommender may properly deserve.

By acting according to the dictates of his own judgment, a man strengthens his own judgment as he proceeds; while a man who subordinates his judgment to other men's is continually debilitating his own. Nothing also is more fallacious than the principle on which we ordinarily defer to the decision of a multitude of counselors. If fifty men pull together at a cable, the pull will combine the strength of one man multiplied by fifty; but if fifty men deliberate on any subject, the result is not the wisdom of one man multiplied by fifty, but at most the wisdom of the wisest man of the assemblage; just as fifty men, when they look at any object, can see only what can be seen by the sharpest single vision of the group; they cannot combine their vision and make thereof a lens as powerful as the sight of one man multiplied by fifty. A banker may, therefore, well resort to other men for information, but he may differ from them all, and still be right; any way, if he perform the dictates of his own judgment, he performs all that duty requires; if he act otherwise, he performs less than his duty. Let the counsel of your own heart stand, says the Bible; and, by way of encouragement, it adds, that a man can see more of what concerns himself, than seven watchmen on a high tower.

As virtue's strongest guarantee is an exception from all motive to commit evil, a banker must avoid all engagements that may make him needy. If he wants to be *more* than a banker, he should cease to be a banker. Should he discover in himself a growing tendency to irritability, which his position is apt to engender, let him resist it as injurious to his bank and his peace; and if he should find himself popular, let him examine whether it proceeds from the due discharge of his duties. A country banker was some few years ago dismissed from a bank which he had almost ruined, and was immediately tendered an honorary public dinner by the citizens of his village, into whose favor his misdeeds had unwisely ingratiated him. The service of massive plate that was given to a president of the old United States Bank was in reward of compliances which soon after involved in disaster every commercial interest of our country. Could we trace actions to their source, these mistakes of popular gratitude would never occur. The moroseness that we abhor proceeds often from a sensitiveness that is annoyed at being unable to oblige; while the amiability that is applauded proceeds from an imbecility that knows not how to refuse.

A banker should possess a sufficiency of legal knowledge to make him suspect what may be defects in proffered securities, so as to submit his doubts to authorized counselors. He must, in all things, be eminently practical. Every man can tell an obviously insufficient security, and an obviously abundant security; but neither of these constitute any large portion of the loans that are offered to a banker. Security practically sufficient for the occasion is all that a banker can obtain for the greater number of the loans he must make. If he must err in his judgment of securities, he had better reject fifty good loans than make one bad debt;, but he must endeavor not to err on the extreme of caution or the extreme of temerity; and his tact in these particulars will, more than any other, constitute the criterion of his merits as a banker.

CHAPTER VII.

DIRECTORS' MEETINGS AND DISCOUNTING.

We may properly open this chapter with some general remarks concerning the duties of bank directors. Whatever may be their shortcomings they usually begin their duties with honest intentions toward their stockholders and the public. The misconduct which may supervene, will proceed from temptations incident to their office, and perhaps from the absence of well-digested notions of their duties. Some years ago, a person was asked whether he would accept the office, then vacant, of director in a bank. After deliberating, he replied, that as the office might result in some benefit to him, he would accept. When the answer was reported to the Board who were to fill the vacancy, they refused to appoint him, lest he should sit at the Board mousing to catch something beneficial to himself, while they wanted a director who would accept office to benefit the bank. A man ought to watch his own interest, when conducting his own affairs, but when he is acting officially, he should lose himself in his public duties. We expect a soldier to sacrifice his life, if necessary, to the discharge of his duty, and we should condemn him for professing a less self-denying creed, how much soever our knowledge of human fallibility might induce us to pardon his short-comings, when death should obstruct his path. Fortunately the performance of bank duties will peril only some forbearance from pecuniary acquisitions, and our creed ought to be self-denying enough to renounce these, instead of avowing them to be the motive of our services; nor is the principle new. The law will not permit a trustee to derive any indirect benefit from his trust, or any judge or juror to decide in his own controversies; and the State of New York has, in its Constitution, consecrated the principle, by prohibiting our legislators from regulating their own compensation, or even the number of days which shall be occupied in legislative duties. In some cities, also, no civic officer can become legally interested in any municipal contract; and who censures not some recent high officers of our National Government, for participating in a private claim, which they officially aided in adjusting and paying. Thus thinking, the president of a large railroad corporation of New York refused to supply iron for his road, though his associate directors, with the complaisance which is as vicious as it is common, offered him the contract. In this case, no contractor could have been more eligible, but the rejector established a precedent that is more profitable for his corporation than the money it would have saved in purchasing the iron of him.

The remuneration of bank directors, consists, too often, in an indefinite claim for bank loans. This claim led formerly to so great an absorption of the funds of country banks, whose capitals are small, that a law was enacted by the New York Legislature interdicting bank directors* from engrossing, directly or indirectly, more than a third part of the capital of their respective banks; a quota which is, in some banks, divided equally among the directors, irrespective of any business merits of the borrower.† This mode of compensation, when founded on ample security for the borrowed money, and when the amount taken, directly or indirectly, is limited to the legal quota, may, in small banks, constitute a less objectionable mode of remunerating directors than any other indirect mode, or than most other direct modes. A man may, however, very properly refuse the office of bank director, unless he can obtain for his services a satisfactory pecuniary compensation; and banks must comply with such a requirement, if suitable men are not otherwise obtainable; but such a contingency promises to be remote, under the desire for accidental distinctions by our citizens, consequent, probably, on their legal equality. But when such a contingency shall occur, a direct compensation will generally be purer than any indirect, and a definite compensation cheaper than an indefinite; and usually money is the most economical mode of paying for services that are not to be deemed honorary.

The law usually regards bank directors as an entirety under the title of a Board. The duties and powers which are usually conferred on the board by the National and State laws may be classed as legislative, supervisory, and appointing. The legislative power consists in creating such offices as the business of the bank shall render necessary, regulating their duties and salaries; directing the modes in which the bank shall be conducted, and generally all that pertains to the management of the stock, property, and effects of the corporation. The appointing power consists in selecting proper incumbents for the created offices; while the supervisory power is indicated by all the foregoing, and by the ability to dismiss the appointees at pleasure. But a man cannot properly supervise

---

* This law, like most other legal regulations of bank directors, was made before the existence of banking associations; hence the directors of such associations are not included therein.

† The National Banking Law limits the amount that may be loaned to any applicant. See Chapter III.

himself in the performance of public services, nor limit and regulate their scope and extent, nor fix his compensation therefor; hence the powers of the board can be exercised efficiently only on persons who are not members of the board. Nor is the inexpediency of uniting in the same person the duties of grantor and grantee, master and servant, agent and principal, a contrivance of man; it proceeds from his organization. No person can sit at a board of directors without observing that agents who are not directors, are supervised more freely than agents who are directors. A practical admission of this is evinced by some discount boards, who, in deciding on paper offered by directors, vote by a species of ballot, while in other boards, the offered notes are passed under the table, from seat to seat; and a note is deemed rejected, if, in its transit, some director has secretly folded down one of its corners. Had the United States Bank been supervised by a board disconnected from executive duties, it would not have permitted its chief officer to persevere in the measures which ultimately ruined the corporation, though its capital was thirty-five millions of dollars. Even the separation of a legislature into two chambers, checks the *esprit du corps*, and pride of opinion which would urge one chamber into extremes, with no means of extrication from a false position. A separation operates like the break of continuity in an electric telegraph, arresting a common sympathy, passion, or prejudice, which, in a single chamber, rushes irresistibly to its object. Still, in many banks (the Bank of England included) the president (entitled governor in the Bank of England) is the chief executive officer, as well as head of the legislative department. The Bank of England is, however, controlled by twenty-four directors, the largeness of which number naturally mitigates the influence of the members individually, and hence diminishes ratably the objection against its executive organization. Such an organization may operate well, where the board consists of a small number of members, yet the good is not a consequence of the organization, but in despite thereof; for, whatever weakens the power of supervision, must diminish its benefits. The joint-stock banks of England are all controlled by officers called managers, and who are not members of the board, though they sit thereat *ex officio* for mutual explanation and instruction.

That the board should legislate, supervise and appoint, but not execute, occasioned probably the exclusion from the directorship that early prevailed, and widely continues, of the person who occupies the office of cashier, and who, with us, was once almost universally the chief executive bank officer. But the executive power, located, should center in only one person; a divided responsibility creating necessarily a divided vigilance. Thirteen men acting as an executive will not produce the vigilance of one man multiplied by thirteen, but rather the vigilance of one man divided by thirteen. The inspection of a picture by ten thousand promiscuous men will not detect as many imperfections in it as the scrutiny of one person, intent on discovering to the extent of his utmost vigilance; hence, large assemblies refer every investigation to a small committee, the chairman of which is expected to assume the responsibility of the examination, while the other members are more supervisors than actors. Here, again, as in most other modes which business assumes by chance apparently, our organization dictates the mode. When, therefore, we want an army of the highest efficiency, we possess no alternative but to intrust it to a single commander-in-chief; and if we want a bank of the highest efficiency, as respects safety and productiveness, we must intrust it to a single executive, under any title we please; but to one man, who will make the bank the focus of his aspirations, and know that on his prudence and success will depend the character he most affects, and the duration of his office, with all its valued associations and consequences.

If the proposed organization is the best that can be devised for a bank, the magnitude of power to be delegated is no proper argument against its delegation, but only a motive for prudence in selecting the delegate. A man of known skill and established fidelity is not always procurable for the proposed duties, especially by small banks that cannot render available a breach of the tenth commandment. But, providentially, the world is not so dependent on a few eminent men, as their self-love and our idolatry may believe. Every well-organized person possesses an aptitude to grow to the stature of the station in which circumstances may place him, and some of the most successful bankers of our State acquired their skill after they became bankers. The like principle is discoverable in all occupations, the highest not excepted. Few of our judges, generals, diplomatists, legislators, or civil executives were accomplished in their vocation before they became invested therewith. Skill is consequent in some degree to station and its excitement, though a vulgar error expects (what is impossible) that official dexterity and competence should be possessed in advance.

On the chief executive should be devolved the responsibility of providing funds to meet the exigencies of the bank; hence, he is entitled to dictate whether loans shall be granted or withheld, and the length of credit that shall be accorded to the borrowers respectively. With him rests also a knowledge of the banking value of each customer; he should, therefore, be permitted to select from applicants the persons to whom alone loans shall be granted. The responsibility should also be cast on him of making the bank pecuniarily profitable to the stockholders; hence, he will be stimulated to obtain good accounts, and to extend business to the utmost capacity that his judgment will justify. On his untiring vigilance should be reposed the safety of the capital; hence, no loans should be granted with whose security he is dissatisfied, nor any except those with which he is satisfied—even the improper negation of a loan being usually a small evil to the bank, how important soever it may be to the proposer. The Bank of England, with a capital of about (including surplus) $90,000,000, intrusts the loaning thereof to the governor alone. He has under him a sub-governor, selected from the directors, while an executive committee, designated by the board, may be consulted by him; but the committee employs itself in digesting matters for the action of the court of directors, rather than in clogging the proceedings and diminishing the discretion of the governor. All the joint-stock banks of England are organized with a like self-depending executive, under the name of general manager, and a bank organized thus to grant loans at all times, during its business hours, will present a great inducement to customers over a bank whose discounts are accorded at only stated days, and after a protracted deliberation by directors—loans being often useful only when obtained promptly. Even the due protesting of dishonored paper, and notifying of endorsers—the enforcement of payment, or the obtainment of security on debts which prove to be unsafe, will all wholesomely fall under the control of the chief executive, by reason that the vigilance of one person can control them better than a divided vigilance; and that the debts having come into the bank by his agency, his self-love is interested in their collectability. He must feel a like responsibility against losses by forgery, overdrawn accounts, the depredation of burglars, and the peculation of subalterns. To secure in the highest degree his vigilance in these particulars, he should be intrusted with the selection of all subordinate agents, even of the notary and attorneys. At least none should be appointed or retained with whom he is not satisfied. His self-respect cannot be too much fostered by the board, and no measure should be enforced, and no loans granted, which can wound his sensibility, or diminish his influence with his subordinates or the customers of the bank. The more he can thus be brought to identify himself with the bank, the more the bank will be exempt from the disadvantages which make corporations contrast unfavorably with private establishments, and which a proverb alludes to in saying that what is every man's business is nobody's. So great is the assimilation to their bank which some managers attain, that a poignancy of solicitude in relation to the debts of the bank, the preservation of its credit and the productiveness of its capital become the greatest evils of their position, especially when they are predisposed to morbid nervousness, which, with disease of the heart, their position induces and fosters. Such a man will obtain from his board all the information it can yield him in relation to the pecuniary responsibility of his dealers; and the directors should give him their opinion—not mandatory, to relieve his responsibility, but to inform his judgment, though he will soon discover that his only safe guide will consist of his feelings founded on personal observations too subtle often to be described, much less enumerated.

His salary should be liberal, for nature will not otherwise produce the activity of mind and body that are essential to his duties. Besides, he must engage in no private business, and will possess neither leisure nor taste to attend minutely to his domestic expenses. No salary can equal in value the devotion of such an officer; still, extravagance is unwise as an example, and unnecessary as a stimulant. The more capable the officer, the more he will appreciate money, and instances are frequent where bank services of the most valuable kind are accorded on salaries that would be deemed unsatisfactorily small by officers whose habits are less suited for the station.

The duties of a board will rather commence than end with the appointment of its executive. Their proper duties are supervisory. Nature aids the discharge of such duties when the supervisor is distinct from the supervised; indeed, one of the most difficult tasks of a supervisor consists in restraining the undue captiousness that is natural to the position. The president of the bank, as head of the corporation, cannot perform supervisory duties too efficiently, and he may well be entitled to a pecuniary compensation therefor. He should deem them under his special charge, but not to supersede therein the modified duties of the other directors. Supervision over the manager's official proceedings will be as salutary to him as proper to the board. Darkness is proverbially unfavorable to purity, but only by reason of the concealment it creates; every other means of concealment is equally productive of impurity. A man can easily reconcile to his judgment and conscience what cannot be reconciled to disinterested supervisors: hence, if an officer knows so little of human nature as to deem supervision offensive, he is unfit to be trusted. That the supervision may be full, it must be systematic. Every director will usually attend meetings of the board in a degree inverse to their frequency, but twice a week, or certainly once, where the bank is not very small, will be as short as is compatible with a due inspection, singly, of the loans, in some regular order, that may have been granted by the manager since the last session of the board. The directors will thus learn individually whether the power to make loans has been prudently exercised; and he will learn the opinion which any of the board may express in relation to the borrowers or their sureties, especially in cities where borrowers are generally known to the board; and a manager may advantageously defer to it the consummation of many loans in relation to which his own information is questionable, or about which he desires time to deliberate. Such a deferring will often constitute a less offensive mode of avoiding an objectionable discount than a direct and personal refusal, though truly the kindest act a banker can perform, next to granting a loan, is to promptly inform an applicant that he cannot succeed, when the banker knows the loan will not be granted.

The supervision of the board must be as comprehensive as the powers of the manager. The revisions of loans will enable the board to ascertain, not merely the solvency of the bank's assets, but whether its business is conducted without partiality, or unwholesome bias of any kind. Nearly every undue partiality possesses concomitants that may lead to its detection; for instance, an unusual laxity of security, or length of credit; with unusual frequency of renewals in a direct form, or an indirect, so as to screen the operations. A manager, properly sensitive of his reputation, and properly diffident of his natural infirmities, will be reluctant to grant loans to his relatives, or special friends; and never to himself, or any person with whose business operations he is connected. To enable directors to judge of these particulars, a regular attendance at the stated meetings is necessary; but memory alone must not be relied on, except to suggest queries, which should always be capable of solution by proper books and indexes, that must be within reach of the directors; who should habitually inspect the books, that the practice may, in no case, seem an invidious peculiarity. In all scrutinies, however, the directors should remember that in mere judgment and expediency they may differ from the manager, and he may still be right, for banking constitutes his business, while to them it is an incidental occupation. Lenity is proper even to his undoubted errors, when they are of a nature which experience may correct; but time will only inveterate bad intentions, and their first unequivocal appearance should produce an unrelenting forfeiture of his office.

The board must understand the liabilities of the bank to its depositors, bank-note holders, and other creditors; also the funds of the bank, and its available resources; so as to judge how far the honor of the bank is safe in the care of its manager. The character of depositors and borrowers are also proper subjects of general scrutiny by the board, by reason that the reputation of a bank is inferable from the reputation of its dealers; not that disreputable people should be rejected as depositors, but a bank is not an exception to the proverb which speaks "of birds of a feather;" and when the customers of a bank are generally respectable in their character and business, we may be sure that the management of the bank is at least ostensibly moral and mercantile.

The ticklers of a bank are books which show in detail the debts due, prospectively to a bank, and the days of payment. The aggregate footing of the ticklers will accordingly exhibit the amount of loans not yet matured, and inductively the amount that is past due. The information which relates to the amount past due is often given reluctantly, but a knowledge of it is vastly important in the proper supervision of a bank; and when tested by the ticklers, the information cannot well be deceptious, or evaded. In knowing the amount of past due loans, the board can pretty accurately conjecture the character of the bank's customers. Such loans should be satisfactorily explained by the manager, and the means he is taking in their collection. The like may be said of over-drafts,* which are rarely permitted by American bankers, though in England they seem to constitute one of the regular modes of advancing money to customers. Whether they shall be permitted is within the proper discretion of the board, and should they occur, inadvertently, the occurrence ought to be manifested to the board. An exemption from losses is impracticable in long-continued operations; yet all grades of intellect are procurable, hence the retention of an officer is unwise when his results are unsatisfactory. Every man can adduce excuses which no person may be able to controvert; but when miscarriages are frequent, or important, the board should assume that something wrong exists and eludes detection, rather than that nature deviates from her accustomed processes, making vigilance unsafe, and skill unprofitable.

The examination of vaults, and counting of money, rarely reveal defalcations, till the defaulter no longer endeavors to conceal his delinquencies. The counting is not pernicious, if the board choose to amuse their vigilance therewith; but we have not attempted to designate modes in which frauds are detectable; the ingenuity of concealment being naturally as great as the ingenuity of detection. Besides, the detection of skillful frauds requires a greater familiarity with banking accounts, and a more laborious inspection of bank books, than can ordinarily be expected of bank directors. For the detection of frauds, therefore, the best practical reliance is a supervision, in the way we have indicated, of the bank's business, and a familiar observation of the general conduct, habits and expenses of the manager, as well as of all the subordinate officers; the latter, however, are more especially within the duties of the manager. The ruin of a bank, by fraud, commences usually in the personal embarrassment of the delinquent, contracted by improper self-indulgences, or the assumption of secret hazards. Men rarely plunder till their conduct is otherwise disorganized, external symptoms of which observant directors may discover. A bank officer, therefore (and the higher his official position the more urgent the

* The term "over-draft" means that the depositor has drawn for more money than the balance to his credit.

rule), who will not keep disengaged from all suretyship and from business that may render him pecuniarily necessitous, is as unfit to be intrusted with a bank, as a nurse who frequents small-pox hospitals, is unfit to be trusted with unvaccinated children. In menageries, animals are kept peaceful by preventing the cravings of hunger; bank executives require a similar assuasive; not by glutting them with great salaries, but by preserving them from expenditures unsuited to their income, and from pecuniary liabilities. A bank manager of undoubted wealth presents therein the best attainable guaranty against misconduct, and is entitled to greater freedom of action in his personal transactions than officers of ordinary circumstances; still we will terminate this first part of our undertaking, by venturing the advice, that when a man wants to be more than a bank manager, especially when he wants to employ much more than his own funds, he had better cease from occupying a station which he is too ambitious, or too avaricious to fill under restraints, which experience shows are alone safe.

We shall now consider the function performed by a bank in discounting paper. First, however,* it is necessary to say a few words respecting *capital*, since it is from the peculiar use made of capital, in the production and distribution of wealth, that the necessity for banks arises.

Capital used in production, is either *fixed* or *floating*. Fixed capital is invested in lands, buildings, machinery, mines, canals, railways and their equipments, telegraphs, &c., all these being used in the creation and distribution of wealth. Floating capital is invested in the things produced, whether raw materials, or articles completed, or in process of completion. It also pays for the labor and other service (wages and salaries) necessary to production and to the distribution of products. The processes of production are very numerous and distinct. Each producer, when he has completed his part of these processes, desires to sell his product, realize his profit, and begin again with fresh materials. The quicker he can do this, and the oftener he can repeat it, the greater will be his profit; for, in a normal state of things, each repetition brings a profit. All the floating capital which he requires is enough to enable him to do this easily, and without friction. If each article were sold for cash, as soon as completed, and no store of raw materials had to be kept in excess of immediate wants, the minimum of floating capital would be attained; and if the fairly estimated profit were always realized, the wealth of the producer would be constantly increasing, and his business might either be enlarged, or a surplus safely withdrawn for outside uses. But immediate sale of products by the producer, and immediate payment for them by the

* This portion of the chapter, to page 58, is from the pen of George Walker, concerning whom proper mention is made in the preface of this work.

buyer, are practically impossible. A long process of digestion must be gone through with before ultimate payment and the final payer (who is the consumer) are reached; and consequently the producer cannot immediately sell, aud the buyer cannot immediately pay. Markets may be dull, or overstocked, and buyers may be either slow to come forward, or come without ready money. Hence, the producer requires additional floating capital to carry his products till sold; and the buyer requires credit till he can get the means to pay for the property bought by its resale. But a sale on credit is to the producer, so far as the use of capital is concerned, precisely like carrying the property without sale. Till he gets back the value of his production, he must depend on other means to carry on his business. He must find the necessary capital elsewhere, or his production stops till payment by the buyer enables him to start again. But a healthy business cannot stop; it must go on constantly and evenly, if the highest economy is to be attained. Stoppage means idle factories, rusting machinery, unemployed workmen. The friction and loss incident to stopping and starting would eat up a large profit, and would destroy the even current of production upon which stability of prices largely depends. The producer cannot stop; he must from some source, get the money to go on with, and fortunately his business furnishes the basis on which to get it. *He must borrow money on the faith of the property sold.* He cannot, it is true, pledge the property specifically, for he has sold it and parted with possession, and hence, I say, he must borrow on the *faith* and not on the *pledge* of it. But though he cannot pledge the property itself, he pledges what represents it, namely, the written promise of the buyer to pay the price of it at a fixed future date. In mercantile language, he gets the buyer's note or bill discounted, and *here comes in the first legitimate function of the bank, a function which underlies all its operations, and is the touchstone of the regularity of its business.*

To reduce it to a definition or formula, I should say that the first and most important function of a bank is, by the use of the capital which it controls, to bridge over the periods of credit which necessarily intervene between production and consumption, in such a manner as to give back to each producer, or middleman, as quickly as possible, the capital invested by him in such products, in order that he may use it over again in new production or new purchases. In this way the interruption of business, which would be a public, as well as a private loss, is avoided. Thus defined, banking is not only one of the most useful, but it is also one of the most safe and healthy of business operations. Its safety lies in the fact that every loan of the character described, is based on property of intrinsic value; and it is *the property* which, in the last resort, pays all the loans predicated upon it in its progress of transmission from the producer to the consumer. It gathers value as it goes, by the addition of all intervening profits incident to handling and resale, and on final sale the consumer pays the first cost and all those profits added to it. This, of course, is on the supposition that the transactions have been fairly profitable. In the case supposed the property has been the real debtor throughout, and the real payer of the discounts. It has purchased the paper which was the subject of each discount in succession, and has finally been exchanged with consumer for the cash which, in effect, pays them all. The several makers of the paper, though debtors in form, are only insurers, or guarantors, in fact. They pledge their respective property to the payment of the loans; but the primary and generally sufficient pledge is the property for which the notes are given. The wealth of the makers is a necessary margin or guaranty, because the property sold may be destroyed, or the value may fall, or some one of its successive holders may, by misfortune or fraud, divert its proceeds from their legitimate application, namely, payment to the last seller. In a great majority of cases, however, no such contingency happens, and the guaranty is not resorted to. The intervening profits are an additional safeguard, inasmuch as each party, when he sells, ought to receive a larger note than he gave when he bought the goods.

From this analysis of the origin of bank discounts it will be seen that the common maxim among bankers—that the safest loans are on mercantile paper—is not only justified by experience, but rests upon the simplest and clearest scientific principles.

In the reign of the first Napoleon, France had a very enlightened finance minister in M. Mollien. In advising the emperor as to the proper administration of the Bank of France, Mollien laid great stress upon the principles which I have just enunciated. "He undertook to show that no discount is regular, except that of genuine bills of exchange, given in settlement of a completed transaction, in which three parties* have coöperated, and by means of which the acceptor is put in possession of property of actual value, equal to the amount of his acceptance."

"The discount of genuine bills of exchange, which represent the *products of labor*, which the wants of consumers have called into being, and which their savings are adequate to purchase, ought to be *exclusively* preferred by banks; it is the real pivot of their organization."

---

* The three parties are, the drawer, the payee, and the acceptor. When the buyer gives his note instead of a bill of exchange on a third party (as is more frequently the practice in certain parts of this country), the property is pledged indirectly, and only two parties engage in the transaction, while in the case of a bill drawn on the acceptor who is also the consignee of the property (as is the practice in the cotton, grain, and provision trades), the pledge is specific, and the paper is paid out of the proceeds of sale.

"He reproached the Bank of France with paying too little attention to the discounts of genuine bills of exchange guaranteed by merchandise in store, which was in demand for consumption, and which the income of the consumers was adequate to pay for."

Keeping in mind the definition already given, and which I now repeat, that the true function of banking is to bridge over the periods of credit which necessarily intervene between production and consumption, by immediately advancing on the faith of the property, to each producer and middleman, his capital invested in the product, and his profit earned in producing or handling it, it is easy to analyze and to test all loans and discounts of a different sort which banks are in the habit of making. The loans which come the nearest in principle to those embraced in the definition, are such as are made upon the specific pledge of property although not yet sold. These may be strictly legitimate, or highly speculative, according to circumstances. When property is on its way to a market, with the certainty or probability of early sale, according to a well established course of trade, it is strictly legitimate to loan upon it, if the loan is made with a proper margin. Of this character are all bills of exchange drawn against produce or merchandise, consigned for sale, either in the home or foreign market. If accompanied by a specific pledge of the property, they are called *documentary bills*, because the title is authenticated by bills of lading, and protected by policies of insurance, which accompany the paper. The merchandise is sold "for account of whom it may concern," that is to say, for account of the bill holder first, and of the owner of the property afterwards. A very large part of the grain, produce, cotton and tobacco business of this country is transacted by means of documentary bills. They have often little else than the value of the property to depend upon, the drawers and acceptors being only middlemen, or factors of small responsibility. If the property is of a staple character, always salable at a price, and the advances are sufficiently below its value, such bills make very desirable paper, for the reasons already given that they do not depend on the solvency or even the good faith of the parties, the property itself, authenticated by its title deeds, being the real security. Foreign bankers make their profit very largely in buying documentary bills at one rate and selling their own plain bills at a higher rate; but it requires large capital and established credit to make a market for bankers' bills. In recent years the margin of profit has been very small, and the liability incurred in making it is immense, as both the bills purchased and those sold have to bear the banker's signature. Foreign bills are not usually dealt in by American bankers, except in the Southern cities, where cotton and tobacco are often consigned directly to a foreign market. The same is probably true to some extent in the grain-handling cities of the West and in

California. It hardly pays to discount foreign bills and send them abroad for collection and remittances of proceeds. To deal profitably in them, a bank must draw exchange, as well as buy it, and the business of drawing is almost exclusively in the hands of private bankers, and of the representatives of European or Canadian banks. It has always been a surprise to many that some of the larger New York banks have never competed for this business. They possess in a high degree the most important qualifications necessary to a good drawer of exchange. They have an adequate known capital, make and publish periodical reports, are examined by official experts, and are conservatively managed by officers and directors conspicuous for their wealth, experience and probity. Some of them have existed for a long time, and have acquired that wide-spread reputation which is a first requisite in a drawer of foreign bills. Such a participation in foreign business on the part of the incorporated banks would have this further advantage, that the banking of this country would be thus allied more closely with the banking and financial operations of the rest of the world. At present there is too great ignorance of, and too little regard paid to, what is going on in the monetary world abroad. It is not considered a necessary part of an American banker's education to study foreign banking and finance, and, as a consequence, all the profit which the banking business should properly derive from foreign commerce, is turned over to private individuals, largely foreigners, or to the representatives of more sagacious and cosmopolitan foreign institutions. One obstacle to engaging in foreign banking, by the incorporated banks, is the great subdivision of capital, and the smallness of the amount controlled by any one institution.

Besides loans on specific property consigned for sale, banks often lend on property withheld from market for a better price. Such withholding is, of course, speculative, and the loans are more or less tainted with that quality. They are not always to be condemned, but they should be made with great caution, and not relied upon to meet the bank's immediate liabilities. Enough available means should always be held in cash, and in perfectly reliable short paper, certain to be paid at maturity, to cover circulation and deposits. Capital and surplus, when not absorbed in Government bonds (as is largely the case with that of the National banks), may be lent on longer and less convertible security. Convertibility, however, is the first requisite in the collaterals to a loan.

The moment such collaterals are inadequate to protect the loan by a forced sale, the debt becomes unsafe. The objection to loans on property not sold, or consigned for sale, is that they have no natural maturity, and however ample the collaterals, they are essentially accommodation loans, and have often to be inconveniently prolonged. The test of soundness in a bank is the speed with which it could liquidate, and return its capital to stockholders.

If loans and discounts could be kept within the limits which have been described, banking would be a very safe and easy business; but it is nearly impossible to avoid a class of transactions of a far more questionable character; and when banks fail, or lose heavily, it is almost always because questionable loans have become the rule, instead of the exception, in their business. The quality of convertibility has been gradually lost sight of (usually in the greedy pursuit of high rates of interest), and, little by little, the assets have become tied up in a harder and harder knot. Commonest among objectionable loans are those on personal security, and accommodation paper without collaterals; such as is not the outgrowth of any business transaction, out of the completion and fruition of which, the means of payment will be derived. Loans made for the purchase or improvement of real estate, whether productive or speculative; loans to provide quick capital for corporations, or for individual business, are not only very objectionable, but unfortunately also very common. However strongly fortified by names, they are always reluctantly paid, and often the cause of anxiety and trouble. It is entirely outside of the province of legitimate banking to furnish money for such purposes. Investments should be the result of savings, and it is very unwise, either for an individual to anticipate his savings by loans at short maturity, or for a bank to help him to do so. So of quick capital; I have shown that all business requires it, and it should be greater or less according to the business. It is the margin which protects from disaster, and guarantees success. It is no part of a bank's business to lend that margin. By so doing, it takes on itself the risk which belongs to the customer, and which is the strongest incentive to prudence. Its duty to him, and its proper relation to his business, begin and end with turning his products into cash, as soon as they are sold—converting his credit sales into cash sales, and thus reducing the necessary amount of his floating capital or margin, without assuming to provide that margin.

A class of loans which has done more than any other to bring our banking institutions to grief, within the last twenty years, is that on railroad bonds. It is very pertinent, in spite of all that has been said and written about it, and while the experience is fresh and painful, to point out the reason why such loans were disastrous, and to indicate the inherent quality which made them so. This leads us to say a few words about commercial, or rather financial, crises, and the steps which lead to them. The soundest maxims and practices prevail in the business world after a crisis and liquidation. Convalescence and repentance go hand in hand, the world over. When business is fairly resumed, in the good time now coming, we shall see every class of business men proceeding with the greatest caution. Miners and manufacturers will be careful not to overstock the market; merchants will sell on short credit, and scrutinize the means and character of their customers; banks will keep their money in the till, rather than make doubtful loans; investors will be content with a low rate of interest, so long as the security is undoubted; speculation and the speculator will be read out of all decent society, and the men who get up pools and corners will be avoided by all who need credit and are careful of their reputation. Contentment, economy, and good morals will prevail, and for a time we shall constitute a model society. But by and by we shall tire of too much virtue; the wheels of industry and exchange will move more rapidly, competition will be sharper, accumulating profits will encourage more luxurious living, luxury will multiply wants faster than the increase of means, higher profits will be demanded and greater risks will be assumed to realize them; speculation, which is oftener the offspring of artificial wants than of the love of gambling for its own sake, will take the place of slow and plodding industry. This will be the progress of things in one direction. A progress more potential and not less dangerous will, at the same time, go on in another. Capital accumulates more rapidly in prosperous seasons, than the chances which offer for its employment. Surpluses accumulate, and with them the channels of investment widen. The first use of a surplus is to increase reproductive capital; but there is a limit to the use of such capital. To augment it too rapidly would lead to over-production and over-trading, and these will inevitably occur before capital consents to seek remoter and slower resting places. But seek them ultimately it must and ought, for otherwise civilization would cling to its old centers, and the extremities would never be opened up or enriched. This process involves the conversion of floating into fixed capital, or to use the more expressive European phrase, the *immobilization* of capital. Capital arising from the profits of business, and invested in lands, buildings, factories, railways, mines and furnaces, is thus immobilized. The degree of immobilization is greater or less, according as the resulting revenue from the investment is more or less remote. If a quick return is yielded, and that return does not involve over-production, the proceeding is wise and healthy. If, on the other hand, the return is uncertain, or very remote, there is great danger that capital, instead of being immobilized merely, may be absolutely lost. It is rarely possible to compute with accuracy the cost of a great undertaking, or foretell the period of its fruition. The disposition to spread present means over a great deal more ground than it can fairly fructify, is as universal as the disposition among farmers to cultivate too much land.

Now, let us apply these principles to our past railway constructions. The two dangerous elements to which we have adverted, speculation seeking illegitimate profits, and surplus capital driven to seek remote investments, coöperated to make it what it was. Men without capital did most of the speculating, men with more capital than they knew how to employ profitably furnished the means. But the means available proved to be sadly inadequate to the undertaken schemes. It became soon apparent, in almost all cases, that to save the *surplus* first invested, the *capital*, vital to business, must be encroached on. Thus, little by little, the working capital of the country—not its savings, but its life—was drawn into the fatal vortex. This working capital is like the grease which greases the wheels of the farmer's wagon. If not seasonably supplied, the heated axle utters its notes of alarm, and if this goes unheeded, the wheel is set fast and the vehicle is stopped. The wholesale construction of railways on credit was a business of which the country had no experience, and this is the only excuse for the gross violation of sound business principles which it involved. The banks were no wiser than the people. They began to lend moderately, on the security of railway bonds, before railways had been discredited, and when they had a surplus of capital to lend; and they ended by lending immoderately on the same security, after its treacherous character had been disclosed, in the vain struggle to save their past loans, or to assist customers whom they were unwilling to see go to the wall. Very largely, also, in 1871-2, and '73, they lent to railways, on railway securities, for the sake of illegitimate interest, by which we mean not such rates as merely violate the usury laws, but such as no healthy business ever did or ever can pay. They were lending to a spendthrift heir on the doubtful security of a post-obit bond. There is no danger that this folly will be repeated in our time, but there are always snares set for the unwary, and the next decade will doubtless disclose its own peculiar temptations, and a period of prosperity will hardly escape the usual dismal ending.

The regular meetings of Boards of Directors in most banks are held twice a week, but in some banks meetings are held daily. The mode of discounting paper varies much in different banking institutions. In many of them, especially in the larger cities, the business head, whether he be the president, vice-president or cashier passes on the paper as soon as it is offered for discount. Customers cannot wait, money is wanted, and they are speedily told whether they can be accommodated or not. But with the country banks a different custom prevails. The paper is offered for discount and is put before the directors, and they decide whether to accept or to decline it. The president of a very profitable bank in New York City once said to the writer, that after his bank had been in existence for ten years it had lost only three pieces of paper, and these were discounted by the board during his absence. He loaned the money, and the directors at their meetings merely ratified the loans made. A board is a very convenient body for referring paper which an officer is unwilling to accept. He does not wish to offend the offerer by declining to discount it, and so it is referred to the board for their action. This is the least offensive way of telling a man that he cannot be accommodated. Of course, many cases are referred to the board for their action which may be decided favorably. The amounts may be very large, or there may be something peculiar about the loans, a longer time than is usually granted perhaps may be wanted, and the cashier or president may not wish to assume the sole responsibility. When banks hold daily meetings the directors decide what paper shall be discounted.

In order to have a correct knowledge of dealers' accounts, the cashier has on his desk a book which contains a record of the average daily balance of every dealer. This is made up at the end of each month, and the average for the month is entered in the Average Book. At the end of the year the average for the twelve months is struck, and usually the Average Book is so ruled as to show the daily average for five to ten years previously. The Average Book is indexed throughout on the margin, with as many leaves as are required for each letter. The names of National banks are usually entered first, alphabetically, then State banks, then bankers, and then the individual depositors from A to Z. Usually there is a new Average Book for each year.

The amount of discounts usually granted to a dealer (the bank's safety, of course, first being assured) is proportionate with his average balances. For example, a dealer whose general average balance is $15,000 would be entitled to accommodation, other things being the same, to five times as large a line as a dealer with an average balance of $3,000. Hence a correctly kept Average Book is an important guide in granting discounts.

Good banking requires a bank to be in a condition to meet every dealer's reasonable needs in proportion to his balances, irrespective of the current condition of the money market.

At Directors' meetings the president is seated at the head of the table, and the cashier occupies a convenient seat near him. In some banks the directors have particular chairs, in others no order of arrangement is observed. The cashier reads the minutes of the previous meeting of the board, and after their approval the board proceeds to other business. The cashier records the names of the directors present, as this fact is worth preserving. The business transacted since the last meeting, as previously stated, consisting of the discounting of paper on the responsibility of the bank manager, is submitted for ratification. Banking institutions are not always so particular as they ought to be in doing this, or in examining the paper taken.

When the wrong practices of Eno, the president of the Second

National Bank of New York, were discovered, it was found that not only did he discount paper on his sole responsibility, but kept it in a vault down town, not belonging to the bank, and the directors never saw it. They accepted his statement of what he did as true, and never troubled themselves to look at the paper discounted. Had this been done, Eno would have been obliged to resort to some other artifice to conceal his fraud; or, what is quite probable, could not have gone so far as he did, without exciting suspicion leading to his detection.

Vigilance is the price of prosperity, and this applies more emphatically to banking than to almost any other kind of busi-

Daily Statement, ...188

	Monday.	Tuesday.	Wed.
Bills discounted............			
Temporary loans............			
U. S. bonds with Treasurer to secure circulation..........			
Other Stocks and Bonds and Mortgages........			
N. Y. Clearing-house Association bonds........			
Sundry securities.........			
Total loans.........			
Legal-tender notes........			
Specie—Gold certificates........			
" Clearing-house certificates........			
" coin........			
Silver coin........			
Arctic National bank notes........			
Notes of other National banks........			
Exchanges for Clearing-house........			
Total cash.........			
Expenses........			
Interest........			
Premiums........			
Taxes paid........			
Exchange........			
Total expenses, &c........			
Real estate, banking house........			
Other Real Estate........			
Deposit with U. S. Treasurer, 5 per cent. fund........			
Due from U. S. Treasurer, Redemption Agent........			
Due from banks........			
Total footings.........			
Memoranda—Legal-tender notes........			
Specie........			
5 per cent. fund and redemptions........			
Total reserve........			
Reserve required........			

ness. No bank manager, however long and ably he may have served a bank, ought to be permitted to conduct its affairs without supervision. Directors who do not direct occupy a false position toward the public, the depositors, the stockholders and the bank manager. The welfare of the several classes concerned in the institution demand that these officials should not neglect their duties.

Before proceeding to discount paper, it is necessary to know what resources a bank has available for that purpose. This information is contained in a Statement from the General Ledger. The following form is copied from the Daily Statement Book of a bank in New York City:

Arctic National Bank of the City of New York.

	Monday.	Tuesday.	Wed.
Capital stock.............................			
Surplus fund.............................			
Profit and loss...........................			
Discount................................			
Interest.................................			
Exchange...............................			
Rents collected..........................			
Total profits........................			
National circulation outstanding...........			
Dividends unpaid.........................			
Individual deposits A to —			
" " — to —			
" " — to Z................			
Certified checks..........................			
Total individual deposits.............			
Banks and bankers' deposits A to —			
" " " — to —			
" " " — to Z.........			
Afternoon mail...........................			
Total banks and bankers' deposits......			
Total footings........................			
Memoranda—Gross deposits			
(*Daily*) Net deposits.................			
Weekly average—Loans and discounts........			
Specie.............................			
(*Reported Saturdays* Legal-tender notes....			
to Deposits.......................			
Clearing-House.) Circulation			

The items are read, or the principal ones, and afterward the offerings, consisting of notes on which the owners are desirous of obtaining money of the bank. Instead, however, of reading these, a record, previously made in a book called an Offering Book, is read to the directors. In this book the names of the offerers are recorded alphabetically, the amount of each note, the time it is to run, the name of the indorser, where payable, and any other particulars relating to it. In small banks the notes offered are read without regard to alphabetical order.

If the amount of offerings exceeds the amount of loanable funds of course not all can be accommodated, even if their notes be desirable. But rarely does it happen when any considerable amount of paper is offered that it possesses a uniform value. Some makers or indorsers are better known, and are preferred to others. What, therefore, happens, is to select from the entire amount offered the most desirable offerings, and to decline the remainder. Yet, often the entire amount offered is not enough to absorb all the loanable funds. Then the bank must look elsewhere to find a way for employing its resources. One way is to buy paper, though in buying it the board may pass on the transaction the same as would be done if offered in the usual way for discount. This business of buying paper is worth a brief explanation.

It is purchased by a bank of a note-broker. But where does he get such paper to sell? Of merchants. Formerly they gave notes only for the merchandise they bought, but in recent times they give notes without reference to the purchase of any special merchandise, in order with the money thus obtained to discount their bills.

Once when notes were for a longer period, and notes were almost universally given for purchases, they were generally drawn to the maker's order, and read for value received "from A B & Co.," or whoever the seller might be. Indeed, some houses were so careful lest the paper might be thought to be *made* paper that they inserted the name of the seller of the merchandise in full. This paper was sold largely in the "street" to banks and others, who bought it with confidence because it represented an actual business transaction. It suited commission houses and importers, because if not willing to hold the paper until maturity, they could realize upon it without the responsibility of endorsing it, and thus go on and sell to a house (whatever their own private opinion of its soundness might be) so long as the paper would sell at a rate of discount not interfering too much with the profit on the goods or the rate of commission. This, of course, was legitimate dealing, representing actual merchandise transactions. So, indeed, is the making and openly selling of one's paper in the market, and the using of the proceeds in "cashing" bills, legitimate, but it is dangerous and liable to abuses. Funds so obtained can be used for any purpose, and the developments in some recent failures have shown that the money was often used for operations entirely outside of the regular business of the maker, or for purely speculative purposes.

As merchants often sell their paper at six or seven per cent. interest, and discount their own bills at seven to nine per cent., of course they make two or three per cent. by borrowing the money for thus paying their bills in advance of their maturity. The broker gets a commission for negotiating the merchants' paper, which must be deducted from the profit of the transaction. After deducting this brokerage, however, there is a considerable profit from borrowing money as just described, and the business has become a very large one.

In some parts of the country, Hartford, Connecticut, for example, the banking capital is much larger than can be profitably employed locally. Providence is another place of the kind. The banks of those cities consequently invest large sums through note-brokers.

The following is the method of conducting the business in the largest cities. A printed or lithographed list of notes is sent to a bank. It may contain a description of a hundred pieces of paper and is marked "This is for bankers' use only." Each piece is numbered. If a bank wishes to see any of the pieces therein described, they are sent on application. There is another way, however, of negotiating such paper, which may be explained here. If a note-broker were selling all the paper given by a certain merchant, the broker would be very careful in offering it for sale. If a banker has twenty thousand dollars of it, for example, and the broker knows that he cannot increase the amount, he will be careful not to offer more. The broker would be equally careful not to put such paper on a printed list through fear that the banker would see it, and concluding that the merchant was giving a large amount of paper, would determine to buy no more. The banker, in other words, might conclude that the merchant was issuing more paper than he ought to issue if his name appeared very frequently on printed lists.

Sometimes the broker has the notes in his possession for sale; in other cases he has simply a memorandum of them. In the latter case he has a printed form, containing the name of the maker, amount, when and where payable, indorser, and other particulars. A list is sent to a bank containing such a description of notes, or a broker, or agent for him, may visit a bank personally and exhibit such a list, or the paper itself, which he wishes to negotiate. Many banks are visited several times a day by these brokers offering the notes of persons for sale.

It may be further added that brokers do not always get possession of the notes until they have paid for them. Several practices exist in this regard. One practice is for a merchant to make notes and then deliver them to a note-broker for sale. The latter may give a receipt or acknowledgment, or he may not. In such a case the merchant has entire confidence in the broker, otherwise he would not give him notes without adequate security. There are some very good reasons for thus leaving notes with a broker when perfect confidence is reposed in him. Very likely he has a class of customers, retired merchants, perhaps, who buy paper occasionally. They frequent his office, and, if he has notes which they can examine, may be led to purchase, whereas they would not do so if the broker had only a memorandum of the paper, and was obliged to send for it before he could sell it and get the money therefor. For this reason, therefore, sales are facilitated by entrusting the broker—and, in truth, vast amounts are left for sale. When Alonzo Follet, of New York, failed a few years since, he had in his office nearly $10,000,000 of notes, and the amount of paper that he had sold annually was about $100,000,000.

Another way is for merchants to leave their paper with a note-broker and get immediately from him a certain amount thereon. A merchant, for example, may leave $25,000 of paper and ask for $10,000, expecting the balance when the paper is sold. The note-broker pays him this advance on account, and after selling the paper and deducting his commission sends the balance.

Another way is for the note-broker to buy the paper, paying therefor at the time of the purchase. A note-broker will go to a merchant and say, "I will take so much of your paper at such a rate." If the rate be acceptable, the merchant will sell it to him and get his money. In these cases the broker expects to sell the paper at a lower rate, and to make more than he would if charging the ordinary commission. Many brokers do wholly a business of this kind—buying paper and selling it at the best rate they can obtain for it.

The broker's commission in the large cities is one-eighth of one per cent.; but for negotiating leather paper, as it is called, one-quarter of one per cent. is paid, and the same rate is paid on dry goods and on tea paper. The rate first named, however, is the most general one for negotiating notes.

In negotiating paper note-brokers sometimes endorse it. Follet, whom we have previously mentioned, guaranteed all the paper he sold, and thus became contingently liable for a very large amount. It was said at the time of his failure that the banks which bought it did not do so on his guarantee, but on the credit of the makers of the notes. A bank president at that time remarked, "If a man were to guarantee the note of the richest man in New York, he would be contingently liable for its payment, but the note would be valuable because the maker was responsible. Follet's transactions were very large, and he handled the paper of some of the best firms in the city. I presume the banks of the city are now buying a million dollars of paper a day from brokers, all bought because the maker is supposed to be good, and not because the broker endorses it."

It may be added that banks do not buy paper of the brokers in preference to discounting that of their depositors; but as we have previously said, these institutions are often unable to loan all their resources to persons who make a direct application for money. Banks must therefore either resort to the note-brokers, or loan in some other way.

This bought paper, as it is termed, is entered in a discount book, separate from the DEALERS' DISCOUNT BOOK, and for distinction the bought-paper book is called CASHIER'S DISCOUNTS. Cashier's Checks are given for the paper purchased, and each day the total payments of the CASHIER'S DISCOUNTS are credited to the "Cashier account" in the ledger. Each check when presented and paid is charged to cashier's account, which offsets the corresponding credit. Paper discounted for dealers is posted in a DEALERS' BILL BOOK, with a title page for each dealer. Paper purchased is posted in a CASHIER'S LEDGER, with a title page for each name on the strength of which the paper is bought, and both books, of course, are indexed. A reference to any name can therefore readily be had, and the amount on hand, if any, at once be ascertained.

The officers, therefore, may tell at a glance what, and how much of any name bought, they may have on hand. Many banks have lying on their president's desk a small book, the leaves of which are made of silicate slate, with two or three leaves for each letter of the alphabet. The names of paper purchased, with the due dates and amounts, are written in pencil on the appropriate pages, and the entries are corrected daily by erasures or additions, as the case may be.

Some banks have adopted a very perfect system of recording the information they obtain concerning the paper they buy. Books are prepared with a page or more devoted to each name. Here are recorded, briefly and succinctly, condensed extracts of mercantile agency reports, extracts from letters that may be received relating to the character and responsibility of the house in question, synopses of conversations with merchants, bankers, and others who have been found to know the firm, &c., &c. A voweled index affords means of speediest reference to any desired name.

Although the buying of paper has long been practiced by the banks, the Supreme Court of Minnesota, in 1872, declared that a bank which was authorized by statute "to carry on the business of banking by discounting notes, bills and other evidences of debt," had no authority to buy paper.* The custom of buying paper has not

* *Farmers and Mechanics' Bank* v. *Baldwin, Banker's Magazine*, vol. 31, p. 630, and see the same volume, p. 510, for a discussion of the subject.

been shaken in the least by this decision. It has been practiced too long and extensively to be overthrown by anything except a legislative enactment.

A common way of lending is on collateral security, that is, on bonds, stocks, warehouse receipts and other evidences of property. Within a few years the banks in the large cities have increased their loans of this nature enormously. They have done so partly because the purchase of paper from note-brokers has proved so hazardous. Within two years mercantile failures have occurred, from which some banks lost heavily in consequence of having large amounts of bought paper. One failure was that of a leather house, whose principal office was in Boston. The banks did not suppose before the failure that the house was floating such an enormous amount of paper. By making their notes, and giving them to note-brokers to sell, it was exceedingly difficult for others to form any judgment of the amount made and negotiated. After that failure, many banks concluded that if loans were made on collateral security their risk would be diminished. They believed that they were quite capable of judging accurately of the value of collaterals offered as security. Many of these loans are made on call, that is, the bank can demand payment immediately, or after one day's notice. Loans on railroad securities as collaterals are regarded with favor by some of the most conservative banks.

The New York Stock Exchange will not list any kind of stocks or bonds unless the instruments or evidences of them are engraved on steel plates. All railroad stocks are required to be issued at a transfer agency and registered at some well-known bank or trust company. This is to prevent a fraudulent over-issue of certificates. The principal New York City banks have the stock exchange telegraph quotations in their banking rooms, and therefore are promptly informed concerning the current fluctuations of the market. On such securities, loans are made usually within ten or fifteen per cent. of the market value. The fluctuations in these stocks thus pledged are carefully watched by a person in the bank, especially appointed for that purpose. It is his duty to demand either more security, or the payment of a part of a loan, in the event of a decline in the value of the security pledged therefor.

In some States, though the rule is not uniform, the law requires that for a collateral to be good security when delivered to the bank. stock must be actually transferred on the books of the company which first issued the same.

Another form of loan is that made on the security of business paper. Thus, a merchant having a number of small notes of his country customers, brings to the bank $15,000 or $20,000 of such paper, and asks, on the pledge of it, for a loan of $10,000, giving his own note at thirty, sixty or ninety days. This custom is more common in Western cities than in New York. It is among the safest of business transactions, if ordinary care and discrimination are observed, for if the principal should fail, his estate will pay something, and the division of the remainder among several parties, with a considerable surplus beyond the amount, leaves the risk of loss very small.

Such are the several ways of loaning the resources of a bank. It may be added, however, that fewer losses occur in loaning to regular dealers than in buying paper. Banks, of course, know more about their dealers than about other persons not keeping accounts with them.

If a single director objects to a note offered for discount or purchase, the board generally will refuse to make the loan. If an objection should be based simply on prejudice, the board probably would not respect it. But if a director should say, "I have a pretty good reason for not buying that paper," his opinion would be conclusive. Directors are chosen partly for the information which it is supposed they will throw on the condition of business, and especially on that in which they are engaged. It is supposed that a director knows more about the condition of persons engaged in the same business as himself, than the other directors, whose occupations are different. This is why their opinions have so much weight. Nevertheless, bank directors are not always disinterested in the performance of their trust. Not long since we heard the following story. A bank director, who was also a member of the Produce Exchange in a large city, attended a meeting of the directors of the bank. Several persons, who also were members of the Produce Exchange, had presented notes for discount, accompanied with collateral securities, principally warehouse receipts for grain. When these offerings were read, one after the other, the director in question objected, maintaining that they were not as safe as they ought to be. When the entire list of offerings had been exhausted, a large balance remained unemployed. The director just mentioned said if no better use could be made of it, he would take it though at a rate which was not very remunerative. His offer was accepted. Immediately he went to the persons who had applied for loans to his bank and loaned to them on the securities which they had offered. Of course he was not the typical bank director. Generally, directors are men of well-known integrity, and though too often neglectful in attending meetings, they freely give their best experience to the bank when they do attend.

Some directors attend meetings with regularity, and take a deep interest in the affairs of their bank. They seek to enlarge its sphere and to increase its gains. There are other directors whose presence is a surprise. A third class appear irregularly, and sometimes are troublesome in their endeavor to learn concerning all the business done at the meetings when they were not present. They are usually retained in spite of their ways for one reason or another. If they attended regularly, most of their questions would be unnecessary. Time would be saved, and the temper of their associates would not be tried. In a large board of twelve or fifteen directors it is hardly possible to have unanimity on all occasions, and yet each director may fill his valuable niche in the institution. Each one, whether pleasant or disagreeable, whether regular in his attendance or otherwise, may through his wealth, or business relations, or knowledge, serve a useful purpose. At all events, they are usually selected with care, and changes do not frequently occur.

It has been said by a banker whose experience is worth heeding that it is one of the duties of the president to protect a dealer when he is unjustly assailed. To do this is also for the advantage of the bank. Beside the general results of the fair treatment of credit, there is this particular result, that the best class of customers which a bank can have consists of those whom it has nurtured from moderate to larger success, and whose experience has been all along linked in agreeable intercourse with its officers and directors. These are not easily seduced to open accounts with other banks; but they are faithful to their old friends and they introduce other dealers.

The New York City banks do not discount paper that runs for a longer period than four months. This is the general rule. It is not always observed; but a man's credit would be unusually good, or ample collateral security would be required, were a loan granted for a longer period. Some banks will take only first-class double name paper, that is, paper having the name of an endorser beside the maker, and would prefer to buy such paper, at four and a-half or five per cent., to buying other paper just as good, perhaps, at six per cent. interest. In any event, a risk is taken, and with the utmost precaution in making loans losses are not wholly avoided.

One of the functions of a good bank manager is to ascertain, in every possible way, the financial condition of his customers. Every well-conducted bank has a book in which everything of importance pertaining to the credit, ability and character of their customers is noted. Papers are diligently read and reports scanned, inquiries are made of persons who are supposed to know about others; all kinds of business are investigated with care; occasionally a considerable sum is paid to an individual for making a special investigation into the affairs of a customer. Very often these investigations and inquiries must be made with great tact and secrecy. If a customer were to find out that he were under a telescopic investigation, he might be offended, withdraw his account, and vengefully exert himself to injure the bank. On the other hand, no faithful bank manager should be negligent of his duties in this regard. No opportunity for inquiry should be neglected. The most successful bank managers are those who are most diligent in conducting these investigations, and in watching all these complicated movements of trade.

Every bank should know as much as possible concerning each of its dealers, and the information obtained should be carefully recorded and preserved. In a large business it would be impossible for any officer to remember the different terms and agreements and understandings had with its various dealers from time to time, and therefore it is the practice of a systematic officer to write or dictate to his stenographer, immediately after an important interview with a dealer, the substance of what has been said. Some banks have found that the most advantageous way is to have a very large scrap-book prepared, in which all records of conversations, statements of condition, agency reports, etc., etc., are pasted. The book should be made with numbered leaves, and with short stubs to which papers can be pasted, and with still shorter stub leaves to fill up the book, so that when it is full the back will not be broken. A voweled index separately bound should accompany such a scrap-book. Between each numbered leaf there should be room for, say, three of the shorter stub leaves on which papers could be pasted. These shorter leaves would be numbered 1, 2, 3, and the entry in the index would therefore be, say, as follows: John Smith & Co., Book No. 1, page (say) $1\frac{2}{85}$, which would mean that on section 2 of page 185, in scrap-book No. 1, there could be found a record of all that was known concerning John Smith & Co. A succeeding administration would therefore be able to know just about as much concerning John Smith & Co. as the officer who directed the entry. Of course, such systems as the foregoing require systematic and regular attention, which usually cannot be given by either the cashier or president, and therefore a clerk must be employed for the purpose. In some large banks a young man is employed as a "*credit* clerk," whose almost exclusive duty is to go about in the various trades for the special information required, and record what is learned in the above-described bought paper books and dealers' scrap book.

Most large merchants outside New York City now make their notes payable there, and have regular accounts with the banks in that city. This is one reason why the banking resources of New York are so rapidly expanding. Another is because the city banks have unusual facilities for lending money.

Bank managers, as well as bank directors, are often importuned to make loans through friendship and other than strictly business reasons. For many years the title page of ·the *Banker's Magazine* has borne the following words, uttered by a successful and eminent banker of Boston, Nathan Appleton: "No expectation of forbearance or indulgence should be encouraged; favor and benevolence are not the attributes of good banking; strict justice and a rigid performance of contracts are its proper foundations." Notwithstanding these plain teachings, many a bank officer, through sympathy and regard for friends and customers, has granted loans which were not warranted either by their condition or by that of the bank at the time of granting them. There are many occasions when a bank manager cannot easily determine what course is the most expedient. A considerate regard for the wants of a customer, his ample security for the loan, the condition of the bank and of trade—these are circumstances which not infrequently render a decision difficult. Of course no extra lights can be provided for these extraordinary occasions. Human experience will not avail much at such times. If the bank manager does not comprehend the situation, so much the worse for him and for all concerned; any lesson he might be likely to learn would come too late to be of any use to him.

Notwithstanding the length of this chapter, we cannot forbear adding the excellent "Suggestions to Managers of Banks," prepared by Mr. Hugh McCulloch, when Comptroller of the Currency, on this very important subject of discounts.

"Let no loans be made that are not secured beyond a reasonable contingency. Do nothing to foster and encourage speculation. Give facilities only to legitimate and prudent transactions. Make your discounts on as short time as the business of your customers will permit, and insist upon the payment of all paper at maturity, no matter whether you need the money or not. Never renew a note or bill merely because you may not know where to place the money with equal advantage if the paper is paid. In no other way can you properly control your discount line, or make it at all times reliable.

"Distribute your loans rather than concentrate them in a few hands. Large loans to a single individual or firm, although sometimes proper and necessary, are generally injudicious and frequently unsafe. Large borrowers are apt to control the bank, and when this is the relation between a bank and its customers, it is not difficult to decide which in the end will suffer. Every dollar that a bank loans above its capital and surplus, it owes for, and its managers are therefore under the strongest obligations to its creditors, as well as to its stockholders, to keep its discounts constantly under its control.

"Treat your customers liberally, bearing in mind the fact that a bank prospers as its customers prosper, but never permit them to dictate your policy.

"If you doubt the propriety of discounting an offering, give the bank the benefit of the doubt and decline it; never make a discount if you doubt the propriety of doing it. If you have reason to distrust the integrity of a customer, close his account. Never deal with a rascal under the impression that you can prevent him from cheating you. The risk in such cases is greater than the profits.

"In business, know no man's politics. Manage your bank as a business institution, and let no political partiality or prejudice influence your judgment or action in the conduct of its affairs. The National currency system is intended for a nation, not for a party; as far as in you lies, keep it aloof from all partisan influences."

In 1876 Mr. McCulloch delivered an address before the American Bankers' Association, closing with a statement of the principles of sound banking, which are a proper sequel to the foregoing.

"*First.*—The capital of banks should be real, not fictitious.

"*Second.*—The managers should not be borrowers, nor should loans be made to stockholders merely because they are stockholders.

"*Third.*—A certain amount of the annual profits should be carried to the surplus—the larger the surplus the better—not only for the safety of the stockholders, liable as they are, under the bank act, for an amount equal to their shares, but for the protection of depositors.

"*Fourth.*—Banks should be kept strong in their cash reserves, as times frequently occur when the strongest stand in need of them. Nothing in the long run pays better than a 'goodly' amount of idle money, especially when specie is the only *legal* money.

"*Fifth.*—As banks are commercial institutions, created for commercial purposes, preference in discounts should always be given to paper based upon actual commercial transactions. Banks are not loan offices. It is no part of their business to furnish their customers with capital, nor should loans be made under any circumstances for operations in stocks, or to furnish facilities for stock operations.

"*Sixth.*—Renewals should only be permitted to secure doubtful debts, or in cases in which more time is required than was anticipated when the loans were made, to complete the transaction upon which they were based.

"*Seventh.*—Such salaries should be paid to officers and clerks as will relieve them from the temptation to dishonest practices; and the services of those whose expenditures exceed their salaries should be promptly dispensed with.

"*Eighth.*—Bank managers should bear in mind that they are not only trustees of stockholders, but that they owe something to the public—that their whole duty is not performed when good profits are made and when solvency is secured, but that they should do all in their power to encourage morality in business and to elevate credit, especially commercial credit, to the highest standard."

CHAPTER VIII.

THE CASHIER.

We have already said that every bank had a leading business official who was either the president, vice-president or cashier. The presidents of the country banks very generally perform only a few duties besides those required by law which cannot be delegated. Here and there may be found a president who is the real head of the concern. In the larger cities the president, in most cases, is the real manager, who is elected to act in that capacity, and on whom the responsibility and success of the bank depend.

The cashier, unless there be a vice-president, ranks next to the president, and has certain specified duties to perform. These are mentioned in the law under which the bank exists. But from what has been already said, he may also be the real head of the bank in conducting its business, and this is often the case, especially in country banks, which form by far the majority of the whole number.

His specific duties may be thus defined. He keeps a record of the meetings of the directors, at which he acts as secretary. The certificates of stock issued to shareholders are signed by him as well as the president, and so are the bank notes which circulate as money. Checks also drawn on other banks are signed by him, unless absent, when they are signed by the president. Drafts and notes sent away to other banks are endorsed by him. These endorsements are usually stamped:

" Pay to......................
or order, for colln for acct
of Arctic National Bank, N. Y.
JOHN SMITH, *Cashier*."

The correspondence of the bank is conducted in the name of the cashier, and when his signature is alone required that of the president may be substituted, but the alternate substitution cannot be made. Formerly a cashier could hold no stock in his bank, and it was regarded an improper thing for him to keep his personal account in it. The pecuniary relations of the president, also, toward his bank were the same. This is no longer the case. The cashier is usually a stockholder, and often a director. Under the National banking system, whereby personal liability to the amount of the stock is borne by everyone, if the cashier owns stock he is supposed to be more interested in the success of the bank than if he had no pecuniary interest.

The cashier is appointed by the directors, and may serve for any length of time. He gives a bond for ten thousand or twenty thousand dollars for the faithful performance of the duties of his office, and which is signed by two sureties. Each clerk also gives a similar bond, and usually for five thousand dollars. These bonds do not cover losses occasioned by misjudgment or neglect, but only fraudulent transactions. The requirement would be unreasonable to hold these officials liable for losses of every kind.

The bondsmen are men of character and wealth. Their names are submitted to the board of directors, or more generally to the officers, for the purpose of making whatever investigation may be needful. If they do not approve of those offered, others must be procured. In the event of a loss, which the bondsmen must pay, it is divided among them equally.

When an official has been promoted he must give another bond, as the existing one does not protect the bank in the event of a fraudulent loss occasioned by him after his promotion. Recently, several cases have come to light of negligence on the part of directors in not procuring new bonds after making promotions. Frauds were discovered, the bondsmen were sued, but the courts decided that the bonds given simply related to the conduct of the principals when holding the offices named in the instruments.

Although the cashier is appointed by the board of directors, and is amenable to them and within their power of removal, he is also the representative of the stockholders. If, therefore, the president or directors should attempt to use the funds of the bank in an illegal manner, it would be the duty of the cashier to prevent them from doing so if possible. His salary, and also that of the president, is varied by the duties and responsibilities assumed. In the larger banks the president, when he is the real manager, gets from five to fifteen thousand dollars a year, and the cashier from ·five to ten thousand dollars. The country banks pay, perhaps, half these figures. These, however, are only crude approximations of the remuneration received.

As the cashier is the ostensible executive officer of a bank, he is presumed to have, in the absence of positive restrictions, all the power necessary to transact its business. Thus, in the absence of restrictions, if he should procure a *bona-fide* rediscount of any paper of the bank, his endorsement would bind it, because he has the implied power to transact such business. But he could not, by virtue of his official relation to his bank, bind it as an accommodation endorser of his own promissory note. Such a transaction would not be within the scope of his general powers, and if a person should accept an endorsement of that nature he could not recover of the bank, in case the note was not paid, without proving that it specially authorized the cashier to make the endorsement. There is no presumption in favor of the delegation of such a power.*

One of the first duties on reaching the bank in the morning is to attend to the correspondence. In some of the New York City banks this is very extensive. Formerly the letters were opened by the cashier, but now they are given to clerks appointed for that purpose. The letters containing cash items are retained by the tellers. Those which must be answered by the cashier himself are termed "special letters," and are laid on his desk in the early part of the morning. These may be applications for discounts, proposals from new customers, orders for the purchase or sale of stocks and bonds, letters asking for advice concerning the standing of persons, opinions concerning the worth of certain bonds or stocks, or complaints concerning the conduct of the business of the bank. The answers are copied in a book kept for that purpose.

The number of letters daily received by a bank having a large correspondence may be from two hundred to two thousand. Most of them are formal, containing a statement of enclosures, and can be easily answered. Printed forms are used in most cases both in sending such enclosures, and in acknowledging their receipt. Mere acknowledgments are not usually copied.

All the checks received in the morning letters which can be sent to the Clearing-house are put in the package which is to be sent there, as will be explained hereafter. The amount thus received daily in some cases is very large, running into the millions.

A cashier of one of the best-conducted banks in New York City has thus described the usual daily routine of his business. After examining a dozen papers to which the bank subscribes, he looks around to see that all the clerks are on hand and are preparing the exchanges for the Clearing-house. By a few glances he can tell whether the work is progressing satisfactorily. If a vacant place is seen, then it is presumed that a clerk is absent, and somebody must be found to supply his place. In the morning, almost all the clerks, except the bookkeepers and the heads of the departments, are engaged in preparing the exchanges. In that bank the letters are so numerous that a large force is necessary in order to get the exchanges ready in time, and a vacancy must be speedily filled if possible. Sometimes he is obliged to assist himself. If a clerk does not appear within ten minutes past nine he is regarded late.

* See the opinion of Ch. J. Waite in *Savings Bank* v. *Parmlee*, U. S. Supreme Court, 1877.

The special letters are brought to the cashier, and those requiring immediate attention are answered at once; others at a more convenient time. Then letters containing remittances are brought in from the bookkeepers. Those requiring special attention are laid on one side, and the instructions they contain are entered in a special letter book for the use of the corresponding clerk. For example, if an advice concerning a payment is requested, it is the duty of the corresponding clerk to make the necessary advice. The last duty which the latter performs in the day is to examine his special letter book, for the purpose of assuring himself that all letters requiring special attention on his part have been answered.

When the directors meet, as we have seen, the cashier meets with them. Besides, he examines loans secured by collateral, to reassure himself of the sufficiency of the security, or perhaps with a view of calling the loan, if the collateral that is securing payment be of a kind which the bank does not wish to hold longer. He also examines the balance books and directs all the detail of the bank, keeping himself informed concerning the business done. Such are the leading features of his daily business, interspersed with frequent calls and interruptions. The afternoon hours are not so pressing, and the duties are more varied.

When the money market is "easy," the duties of a cashier are very agreeable. The departments of the bank move along harmoniously. The dealers call and transact their business, and go away in good humor. If they want to get notes discounted this is done promptly. Very often social topics are pleasantly blended with their negotiations. But when the market shows signs of tightening, then these pleasant daily scenes are quickly changed. The amount of paper offered for discount is suddenly doubled, and the amount discounted is reduced one-half. Merchants are not satisfied with their usual preparations for future payments. They are determined to get more ready money, if possible, and eagerly demand more loans. These are the times that test the ability of the bank manager, and which prove his fitness or unfitness for his position.

One of the duties of a cashier is to increase in every proper way the business of the bank. The banking business in this respect does not differ from any other. The profits in the business in most banks are made on the deposits. To increase these, therefore, is the ambition of all concerned in the enterprise, and especially of those who are the most active and responsible in its management. New accounts are eagerly sought. While, however, this is true, no well-conducted bank will blindly open an account with any person. He must be properly identified and introduced, and his character must be ascertained. Some banks will not take the accounts of persons introduced by a clerk of their own, for the reason that it is possible for him to be a confederate in some plan with the introducer to defraud the bank. The clerk might be enabled to give him a fictitious credit or in some way assist him in defrauding the institution. If, therefore, a clerk should introduce a customer, an additional introduction would also be required. If he were a merchant, the introduction of another merchant would be needful. If the applicant were not engaged in business, he might present such facts as would satisfy the cashier concerning his worthiness without further investigation. If the cashier should decide to open an account with him, he would be required to sign his name in a book kept for that purpose. All that the applicant has said concerning himself, and whatever can be found out about him afterward, is recorded in a book which has been already described.

It is not possible for the cashier to supervise the books of a bank personally, but he should look at them frequently enough to satisfy himself of their correctness. Clerks sometimes get careless and negligent, and may carry over their work from day to day, or portions of it, if they are not watched. A supervision of this kind is needed in order to maintain the best discipline. Without it, clerks too often become careless and inattentive and delay their work in various ways. A cashier should have an intimate knowledge of the theory of accounting maintained by his bank, so that when he examines any book he will be able at once to understand it. We do not suppose that every bank has such a cashier, but unquestionably it should have. Bank-booking is generally quite simple, and no very high order of ability is required to master it. Banks differ from one another in many details of doing business, but in no case are these difficult to comprehend.

CHAPTER IX.

THE PAYING TELLER.

Having described the duties of the cashier, we will describe those of the paying teller, which are regarded as next in importance. He is frequently called the first teller. Whenever the cashier is promoted, the paying teller usually succeeds to his place. It is sometimes maintained, however, that the general bookkeeper and the corresponding clerk ought to have an equally good chance for the office.

The paying teller receives a higher salary than any other clerk, and the general bookkeeper the next highest. The paying teller's salary is larger, because he is trusted with more funds, and because the responsibility put on him to scrutinize signatures and to pay money is peculiar and very great.

To him is committed the custody and disbursement of the funds of the bank. The amount of money in his keeping in a large bank may amount to several millions of dollars. In such a bank several apartments in the vault are appropriated to his exclusive use. A cashier said to the writer not long since that in his bank an average amount of two million dollars was kept. The responsibility of keeping it was too great for one man. The vault where it was kept was divided into compartments. The paying teller had three, the receiving teller one, the note teller one, the collection clerk one, the discount clerk one, and the loan clerk two, and one was assigned to the cashier. Two locks were placed on each of two of the three compartments assigned to the paying teller. The combination of one lock was known only to the cashier, and the combination of the other only to the paying teller. Consequently neither person could open the compartments without the knowledge of the other. In these compartments was kept the greater part of the reserve of the bank. In the third compartment, which had only one lock, the paying teller kept the balance of his cash, which changed from day to day, and which necessarily must be under his control. The cashier knew every combination except those of the paying teller.

The paying teller is therefore the sole guardian of his cash. Nobody ever thinks of invading his compartments; but there are times when this may be necessary. He may be taken sick, and in that event another person must open the compartments to get the funds for carrying on the business of the bank. There are times, too, when investigations are made, annually or otherwise, all the compartments are opened, and their contents are examined. But, except on such occasions, or when fraud is suspected, the teller's compartments are not opened unless he is present. The reader can well understand why such strictness prevails. If the cashier were accustomed to going to them, if any loss should occur, it might be very difficult to trace. The paying teller, therefore, has sole charge of his compartments, and alone is responsible when losses arise.

The paying teller reaches the bank about nine o'clock in the morning. He unlocks his compartments, and the porter assists him, if necessary, in carrying to his desk the money which is likely to be wanted during the day. His compartment is then locked, and he returns to his desk.

The different kinds of money paid by him are familiar to every one. It consists principally of United States notes and National bank notes. The former are issued by the Government, and are more frequently called "greenbacks;" the latter notes are made by the banks themselves. Then there is coin,—gold, silver—"the dollar of the daddies,"—and minor coins. Silver certificates are also paid, and less frequently gold certificates. They represent the amount of gold or silver specified on their face in the possession of the Treasury department, and which can always be obtained by presenting these certificates to the United States Treasurer at Washington, or to any assistant treasurer.* To facilitate payments, the money drawer is divided into sections which contain notes of different denominations. A package of fives contains two hundred and fifty dollars. A package of tens five hundred dollars. A package of twenties one thousand dollars. There are other packages for varying amounts. When a check is presented for the amount of any packet, it is delivered without recounting. For intermediate amounts, of course, the packets must be opened.

All payments of money are made by one teller; consequently all the exchanges sent to the Clearing-house must appear in his accounts. It may be stated here that this is composed of the checks on other banks taken on deposit, and also those which are received in letters from other banks. Formerly, it was the duty of the paying teller to receive the exchanges in the morning, and to prepare them for the clearing house. This, however, is now the duty of the third teller, though sometimes performed by the second or receiving teller. In the largest banks the business, of course, is more subdivided than in the smaller ones. But in all cases the exchanges, by whomsoever prepared, are charged to the first teller. On this topic more will be said hereafter.

* There are nine assistant treasurers in the United States.

At ten precisely the teller is ready for the business of the day, which consists in paying checks of depositors of the bank. These checks are usually given by depositors to other persons, but they also draw money themselves from the bank. In any case, an order or check is necessary to get it.

It is a good rule when drawing a check on a bank or banker to make it payable to the order of an individual, firm, or institution, as the case may be. By this means the drawer is saved from the risk of loss, in case the holder of the check loses it—a risk to which all holders of checks payable to bearer are subject.

In paying a note or acceptance to a bank or banker, instead of drawing bank notes for the amount, the payer should request the paying teller of the bank in which his funds are deposited to certify that his check is good for the amount, and hand it to the bank or banker who holds the note or acceptance. The check in all cases should be made payable to his or their order for the amount of the same.

When making up a list of checks for deposit, the depositor should endorse them all, whether payable to bearer or order, with this phrase:

"For Deposit."
A. B. & Co.

Or, "For Deposit at Arctic Bank."
A. B. & Co.

By this means the depositor protects himself from risk of loss by losing any of the checks; for though payable to his order, and endorsed by him, they cannot be collected by any person except the clerk of the bank in which the deposits are made, and consequently they would be valueless in the hands of a stranger.

In the case of checks payable to bearer, the safer plan is to write across their *face* "See endorsement," or "For deposit." In England, the custom prevails of crossing checks payable to bearer. This crossing consists simply of drawing across the face of the check two parallel lines, between which are written the words, "& Co.," after a blank space. The check can then be collected only through a bank or banker.

To obviate the trouble of writing in full the words, "For deposit," or "For deposit at Arctic Bank," a stamp may be used, leaving only the signature of the party to be written underneath by himself.

A banking firm in San Francisco have the following rules printed on the inside of the front cover of their check books in order to impress on their customers the importance of using every precaution against fraudulent alterations or forgery of checks:

GUARD AGAINST FRAUD!

Draw all your checks from your own book.

Number your checks in regular succession.

Write plainly. Use plenty of good black ink, and allow it to penetrate the fibre of the paper before blotting.

Begin writing and figures close to left-hand margin, and leave no space for additions or alterations.

See that the figures correspond with the body of the check, and that dollars are plainly separated from cents, thus: 100\frac{75}{100}$ or 100\frac{x}{100}$.

Keep this check-book in your safe when not in use.

Deposit your pass book regularly for monthly settlement.

In a recent address by an experienced banker,* he says that "a good bank clerk is one who, being thoroughly trustworthy, has a natural aptitude for figures, who is ready of hand and quick of eye, who can handle money neatly and expeditiously, and see in an instant whether what he handles is good or otherwise. A first-rate teller will detect a forged note or spurious coin by its very touch, even while he is handling thousands. Those who handle checks must acquire a rapid power of observing signatures, and be able to detect in an instant any attempt at fraud or forgery."

About half-past ten the exchanges from the Clearing-house are brought in by the messenger. If the paying teller examined the checks received he would be obliged to neglect other work, for they frequently amount to several millions. Three men are often sent by a bank to the Clearing-house. One man, a messenger, carries the exchanges, another guards him, and the third is the settling clerk. The settling clerk sits at a desk assigned to him. The messengers start one after another in the manner fully explained in the latter part of this work. The settling clerk receives the envelopes, containing the checks on his bank, from the messengers of other banks as they are passed in to him. He keeps these in a certain order, and enters the amount from each bank in the appropriate place in a statement prepared for that purpose. As soon as the proof is made the balances are struck, and the messenger and assistant return to the bank. The settling clerk remains to make the final proof, and then he returns. The messengers bring with them the record of the balance, which is generally correct. Sometimes, but not often, a small variation is discovered after further examination, which is always made.

When the debit exchange is thus received it must be carefully examined. From what has been said already the reader will understand that it consists of checks drawn on the bank to which it has been returned. The signature, endorsement, and whatever pe-

---

* Mr. George Hague, General Manager of the Merchants' Bank of Canada.

culiarity a check may possess, must be examined before charging it to the drawer. This work is done during the intervals of other business, and not so much haste is required in completing it as in preparing the credit exchange for the Clearing-house, because that must be there by ten o'clock, otherwise a bank is fined for tardiness.

The assistant bookkeepers check out the exchanges, though this work is sometimes done by the bookkeepers who post them in their ledgers, and bring the totals of their postings to the paying teller, who compares the record with the amount brought from the Clearing-house, which must be the same.

Having now considered the duties of a paying teller with respect to preparing his exchanges, we proceed to consider another very important function performed by him, namely, the certifying of checks.

This consists in writing or stamping on a check words to the effect that it is "good," which signify that it will be paid on presentation.

When a depositor has enough money in the bank to pay the check presented for certification, the duty of the paying teller is a very simple one; he will not hesitate to certify such a check. Requests of this kind are often made in order to render a check more negotiable. A person, for example, may be unwilling to receive a check if drawn in the ordinary manner; but if certified by the bank on which it is drawn, no one will hesitate to receive it.

The paying teller is often asked to certify checks for a much larger sum than the drawer may have on deposit, and the question then arises, "Shall I grant or refuse the request?" This is often a very delicate question with him. When observing the National banking law his duty is very plain, for he is not permitted to certify beyond the amount which the depositor may have in the bank. Under the State bank system, however, no such regulation prevails.

Whenever the request is made the drawer expects to make deficiency good within a short time, generally before the close of the day. The paying teller is given a very wide latitude in granting or declining these requests. Usually he acts on his own authority, though, of course there is nothing to prevent him from getting the opinion of the cashier or president. In all cases the question is decided very quickly. If the person asking for the favor is an old customer, and has always been prompt in fulfilling his engagements, and whose account is a large and desirable one, the paying teller would not hesitate to certify. If he were a new dealer, and not well known to the paying teller, he would refuse. A good authority says, "The discretion of the teller in certifying checks is for the most part independent of his superior officers, and they are averse to interfering with it. In doubtful cases he refers to them for special instruction. Dealers apply to them also to reverse his judgment, but not often with success. Either of them would be likely to answer, 'The teller understands his business better than I do.' Such is the influence acquired by a competent and judicious clerk in this post that he obtains a degree of respect of the customers of the bank a little less than is accorded the president or cashier."

In the absence of the paying teller the receiving teller occupies the place, and the same authority to certify.

Certified checks are generally returned in the debit exchange on the following day through the Clearing-house. But very often they are remitted to other places and do not appear for redemption for a considerable time. They are charged, however, to the drawers immediately, for certification is regarded equivalent to payment.

The city banks have a book in which these are recorded. The aggregate is posted to the credit of an account called "Certified Checks," which is balanced by the separate charges as the checks come in. When the checks are paid they are entered on the debit side of this account; consequently it always shows the balance of certified checks outstanding. Formerly the dealer's ledger account was not charged with such checks until they were received for payment. They might be out so long as to be forgotten by the teller and the bookkeeper, and it was not difficult to practice a fraud on a bank by checking out deposits to such an extent as to leave an insufficient sum for the redemption of a certified check when presented. The losses to which the old methods gave rise led to the adoption of the existing plan of posting certifications.

A great variety of checks are drawn and presented for payment. Every check requires more or less examination. One of the most common defects is the lack of a proper endorsement. Checks are not infrequently given to persons who know but little about such matters, and who forget to fulfill this requisite, or who, perhaps, are ignorant of the fact that a check is made payable to their order. Sometimes checks are post-dated, and are presented for payment before the time fixed by the drawers. Sometimes the dates are altered, and the teller must be satisfied whether the alteration is material or not. Sometimes a check is drawn for a larger amount than the depositor may have on hand, or the paying teller may think so, and it is necessary for him to ask the bookkeeper what the balance of the depositor's account may be before paying it. Many irregularities and delays and inquiries may arise beside those mentioned.

All checks that have passed the paying teller's examination are given to a clerk for entry on his check list, and are charged to their respective accounts in the ledger, except by those banks which use the Boston system of ledgers, to be hereafter explained, in which the check list is not used.

In paying checks the teller must think of three things: first, is the signature genuine; secondly, is the account of the drawer good; and, thirdly, is the person presenting the check entitled to receive the money.

Much might be said under the first head. A great many forged checks are presented and paid. It is one of the terrors of banking. All kinds of devices have been invented for preventing forgeries. Various kinds of paper have been tried. The use of green ink on the United States and National Bank notes was to render their forgery more difficult. And indeed it has proved one of the most effective of preventives. Private marks in signatures are sometimes used. This must be said, however, concerning them: if a forger finds out what the private mark is and successfully counterfeits it, the paying teller is more likely to be deceived than he would be if no such mark were employed.

One of the universal precautions observed by banks to prevent forgeries is to require every depositor to write his name in a signature book. With this the paying teller compares doubtful signatures. Every drawer should always sign his name in the same manner, or, if varying it, should acquaint the paying teller with the variation.

The paying teller must also satisfy himself concerning the genuineness of the endorsement on every check presented for payment.

The second inquiry is, has the drawer a sufficient deposit to pay the check. In every large bank several hundred depositors transact business with it. They have various times and methods of depositing. Some draw many checks daily, and some only a few, or at rare intervals. The deposits of a bank, therefore, are constantly varying in amount. How then can a paying teller recall the condition of every depositor's account?

We cannot describe how a paying teller performs this important part of his work any better than Gibbons has done. By carefully examining the deposits and checks of a dealer, it is easy to judge whether they are the proper returns from his business, or whether they are mostly transfers between different persons and accounts; also to what extent his balances are maintained by loans and transient accommodations. It is not difficult to ascertain whether a man uses his credit excessively or with prudence; nor to get information of his personal habits, associations, and general character. The contact of the teller with merchants in all branches of trade affords many opportunities of inquiry which, with those in possession of the bank officers, enable him to classify the dealers, and thus to assist his memory.

In the first-class stand those of known large capital, who never give out their own notes. They may sell on credit, but they always buy for cash. Their deposits in bank are generally far greater than their immediate wants. When their checks are presented, the teller may safely pay them without reference to the condition of their accounts; for if they should even appear overdrawn at the moment, he knows that they will make an ample deposit before the close of the day. In addition to this, they are likely to have a considerable amount of promissory notes lodged in the bank for collection, which are collateral security.

The middle class of dealers are the most numerous. Less independent with regard to capital, and relying on the bank for loans, they are yet generally safe and trustworthy. They will not transgress its rules, lest they forfeit its confidence. The teller pays their checks commonly without examining their accounts, depending on their integrity and self-interest to rectify possible errors by overdraft or otherwise.

Next come the retail shopkeepers, mechanics and small manufacturers. Many of this class keep accumulating accounts, and seldom call for loans; or if so, to a very moderate extent. Separately, their deposits are not large, but in the aggregate, they add materially to the loaning facilities of the bank. They draw but few checks, and their accounts are not liable to sudden changes. The teller soon acquires such a knowledge of them as to remember which need watching; and the bookkeepers aid him in this by an alphabetical list of balances. An old bank gradually expurgates its ledgers of troublesome accounts, while a new bank, from competition for business, or non-acquaintance with the character of dealers, is likely to fall heir to them.

By these precautions the paying teller is able to tell what checks ought to be paid and what ought not to be. Now and then an overpayment is made, but rarely. But a method of getting money from a bank is sometimes practiced, which though illegal is successful. Two persons who keep accounts in different banks may exchange checks, and each person deposits the check of the other. Afterward, they draw out money on their own checks. Of course, if the checks originally given were paid, no loss would ensue to either bank, but in case they are not paid, the banks lose. When a check is thus deposited, if the deposit teller should have any doubt concerning the payment of it, he would inform the paying teller of the fact, and that eventually when the depositor presented his check for payment he would get no money. Such a thing would not happen with a new depositor, for a bank would not be likely to pay out money when it had received none. But when a person has been depositing for a considerable time, if he should thus slip in the check of another, the payment of which was doubtful or impossible, he might be able to check against it and in that way defraud the bank. This process of exchanging checks and drawing against them is called "kiting," and the persons who practice it are regarded dangerous by a bank. No one would be likely to succeed a second time with the same institution; indeed, when a person is detected of doing it, his account is closed, and the bank refuses to have further dealings with him.

Merchants in distant cities usually make their notes payable in a New York City bank and remit the money to pay them previous to their maturing. These remittances contain a letter of instruction which is delivered to the paying teller who pays the obligation when it is presented. After canceling it, the note is returned to the person who sent the money.

Before paying an endorsed check the holder must be identified. A great many persons holding such checks present them for payment and are surprised to learn that identification is necessary. A check drawn "payable to bearer" requires no identification, and if a bank should pay it, in no event would it be the loser; but if it should pay a check payable to order to the wrong person, then it would be required to pay a second time. It is to guard against payment to the wrong person that checks are drawn payable to order. It is a form of security which should not be omitted. Even if a check should be lost or stolen, and the endorsement of the person to whose order it was payable was forged, and payment was demanded and made, the bank would be required to pay a second time to the rightful owner of the check. As this is the law, banks cannot exercise too much care in paying checks to the persons who are entitled to the money, and no one can reasonably complain if the utmost precaution is observed in making needful inquiries concerning those who present checks for payment. Nevertheless, such inquiries are sometimes vexatious and annoying. It is not always easy to find a person who is willing to go to the bank, or who can, to identify the checkholder. A great many suits have arisen from time to time concerning the liability of banks for the payment of checks to the wrongful person.

Endorsed checks paid to the Clearing-house are regarded as guaranteed by the bank from which they come. Any bank will guarantee the endorsement of a dealer who is well-known to it.

Drawers sometimes direct that checks which they have given be not paid on presentation. As a check on a bank is an order for the payment of money belonging to the drawer, he has the right to revoke it, and if such a revocation is given, and the bank does nevertheless pay, it assumes a new risk. It is therefore very important to keep a record of the checks whose payment has been stopped. Books are prepared for this purpose, one for each ledger, and arranged alphabetically, so that the dealer's page may be referred to as quickly as possible. The direction to stop payment must be in writing, and all the particulars concerning the check on which payment has been stopped must be carefully entered with full extracts from the letter giving directions to the bank concerning the matter. Some banks have a form which they send to their dealers to be filled out when they wish to stop the payment of a check.

As soon as payment has been stopped, the notice is sent to the paying teller. He examines it, and puts his initial on it, and turns it over to the bookkeeper, who records the fact. He is the person to watch the matter, because he has the record. As soon as the check is presented through the Clearing-house, he compares the stop-check list with those received, and arranges them alphabetically, and runs them over, and can speedily determine whether any check has been stopped. In some banks as soon as a check of this kind appears, he takes it immediately to the cashier. Nothing important is done without his action.

There are other ways by which the bank may pay and receive checks than by the first teller. First, the note teller may receive them in payment of a note. Secondly, the receiving teller may take them on credit; and, thirdly, the runner in payment of a draft. For example, if Smith has a balance of $5,000 in a bank he may draw that sum from the paying teller, or he may give his check for it to another person for deposit in the same bank, or he may take up a note with it at the note-teller's desk, or he may pay a draft to the runner with it. Hence he may draw out $15,000 though having but one-third of this sum on deposit. Of course such a transaction is fraudulent and rarely happens. But it is possible.

If checks are not paid when sent through the Clearing-house they are chargeable to the depositor's account. But if a check is deposited in the same bank as that on which it is drawn it is paid when taken by the receiving teller, as truly as if the first teller paid money in discharge of it. In such a case if the check should not be good, the bank might be obliged to look to the drawer of it and not to the depositor. So, if a dealer A took up his note with the check of another dealer B on the same bank, the bank would look to the drawer of the check and not to the dealer for the money.

When the time for serving dealers has expired, the paying teller makes up a statement of the day's business. This is called a Proof. This proof is a test of the accuracy of the day's transactions. The footings of cash on hand must agree with the "balance of cash." If there is any discrepancy it must be hunted for until found, and the necessity of going over figures and recounting cash, after the close of a hard day's work, is often an exasperating trial of the teller's patience.

On the next page is the paying teller's Proof of the Arctic National Bank for July 24th. The form of Proof differs in banks. Some tellers have a simple form, like that given here, others have a much more elaborate form:

FIRST (OR PAYING) TELLER'S PROOF, ARCTIC NATIONAL BANK,

Thursday, July 24, 1884.

				PAID.		
Balance of Cash brought forward from previous day			2,830,269 56	Second Teller's Exchanges sent to Clearing-house	840,305 80	
RECEIVED.				Third " " " "	125,717 15	
From Second Teller, Office List*	25,275 43			Morning Additions by Mail	103,911 25	
" " " Gold	6,189 00		31,464 43	Debit Balance Paid	106,072 39	1,176,006 59
" Third Teller, Office List	35,345 57			*Checks paid, viz.:*		
" " " Gold	13,190 00		48,535 57	Individual, A to L	327,659 44	
" Second " C.II. Exch.	840,305 80			" M to Z	209,811 70	
" Third " "	125,717 15			Banks and Bankers, A to L	195,268 84	
" " do., checks by morning mail	103,911 25		1,069,934 20	" " M to Z	202,193 68	
Exchange from Clearing-house			1,176,006 59	General Ledger	120,451 35	1,055,385 01
				SECOND TELLER'S DEBIT.		
Cash on Hand, July 24, 1884.				*Cash, viz.:*		
Legal tender notes	1,270,390 00			Legal Tender Notes	5,750 00	
Arctic National Bank notes	73,215 00			Gold Certificates	20,000 00	
Other " " "	618,440 00			Gold Clearing-house Certificates	100,000 00	
Gold, in vault $750,000 00				Gold Coin	5,000 00	
" in trays ... 11,455 00	761,455 00			Silver Coin	450 00	
Silver, in vault 17,500 00				National Bank Notes	12,500 00	
" in trays 1,179 50	18,679 50			Checks on other Banks, etc.	38,500 00	182,200 00
Sundries	439 25			Total Payments		2,413,591 60
			2,742,618 75	Balance of Cash, carried forward to next day		2,742,618 75
						5,156,210 35
			5,156,210 35			

* Checks on private bankers, or on other cities, which cannot be used in the Exchange, with mutilated bills, etc., constitute the Office List.

THE RECEIVING TELLER.

CHAPTER X.

This official ranks next to the paying teller, and usually succeeds him when he is promoted.

The accounts of a bank may be divided into the following classes: general accounts, individual accounts, banks and bankers' accounts, city dealers' accounts and collection accounts. The general accounts are such as stock, expense, bills discounted, profit and loss, cash, interest, exchange and some others.

The receiving teller receives all kinds of money and checks from the depositors. The book in which these deposits are entered is called the RECEIVING TELLER'S CASH BOOK. He has two books of the same kind for alternate use by the teller and the bookkeeper.

The original entries of individual deposits are made by the receiving teller, and the other entries are made by the note teller. The latter also receives the money paid for notes lodged for collection. Both clerks are receiving tellers, the receiving teller is called the second teller, and the note teller the third. This rank they hold in the order of promotion.

The deposits of merchants consist of the various kinds of money and checks already described, and other documents representing money. The depositor is required to state the details of his deposit, and a form is given him to fill up, which saves labor in making the necessary statement. This blank is called a deposit ticket. A teller will not receive money without it. The practice is different in country banks, as will be hereafter shown. If his cash does not prove at the end of the day, he re-examines these tickets and generally can find out where the error is. After proving his cash, the tickets are put into a bundle and marked and stored for future reference.

A bank located in a large city has an exchange drawer or rack which is divided into numerous boxes. The checks of neighboring banks received for deposit are assorted, and those on each bank are put into their own box.

The footings of the checks thus received are copied on the general list, and added together constitute the deposit teller's portion of the exchange which goes to the Clearing-house.

There are no complex calculations in the accounts of the receiving teller. His duties are simple, and a high order of intelligence is not required to fulfill the duties of the place. Most of the deposits, especially in the banks in the large cities, consist of merchants' checks, which are given in discharge of obligations or purchases. Some of these are certified before deposit and some are not. Whenever the depositor is well known, his checks are received without previous certification. But in other cases a certification is required.

The reader should not confound the business of certifying with that of over-certifying. There is no legal objection to certifying a check to the amount of the depositor's balance. The National banking law prohibits the certifying of checks only in excess of the depositor's balance. The former kind of certification is very necessary. Many persons whose financial standing is not known give checks outside the banks on which the checks are drawn. When, therefore, the check of an individual bears the certification of the bank on which it is drawn, it will readily pass in making payments, or be taken on deposit in any bank. But the check of an unknown person would be received with hesitation. It might be good, and it might not be. The certification of a check by the bank on which it is drawn adds much to its negotiability.

The receiving teller of a bank may have reasons for requiring checks to be certified of which the dealer may be ignorant and perhaps cannot be informed. Sometimes a very considerable degree of tact and caution are necessary in determining when certifications should be required. Dealers should not be offended unnecessarily, yet the safety of the bank must be regarded at all times. To protect it, and to retain the friendship and good will of dealers, is sometimes a difficult thing to do. Some persons are richly endowed with tact and power of discernment; they always know what to say, and how to say it, when to be silent and not excite distrust or arouse the ill-feeling of dealers. By other persons such a knowledge of men and things is never acquired, though their knowledge in many ways may be great and useful.

The receiving teller should know the condition of all accounts. To do this he must ask the bookkeepers what is their average run; he should personally examine the ledgers, and also the deposits and checks, and make all other inquiries of persons in the bank or elsewhere who are likely to throw any knowledge useful in his department of the business.

The receiving teller should examine the signatures, endorsements, dates, and other features of checks, the same as the paying teller. Dealers who are perfectly honest may be cheated by others, and deposit fraudulent or "kiting" checks. The depositor should endorse his name below all others on the back of each check. The receiving teller should notice especially this last endorsement, for it is the key to discovery if anything wrong should appear in the future history of the check. At times, when checks are rapidly received for deposit, it is impossible to examine them carefully, and hence the greater need of looking at the endorsement of a depositor. When checks are finally paid where they are made payable, errors are sure to be detected, and of course the bank receiving them ought always to know from what source they come, in order to know what to do with them should any imperfection be discovered.

Reclamations between banks occur daily. Checks are dated ahead, or the dates are obscure or omitted. They lack intermediate endorsement, or they are endorsed by attorney without adequate proof of his authority. The sum in the body of the check may not correspond with the figures below, or may be entirely wanting. Checks sometimes are paid without signature. The paying teller recognizes a familiar style of writing and the omission of the name may not be detected. Sometimes they are thrown into the wrong box, and are taken to the wrong bank. These and many other errors happen. As soon as discovered the checks are sent back to their proper places for correction.

Merchants sometimes keep accounts with more than one bank. This is done for several reasons. One reason is to obtain larger discounts. Some persons think that greater secrecy can be maintained than by doing all their business with one bank.

There is a protective feature in many accounts which prevent banks from losing by overdraft; we mean when dealers have notes deposited for collection. For, when paid, they are posted to the credit of their owner, and may make up a deficit in his account. Bank officers will sometimes admit temporary overdrafts in anticipation of the maturity of collection notes; or, what is better, make transient loans, holding them as collateral, by which the irregularity of overdraft is avoided. The receiving teller takes no cognizance of this source of recuperation unless he finds a necessity to resort to it.

The word "foreign" is applied by banks in New York City to all others. Most of the banks located there receive, on deposit, individual checks on banks at a distance. Merchants in Buffalo, for example, remit their checks on banks in that city to their creditors in New York, and there they are received as cash, perhaps, deducting enough to cover the exchange and the expense of collecting. They may be returned not good after several days, and, in such a case, the depositor must promptly redeem them. The interval between their deposit and their return is long enough to permit the dealer to close his account and leave the bank in the lurch. It follows that the receiving teller is practically discounting paper all the time.

Drafts on individuals and on private bankers in New York are received on deposit, but this throws on the bank receiving them the trouble of collecting them, while rendering it responsible for endorsements in which it has no interest. Dealers, therefore, are required to scrutinize and to collect them on their own behalf.

The deposit teller must examine the bank notes received, lest counterfeit ones be taken. When the State banks issued notes there was such a great variety of them and they were often so poorly made that it was an easy thing to make counterfeits and to put them into circulation. It has been far more difficult to counterfeit the Government issues, and those of the National banks.

There are publications whose special function consists in describing counterfeits, and the deposit teller should study constantly such sources of information. "A man sent us a bill," said a cashier to the writer, not long ago, "that had been stolen before signature. Our clerks picked it out at once; they had been notified concerning it." The National Bank Act requires that every National bank officer receiving a counterfeit or stolen bill shall cut it, or brand it, or stamp it "counterfeit" or "fraudulent," as the case may be. With the note in question the cashier said he did not wish to do this, because he might lose ten or twenty dollars. So he notified the depositor that the bill might be returned to him and sent it to the Comptroller of Currency at Washington for redemption. When it came back it was cut in many places, and stamped, "stolen," "stolen;" "bad," "bad." As soon as received the cashier sent it to the depositor, and wrote to him that the bill could not be credited on his account. He was very angry, and said he would like to know what conceited fellow in the department undertook to say that the bill was stolen. How could he know that it was? The cashier simply replied that the clerks had picked the bill out when it came over the counter, that the information was derived from a counterfeit detector, a copy of which was sent to him.

Not infrequently a claim is made by some depositor for a larger sum than that with which he is credited. How these differences arise is often mysterious. The deposit teller then makes a general and thorough revision of all his figures, checking them off by his deposit tickets and going over his additions. If the error cannot be discovered in this way, he sends a letter to each dealer whose deposit may possibly have been erroneously entered, and if the error still remains undiscovered the cashier is informed, and perhaps the directors at their next meeting. The search is continued as long as there is any chance of detecting their error.

Gibbons says there is a loose practice with some banks with respect to a deficit or excess of cash in the daily accounts of their tellers. Small sums accrue, which are thrown together in a box or drawer and applied to the payment of small deficits. These are not noted on the face of the day's transactions. He objects to this mode of conducting a banking business, and well he may. Nothing short of exactitude should be allowed in commercial accounts, and especially in a bank. A ledger account should be opened with each teller, in which any surplus should be credited under its actual date, or any deficiency charged, and this might be periodically balanced by a transfer to profit and loss.

When deposits are made the depositor sometimes waits until the counting is finished; on other occasions he leaves immediately. Some banks, though, require the dealer to wait until his deposits have been counted in his presence. Sometimes deposits are left containing the dealer's count on them; if they are, when the recount is made, should there be a deficiency, the depositor must abide by the teller's count.

Depositors have a book in which is written on one side the dates and amounts of their deposits, and on the other the amounts that have been checked out and the dates when this was done. The depositor presents this book whenever he makes a deposit, and the amount is written therein. It is the general practice to write up these books at varying intervals of a month or more.

The receiving teller rarely receives forged checks, as he transacts business only with the regular dealers. Of course a dealer may determine to be a knave, and to practice a fraud on a receiving teller, but happily such cases are very infrequent.

Toward the close of the day depositors multiply in number. "First come first served" is the rule; a row is formed, and the last comer must take his place at the end farthest away from the receiving teller. Formerly, when the State banks issued notes, and counterfeiting was a more general practice, the business of assorting and counting bank notes was a more difficult practice than it is at present. No assorting is done now when notes are received. The teller merely watches sharply for counterfeits. Afterward the notes are assorted into packages of various denominations without regard to the bank issuing them. Such is the perfection of the National bank-note system, that the note of one bank is as good as that of another, and hence there is no occasion for noticing their parentage.

The checks on country banks are handed over to the corresponding clerk, who lists them in his letters and in mail blotters for charge to the appropriate banks in the collection ledger, unless they are on dealers of their own bank. In that case they are often charged directly to the general account of the dealer.

CHAPTER XI.

THE NOTE TELLER.

The note teller receives the letters and the money for all promissory notes liquidated at the bank. In small banks his duties may be blended with those of the receiving teller. And again the duties of both may be performed by the paying teller. In other words, one person may perform the duties assigned in a larger bank to the three beside several assistants.

There are two kinds of notes. Those which are discounted by the bank, and those which are deposited by the owners for collection, and for which they are to receive credit when they are paid The former are called bills discounted, and the latter collection notes.

In large banks at the present day the note teller does not have charge of the notes until the morning of the day of maturity. The bills discounted are handed to him early on the morning of the day of their maturity by the discount clerk. They are usually strapped together, and the total amount of the notes is stated in pencil on the strap. When collected, this total amount is credited to "bills discounted" in the general ledger. Should any of these notes not be paid, of course the amount to be credited to "Bills Discounted" will be just so much diminished.

The collection clerk each morning hands to the note teller the notes he has maturing, and with a ticket for each note, or with a ticket for each owner of notes.

When the notes are entered they are arranged by the note teller in the order of the names of the payers. The note teller is now prepared to receive payment of the notes whenever debtors appear. The notes payable at the bank are retained by the teller in his drawer, and those payable at other points in the city are sent out by messengers for presentation.

The note teller reaches the bank in time to make the entries of remittances by the morning's mail before the institution is opened to the public. The following is the usual form of letter received now-a-days, with abbreviations:

DELAWARE RIVER BANK,
Philadelphia, June, 30, 1884.

H. MORSE, Esq., Cashier.

Dear Sir:

Enclosed find for our credit:

Peters, Cashier	.....on Com.		$9,400 00
Ruffin,	"	" Am.	10,000 00
Luther,	"	" Am. Ex.	1,575 60
Simpson,	"	" Met.	14,263 70
Corse & Co.	.....Third Nat.		1,800 00
Kerr	.....Phx.		2,740 00
			$39,779 30

We add for collection:

Brown	......on Thompson	3 ds.	$1,250 00
Green	......Burr & Co.	10 ds.	3,263 20
Wilson	.....July 10.		2,249 75
White	.....90 ds.		242 90
Kent	.......Albany	July 25.	506 00
Mother	.....Buffalo	Aug. 3.	1,000 00
Gray & Co.	Hartford	sight.	2,600 00
Roberts	.....Port.	10 ds.	1,050 00

Yours truly,
J. JONES, *Cashier.*

To explain them fully, these items for credit mean checks as follows:

J. Peters, Cashier, Sussex Bank of Milford, on N. Bk. of Commerce, N. Y. $9,400 00
T. Ruffin, Cashier, Bank of Fullerton, on Bank of America............. 10,000 00
Corse & Co., Richmond, Tenn., on Third National..................... 1,800 00
And so on.

The collection items are drafts or notes, thus:

A. Brown & Co., draft on Thompson Bros. at 3 days' sight............ $1,250 00
P. Green & Sons on Burr & Co., 10 days' sight....................... 3,263 20
Wilson & Co., note due July 10...................................... 2,249 75
Kent Bros. (payable at Albany) July 25.............................. 506 00
Draft on Gray & Co., Hartford, sight 2,600 00

This letter is given to the note teller, who writes his initial as his receipt for each check that he takes from it for credit to the remitting bank. In the same way, all letters containing cash documents are passed into his hands, and the proper entries are made from them. In the Boston system of bookkeeping, which will soon be explained, the entries are made from the letter itself. The total footing of the letter is first posted in the Note Teller's CASH BOOK, the letter is then handed to the bookkeeper who again posts the total opposite the dealer's name, and afterward the letter is handed to the corresponding clerk, who brings all the letters to the cashier for examination. In many banks, the president goes through the letters received the previous day; in other banks, the president is shown every unusual letter. It is important by this system to have the letters footed, because the letter is the original entry, and every footing is from the letter. The totals of the letters are posted by the note teller, and again by the bookkeeper, and they compare the footings.

Some banks send notices of the time when a note falls due. Formerly this was done more generally than it is now. The business has become too large for banks to continue it. Persons who give notes are supposed to know when they become due, and should be prepared to pay them without notification. In some cities the custom seems to prevail of making notes payable at any bank in town. Especially is this the case in Boston; where it prevails notices would seem to be necessary. In New York City, however, it is customary for merchants and other persons to make their notes payable at a specific place, and to have the money there to pay them at maturity.

When notes are paid, a certified check may be used, or money. A teller should preserve the notices and memoranda of his transactions in the order of their occurrence until his cash is proved at the end of the day. They may serve a useful purpose in refreshing his memory or in detecting any error that may happen.

When a note is paid, the bank stamps thereon a notice like the following:

"Paid at the Merchants' Bank."

Of course a great many incidents and irregularities happen in connection with this department. The persons who ought to pay perhaps forget where the note is payable, or when, or the amount. Sometimes the notice is delivered to the wrong person. Some merchants write their notes payable at the bank where they keep their account.

After the last payer is dismissed the note teller closes his gate erases from the Cash Book and DISCOUNT TICKLER the notes that remain unpaid, and delivers them to a Notary Public for protest, except where no endorser is to be held.

The protest consists in presenting the note at the place of business of the drawer, or wherever it is made payable, and demanding the money for it. If this be refused the note is attached to a printed legal form, containing the following particulars: First, a true description of the note, so as to ascertain its identity; second, an assertion that it has been duly presented to its maker, or place of payment, at maturity, and dishonored; third, the holder, or the person giving the notice, looks to the person to whom the notice is given for payment and indemnity. This statement is essential to establish the claim or the right of the holder or the party giving notice, for otherwise he will not be entitled to any payment from the endorser. It will be sufficient, indeed, if the notice sent necessarily or even fairly implies by its terms that there has been a due presentment and dishonor at the maturity of the note, but mere notice of the fact that the note has not been paid affords no proof whatever that the note has been presented in due season, or even that it has been presented at all. The note is returned to the bank on the following day. The Notary sends notice of the protest to all the endorsers and to the drawer of drafts, which advises them of their liability for the payment in case of the continued default of the first debtor. If the notes should be paid when presented by the Notary he returns the money to the bank on the next morning.

CHAPTER XII.

THE DISCOUNT CLERK.

As we have seen, the profits of banking are composed of interest on money—in other words, of interest, discount and exchange.

The loans are called discounts, because the interest is paid in advance and deducted from the amount due to the borrower. But if a bank were to deduct seven dollars from a hundred dollar loan, payable a year after date, the bank would receive seven dollars for a loan of only ninety-three dollars. If the bank paid the borrower $93.46, this sum at seven per cent. interest for a year would amount to a hundred dollars, the sum expressed in the note. Banks are permitted by law to deduct interest in advance in this manner, at the rate prescribed, without rendering themselves liable for usury The difference, therefore, between interest and discount in bank practice is, the former is a sum of money payable for the use of money at the end of a given term, while discount is the money reserved from another sum at the beginning of the term for which it is loaned.

When a bank discounts a note the interest is deducted at once, and the borrower receives credit for the balance.

The OFFERING BOOK, containing a record of the notes offered for discount, we have described elsewhere. The form of Offering Book, however, is not the same in all banks. Some dispense with the balance column, and some add another, showing the liquidations before the next discount day. Some banks enter in this book loans already made to the borrower so that directors may have before them, when they meet, all the essential facts necessary to transact their business intelligently.

Accepted paper is now taken by the discount clerk, who first examines the notes for filling and general character, and then "times" each note, *i. e.*, writes in pencil on the back the due date of the note. The notes are then entered in what is termed the " DEALERS' DISCOUNT BOOK," which usually is ruled to permit, first, the maker's name, then the endorser's, the place of payment, due date, and the number of days to run, discount, amount of exchange charged, and net proceeds. For the latter amount there is a separate column for each of the ledgers, so that all the amounts belonging to any one ledger appear only in one column. From this discount book the discount clerk makes his statement, and posts his ledger, or bill book, and his Ticklers. Before putting away the notes he "checks" them back on the "Ticklers." These "Ticklers" are very important books. Why they have been so called is scarcely known, but probably from the habit of ticking or checking off the entries. There is usually one tickler for each month in the year, and one or more pages for each day, with the pages on the left side reserved for notes payable in the city, and those on the opposite side for notes payable out of town. The total footings of these Ticklers will present the total amount of "Bills Discounted," and the proof of these total daily amounts is taken at least as often as once each month, and proved with the General Ledger.

There are discount ledgers, which are opened in the same manner as personal ledgers, but embrace the accounts only of customers who get notes discounted. They contain a record of every note discounted, the date of discount, the endorser or security therefor, and the time of maturity. They also show the liability of each customer as endorser for others on discounted paper. It is desirable to keep this record to guard against losses. If two dealers should exchange notes or endorsements and put them in the same bank, these books would bring the fact to light. They are placed on the directors' table on discount days.

From these ledgers the discount clerk ascertains the amount of discounts set down in the Offering Book. He keeps daily supervision over them, cancelling the paid notes as fast as they mature, by drawing a line across the figures without obliterating the record.

Some banks number their notes on the back and end with red ink, and file them in packets. A good many banks, however, do not number their notes, and are careful not to mar them, even by a pin hole, so that if, for any reason, they should wish to dispose of them, this could be done without the paper showing any indications of having been in the possession of a bank. For the same reason also, it is not desirable for a bank to have a note made payable to its own order. When thus made, it would appear on its face to be given in liquidation of an obligation of the maker to the bank. It is, therefore, desirable that notes be made to the maker's order, and endorsed to the bank if taken direct from him.

Notes are also transcribed on the Discount Ticklers; each note is under the date of its maturity, with a number and name of the payer and amount. The Ticklers, which, as previously explained, are books of monthly duration, continue to receive additions by new discounts until within a few days of the transpiring date. They are kept added in pencil until that time and are finally closed in ink.

In some banks notes are filed without number. Those of each

day are kept in a separate packet, and the packets are arranged in a consecutive order of dates. This plan is regarded more convenient when there are very many notes.

The discount clerk has the possession of the greater part of bills receivable. in which the resources of the bank are invested. These are in his custody, are deposited by him at night in a compartment of the vault assigned to him, and taken out on the next morning by himself. If any of the officers wish to examine notes they do so in his presence, or require him to show them. By this method his responsibility is kept distinct from that of the other clerks and officials.

The discount clerk is in frequent intercourse with the customers of the bank. The offerers apply to him after adjournment to find out what disposition has been made of their application. We are now speaking of the larger banks where such a clerk is employed. In a small bank the cashier may transact the entire business described in this chapter. When he appears at his desk to answer the questions of applicants on occasions when the money market is tight, his duty is by no means a pleasant one. Customers press toward his gate at the earliest moment, to ascertain whether their offerings have been accepted or rejected, and the letters A and R enable him to give a very short answer. When notes are rejected they are returned to the offerer in the original envelope.

The discount clerk, as will be seen from the foregoing description of his duties, does not receive or pay out any money. It is not easy therefore for him to perpetrate a fraud on the bank. Gibbons relates an instance which occurred in the second Bank of the United States. The discount clerk selected some notes after they had been discounted and filed away, which he thought would be least likely to be wanted before maturity, and through the help of an outsider, hypothecated them for a loan of money. When the time of maturity drew near he selected others of longer date, and substituted them for those first abstracted, which were restored to their proper places in the files. The trick was discovered by the maker of one of the hypothecated notes, who called at the bank to pay it before maturity.

Sometimes a bank will rediscount a portion of its notes with other banks. It may desire to get possession of more funds, in order to pay the demands of depositors, or through fear of an increased demand. In other words, the loans which it may have made are transferred to another institution.

Discounted notes payable in other cities are transmitted by mail, and when advice of their payment is received a journal entry is made, charging the collecting bank and crediting "Bills Discounted" in the usual commercial form. Discount notes which are payable in other cities, are transmitted two or three weeks previous to their maturity.

CHAPTER XIII.

COLLECTIONS.

An immense number of notes are given in liquidation of purchases and other obligations, and which sooner or later are delivered to banks for collection. Our readers will understand from what has been already said, that many of the notes thus received by the depositors of a bank are offered for discount, and the mode of procedure with regard to them has been explained. But the remainder are lodged for collection, and their future history needs explanation.

They are first entered by the collection clerk in the customers' book, after careful examination. Informality of endorsement, obscurity of date, or other accident might render the bank liable to the holder, although it was acting merely as a collection agent. The clerk must scrutinize every note carefully before entering it, and must always require the final endorsement of the owner, so that it may not be placed to the wrong credit when due. Banks generally will not receive for collection notes that have been disfigured or changed after issue by the drawer; nor will they receive them from strangers on any terms.

Promissory notes are transferred by endorsement from one merchant to another in settlement of debts, until the time of their maturity, when, of course, they must be presented for payment. There are several varieties of endorsement which may be briefly mentioned. An endorsement may be (1) in full, or (2) in blank; it may be (3) absolute, or (4) conditional; it may be (5) restrictive; it may be (6) without recourse on the endorser; and there may be (7) joint endorsements of the instrument; (8), successive endorsements, and (9) irregular ones. An *endorsement in full* mentions the name of the person in whose favor it is made, and to whom, or to whose order, the sum described in the note is to be paid. An *endorsement in blank* consists simply of the name of the endorser written on the back of the instrument. "The receiver of a negotiable instrument endorsed in blank, or any *bona fide* holder of it, may write over it an endorsement in full to himself, or to another, or any contract consistent with the character of an endorsement, but he could not enlarge the liability of the endorser in blank by writing over it a waiver of any of his rights, such as demand and notice."* By an *absolute endorsement* the endorser binds himself to pay on no other condition than the failure of the prior parties to do so, and of due notice to him of their failure, while a *conditional endorsement* contains some other condition to the endorser's liability. An endorsement may be so worded as to restrict the further negotiability of the instrument; it is then called a restrictive endorsement. The words "for collection," which are frequently written on notes that are put in a bank to be collected, render the endorsement restrictive. The endorser in such a case may prove that he is not the owner of the note, and did not mean to give a title to it or its proceeds when collected. Such an endorsement merely makes the endorsee agent for the endorser in collecting the note. The sixth kind is a *qualified endorsement*, or *endorsement without recourse*. This consists in writing the words "without recourse," or "at the endorsee's own risk" on the back of the note. The endorser is then a mere assignor of the title to the note, and is relieved of all responsibility for its payment. A *joint endorsement* is made when a note is payable to several persons who are not partners. *Successive endorsements* are those made by several persons on a note, the legal effect of which is to subject them as to each other in the order they endorse. The endorsement imparts a several and successive, and not a joint obligation. Lastly may be mentioned *irregular endorsements*, which may originate in various ways. But in all cases an endorser guarantees the genuineness of all the preceding endorsements.

The clerk marks on each note the date of its maturity. If he should mark it one day too late, and the drawer should fail to pay, the bank would be liable to the owner, because the notice of the protest to the endorsers would be too late to hold them. A careful clerk will revise his "timing" of notes so as to guard against any error of this kind.

Dishonest customers have been known to mark a wrong date of maturity on notes for the purpose of "catching" the bank; in other words, of making it liable. The bank could not escape by showing that the wrong date was the customer's, without proving that he intended to render the bank liable. It must be exact in its own business, and cannot escape by showing that it adopted the errors of others.

After the notes have been "timed," they are numbered on the back and end, and recorded in the COLLECTION REGISTER, a page of which is herewith given. From this book the notes are copied into the Ticklers.

Notes should be deposited ten days or longer before maturity, so that there may be time enough to pass them through the several

* *Daniel on Negotiable Instruments*, § 694.

books in the bank, and to serve notices on the payers, though this practice, as we have already remarked, is not so general as it once was. Merchants, however, are constantly receiving short-time drafts, and these cannot be deposited long before the time of payment. Other circumstances often prevent their deposit until very near the time of maturity, for example, the pledging of them to secure loans.

The clerk of this department is responsible for the safe keeping and production at all times of any note or draft deposited in the bank. If payable in the city where the bank is located, he can produce it; if sent elsewhere for collection he can show what he has done with it.

Notes or drafts which are payable in another place are in some banks recorded in a FOREIGN COLLECTION REGISTER. In those doing a smaller business the regular Collection Register may be made to suffice by a special column ruling. In the Foreign Collection Register are recorded the place of payment, and the name of the correspondent to whom the paper is sent for collection, with the date of its transmission. In a small bank a column is provided in which to record the fact and date of payment, or of return if unpaid. In other small banks, the Foreign Collection Register may contain the only record of such paper, obviating entries against the collecting bank, until payment is advised.

It is the practice of many banks to make their collections for a district or county through one bank which has established correspondence with all parts of it. But the large banks desire so far as possible to make their collections direct. Their notes are then presented more promptly, returns are received more quickly, and country business is cultivated more successfully by thus having reciprocal accounts.

When a bank is employed by another to collect notes within a particular district, the clerk opens another book and records on the page appropriated to the National Bank of Albany, for example, all notes that fall within the circuit allotted to it. He stamps or writes on the back of each note below the other endorsements,

"Pay National Bank of Albany, Albany, N. Y.,
on order, for collection for account of
Arctic National Bank, N. Y.
THOMAS JONES, *Cashier.*"

After the letter enclosing the notes has been copied it is sent by mail to the collecting bank.

When drafts or notes for collection are payable at places where the bank has no regular dealer, they are sent to a bank in such place "for collection and remittance." If there is no bank or banker of established credit there, the collection would not be received. When the note or draft is paid, the collecting bank remits at once a check for the amount, less the charge for exchange, if any. The check will be on a bank either in a city from whence the collection has come, or on such other point as instructed by the bank owning the paper. The bulk of checks remitted for collections are drawn on New York, and many on Boston or Philadelphia. Such collections are desirable at points where a surplus of exchange is created, as they afford a means of working it off at a small profit.

The usual form of letter transmitting collections is as follows:

BUCKEYE BANK, DAYTON, O.
July 5, 1884.

E. SIMPSON, Esq., *Cashier*,
   Tuscaloosa, Iowa.

      Dear Sir:—We enclose for collection and remittance, O. Kane on Smithers & Co., sight.......$750.
Patterson & Brown..........Aug. 20.....$1,000 & exchange.
   Yours respectfully,
F. BANDERS, *Cashier*.

CHAPTER XIV.

THE BOOKKEEPER.

Mathematical accuracy is one of the prime virtues of an accountant. It is nowhere more important than in bank bookkeeping. While the affairs of a bank are running along smoothly its customers are given little opportunity to judge of the capability and thoroughness of those who manipulate the books of accounts. But when the institution comes to grief, and the creditors are waiting in painful suspense to learn the fate of their deposits, the opportunities for determining how well the books have been handled are excellent. It is at such times that the public are taught to appreciate the value of accuracy, system and promptness. When it requires days, and, as is sometimes the case, weeks, for the bookkeepers to make up a statement of the condition of a suspended bank, the inference may be fairly taken that something is radically wrong. It may be the imperfections of the system in vogue, or possibly a weakness in the brain of the bookkeeper.

A good theory to follow in bank bookkeeping is one which each day presumes that the bank is to suspend payment before time for the doors to open the next morning. And not only so, but also one which presumes that the directors or proprietors are to require a complete financial exhibit of the bank's affairs within twenty-four hours from the time the suspension is announced. There can be no good reason why a complete statement should not be presented within a few hours at any time, if no crookedness has been practiced. It is not only important that the work of each day should be finished before the doors open on the morning of the day following, but that the work should be so performed as to enable the bookkeepers to make up a full exhibit without delay. Even in cases of defalcation and crookedness on the part of any one individual where several officers and clerks are employed, there would be no reasonable excuse for requiring days, and often weeks, in preparing statements for the public. Simplicity in method and an efficient clerical force will obviate the present prevailing difficulties.

It is not good economy for the manager of a bank to expect one clerk or bookkeeper to perform the labor of two. There can be as much of a mistake in employing not enough as too many. But, before considering the number to be employed, the fitness of each for the position should receive attention. Above all things, know that each and every person doing clerical work in a bank is thoroughly qualified. Then see that the force is sufficient to have the work kept closely up, and require in all cases that no part is neglected. We would say to the bookkeeper of a bank: Demand that you be allowed a sufficient force to do the work punctually and in the best manner. If your request is refused it is better to resign than take chances in doing your duty when you know that important parts must be neglected. Banks show, as a rule, more wisdom in this respect than commercial houses. Yet there are but few banks in which an improvement might not be made by an addition to the regular force. This improvement would redound to the advantage of stockholders as well as the bank's customers.

The method of bookkeeping practiced in a bank may have much to do with the force necessary for performing the work properly. We cannot undertake in this treatise to go into the details of all the different systems in vogue. It is our aim, however, to give such explanations of the methods in most general use as will enable the reader to understand the principles and be able to choose a plan best adapted to his special needs. Important changes and improvements in bank as well as commercial bookkeeping have taken place within the past ten or fifteen years. A few years ago banks received a fair revenue from the sale of exchange. Remittances from one part of the country to another are still made almost entirely by means of bank drafts, but since the establishment of a currency which is at par throughout the United States, the rate of exchange cannot much exceed the cost of transmitting money by express, and the business of dealing in exchange by banks is no longer considered an important item of revenue. The change has had its influence upon bank bookkeeping.

The tendency has been, in bank bookkeeping, to abridge the work. There is still room for improvement in many institutions in this direction. It is a good idea, in all places where possible, to avoid rewriting items and amounts. We will first turn our attention to

ACCOUNTS OF DEPOSITORS.

The depositors' accounts, in an institution doing a general banking business, absorb much the greatest attention of the bookkeepers. Eternal vigilance is a prime virtue in their manipulation. Considering their numbers, the infinite multiplicity of items they represent, and the vast sums received and disbursed upon them, the small number of mistakes made in their keeping is worthy of consideration. It demonstrates the possibility of wonderful accuracy. The errors, at least those discovered, will not average one in a thousand transactions.

There is, perhaps, an unusual degree of accuracy exhibited in the work upon this class of accounts. The reason is obvious. An error, no matter how slight, is almost certain to be discovered by the depositor. Whether or not the error is reported to the bank officials, such a discovery is painful to the bookkeeper. It forms a basis for suspecting other blunders; it may, too, involve serious difficulty. These are some of the penalties constantly in view, and they, no doubt, exert an influence.

In all branches of an accountant's work the probability that an error, if made, will be discovered by some one other than himself will invariably cause some weight upon vigilance and thoughtfulness. Where an error, if made, will be detected by its author, as is the case in some parts of the bookkeeper's work, and may be corrected before reaching others' eyes, a feeling of indifference is more apt to manifest itself. This suggests the importance of rotating the force employed in large banks, so that the work of each one will be examined by some one of the other employees. In England it is almost the universal practice to have a professional accountant go over, at stated periods, all the work of a bank. The plan is not much followed in this country, but it is being discussed in many quarters. Experience has shown that the examinations made by Government officials are not a sufficient guarantee to stockholders and depositors that the published exhibits are faithful showings of the banks' condition.

One cause that has had a tendency to bring about a high standard of accuracy in the treatment of depositors' accounts is that of special study in this direction. Much attention and skill have been directed to devising plans for keeping this class of accounts. We will presently illustrate some of these inventions. But let us first consider the elementary functions of a depositor's account.

THE DEPOSIT SLIP.

In the tenth chapter of this work are described the duties of the receiving teller. Depositors come oftener in contact with the receiving teller than with any other employee. It is this teller who receives the deposits. On page 92 appears a brief description of the depositor's pass-book. When making a deposit the depositor fills out a printed blank, upon which he writes his name and a description of items making up his deposit, thus:

Deposited by

George Washington

IN THE

NATIONAL BANK OF VALLEY FORGE.

PHILADELPHIA, *July* 4, 1886.

	Dollars.	Cents.
Bills...............................	650	
Checks.............................	310	
	280	40
	725	50
	1,965	90

This "Deposit Slip," with the funds to be deposited and the depositor's pass-book, are handed to the receiving teller. The bills are counted and the items examined and checked off by the teller, who charges the bank in the depositor's pass-book with the full amount of the deposit, and files the slip ready for the bookkeeper. These slips are the bank's vouchers for the transaction.

THE DEPOSITOR'S PASS-BOOK.

The depositor's pass-book is a small account book. Upon the left-hand page, or debit side, the deposits are entered; the right-hand, or credit pages are used to enter up the checks of the depositor. It is the bookkeeper's duty to write up and balance the depositor's pass-book when left at the bank for that purpose. The depositor's account in the bank's ledger furnishes the data for writing up the pass-book. In the ledger account, however, the deposits which, in the pass-book, appear on the debit side are entered on the credit side. The checks are entered on the debit side of the ledger account. The reason of this transposition is, that the

THE ARCTIC NATIONAL BANK in Account with RICHARD WHITTINGTON.

Dr.					Cr.
Jan. 2.....	E. K.............	10,000	1,324 05	175 20	100
3.....	J. C.............	400	208 40	960 50	46 75
4.....	E. K.............	2,000		2,100	10 50
				137 10	305 10
			12 *Vouchers returned.*	5,420 50	1,240 80
			Balance......		371 10
		12,400			12,400 00
Jan. 5.....	Balance........	371 10			

The letters opposite the dates on the debit page are the initials of the teller who received the deposit. On the credit page are several columns in which the amounts of the checks or vouchers are entered. These checks are returned with the pass-book to the depositor. The balance, after having been added to the footings of the checks, is carried to the debit of the account preparatory to continuing the transactions.

pass-book represents the depositor's account with the bank, while the bank's ledger shows the bank's account with the depositor.

DEPOSITORS' LEDGERS.

The postings to the depositors' accounts are sometimes made direct from the deposit slips on the one side, and from the checks on

Form of Depositors' Ledger.

Brown & Bacon.

| | | | Jan. 2.... | Dep......... | 500 |
| | | | | Col......... | 842 25 |

John Adams.

| Jan. 2..... | C'ks......... | 423 10 | Jan. 2.... | Col......... | 500 |

Henry Smith.

| Jan. 2..... | C'ks......... | 312 50 | Jan. 2.... | Dep......... | 250 |

C. C. Brown.

| | | | Jan. 2.... | Dep......... | 1250 |

the other. The checks and slips, when thus posted, are first entered in a journal or register for the purpose of proving the cash and accounting with the tellers. This journal or register forms a part of the general books of the bank. The ledgers containing the depositors' accounts are auxiliary to the general books. We mean by this that a statement of the bank's condition is made up independently of the depositors' ledgers. One account in the general ledger serves to show the liability of the bank to its depositors. In some banks the postings to the depositors' accounts are made from other books, usually called "journals." In some systems two journals are used, and in others only one. We give, in this connection, some illustrations of these journals. Though still used to some extent, the forms shown under the title of "debit journal" and "credit journal" have been mostly superseded by more modern devices. The form under the title of "deposit journal" is used by many country banks. It is simple, and well serves the purpose for which it is intended.

DEPOSITORS' LEDGER WITH BALANCE COLUMN.—FORM 2.

Richard Whittington.

Jan. 2...	Deposit...................		10,000	
2...	100, 46 75, 10 50, 305 10....	462 35		9,537 65
3...	Dep......................		400	
	1240 80, 175 20, 960 50......			
	2100, 137 10...............	4,613 60		5,324 05
4...	5420 50, 1324 05............			
	208 40....................	6,952 95		*1,628 90

The first column contains the debits or checks, the second column the credits or deposits, and the third column the balances. The balances are carried out every day after the deposits and checks have been entered up.

In the large city banks where the depositors are so numerous as to require a classification of the accounts, several books are kept for summarizing the checks and deposits. The depositors' accounts are grouped thus: Names commencing with A to D, E to K, L to R, and S to Z. The checks and deposit slips are assorted so as to be entered up under the several classes or groups in separate

* This balance is printed here in italics to represent an overdraft. In practice it would be written in red ink.

journals or registers. The work of writing up must be commenced in ample time for entering the last check paid and the last check deposited almost immediately after the tellers close their windows.

DEPOSITORS' LEDGER WITH DOUBLE BALANCE COLUMNS.—FORM 3.

Richard Whittington.

	462 35	305 10, 10 50, 46 75, 100...........	1/2	10,000	9,537 65
	4,613 60	2100, 137 10, 960 50, 175 20, 1240 80.	3	400	5,324 05
1628 90	6,952 95	208 40, 1324 05, 5420 50...........	4		

This represents a Depositors' Ledger with two debit and two credit columns; one column for itemized checks and one column for dates. The first column on the left shows the debits' balance or overdraft; the second column the totals of checks; the third, itemized checks and other explanatory remarks; the fourth, the dates; fifth, credits or deposits; and sixth, credit balances.

In the work of writing up there is precaution taken to leave sufficient space after the name has been once entered to add subsequent checks. This does not apply so much to deposits, as cases of more than one deposit to a name in a day are exceptional.

Form 4, or what is commonly known as the Boston method, possesses some advantages which have influenced its adoption in many places. It is intended to serve as a day-book and ledger combined. The asset balances are entered in *red*, and the liability balances in *black* ink. In our illustration we give a page, or portion of a page, showing the closing entries for two days. It will be seen that the depositors' accounts run horizontally across the page (two accounts occupying a compartment). First comes the balance brought forward from the page where the name previously appeared. Then there are two narrow columns under the heading "Checks in detail." The first of these columns belongs to the second account in the compartment, and the second column to first account in the compartment. The next two columns are for the totals of checks and deposits. The sixth column is a space for explanations upon the deposits or other credits. The seventh column contains the

DEPOSITORS' DAILY BALANCE BOOK.   III

balance at the close of the day. Following this, still to the right, the same is repeated under another day. A page nineteen inches in width will give space for three days' transactions. Running across both pages of the book, six days' business is recorded before the name is re-written. The object of dividing the page into compartments with horizontal lines, and placing only two accounts in one compartment, is to aid the eye in its sighting across the page from the side where the name is written.

In footing the balance columns the overdrafts are deducted, making the footing show, not the total liability of the bank for deposits, but the "net total deposits." This is one of the objections to be urged against the system. The overdrafts of depositors are assets. They may be serviceable in paying depositors, and they may not; they are certainly not as reliable as money in the vault. And, besides, a statement of a bank for the benefit of stockholders ought to show the total deposits and the aggregate of overdrafts as two separate items.

After footing the balance and total columns of the depositors' accounts for the day, a general statement may be written up by adding capital stock and other general accounts, if not too numerous. The column entitled "Total checks" may, in entering the impersonal or general accounts, be used for all cash disbursed. The "Total deposits" column may contain all cash receipts; in this way the balance book will serve to take the place of a general ledger.

One advantage of this method which recommends it is the easier locating of errors. Each page is susceptible of proof in itself, and thus an error may easily be pinned down to a small number of entries.

DEPOSITORS' BALANCE LEDGER.

The illustration presented under the title "Depositors' Balance Ledger" represents a portion of a page of a book extensively used by the large banking institutions of New York, and in some other cities. Practically speaking, it is a skeleton ledger, kept for the convenience of the paying teller. During banking hours it is never far from his counter, and the standing of any depositor's account can be ascertained in a few seconds at any time. This book has no connection with the depositors' ledger kept by the individual bookkeeper.

In the Boston method the daily balance book is the only ledger used for keeping the depositors' accounts. Thus, it will be seen that the two books have a widely different purpose. In many banks where the balance ledger is used the regular accounts of the depositors are kept by the individual bookkeeper, or bookkeepers (for there may be several of them), in ledgers of the usual form.

A complete explanation of the skeleton ledger is difficult in a small treatise which will not permit the introduction of ruled forms showing different colored inks. A page about eighteen inches square will give space for thirty accounts six days. The two pages of such a book will serve thirty accounts thirteen days. Two writings of an account will thus carry it through a month. The lines upon which the names are written are about five-eighths of an inch apart, and they alternate in color, first blue and then red. The change of color serves to guide the eye correctly across the page, or the two pages. For each day there is a pair of columns, the

DEPOSITOR'S BALANCE LEDGER.—FORM 5.

Names.	Aug. 1.		Aug. 2.		Aug. 3.		Aug.
N. Y. Tribune Ass'n.	210 40 318 60 27 50	*18400 10* 1415 60	'1540 835 15	*19259 20* 1410		*18194 05*	
R. Wells............	1210	*4200*	1840	*2405*	355 50	1840	
P. White............	460 375 *580 50* 250	250 1840 50	270 50 650	*1010* 375	350 70 10	*1385*	
	580 50	*22600 10*		*22674 20*	*355 50*	*19579 05*	

first, or left-hand column, being for debits or checks, and the second, or right-hand column, for credits or deposits; the balances are carried forward in pencil. The calculation in carrying the balances forward is done mentally. It would be surprising to one not expert in this work to observe the rapidity with which the bookkeeper performs these mental calculations. With three amounts on one side and two on the other, the items ranging in value from the units column to several thousand, the calculation is performed mentally, the balance struck without a moment's hesitation, and placed in its proper column for the next day. For example, the following represents a day's transactions:

Debit.	Credit.
7,462 25 35 60 379 84	12,620 39 284 60

The balance, 5,027.30, is dotted down with surprising rapidity. In footing the columns the pencil figures only are taken to get the total balances. The amounts in ink, when footed, show total drafts and total deposits for the day.

The plan followed by which the entries find their way from the tellers' counters and the exchanges, to the depositors' ledger and balance book, varies in different banks. The volume of business has much to do with the system in use. It is well worth the space here to give a description of the plan in vogue in the National Park Bank. This bank is a representative institution with over ten thousand active accounts on its depositors' ledgers. There are two receiving tellers. A depositor presents his book with deposit enclosed. If currency or specie form a part, it is counted and dropped into the till or money drawer. The checks and other items are not carefully examined. If the currency and coin are correct, the amount according to the deposit slip is entered in the pass-book. The deposit slip, the checks, drafts, or other items are kept together until a checking clerk takes them away. These items of the deposit slip are then carefully examined and re-checked upon the deposit slip. If an error is discovered the correction is made upon the slip. The checks, drafts, etc., are now classified and passed over to other clerks. Some go to clerks who enter them up ready for passing through the Clearing-house. Others must be sent out for collection by the bank's messenger. The checks of the bank's own depositors and correspondents go to clerks who enter them up preparatory for the bookkeepers. This is followed up so closely that, at the hour for closing the receiving teller's window, every check, draft and other item of the day has been charged up at the checking counter. The items in the balance ledgers are taken from the books kept up by the checking clerks, and the individual bookkeepers also make up their ledgers from the books kept on the checking counter.

There are four sources from which the balance ledger bookkeepers obtain the items of debits to the accounts in their charge. These are—first, through the Clearing-house; second, through the paying teller's department; third, from the receiving teller's department; and, fourth, through the note teller's department. They have been classified and entered up at the checking counter, so that he has only to write down the totals. There are some institutions having accounts with the Park Bank which draw as many as forty checks in a day; many draw twenty to thirty. This will explain why a method like that described in connection with the Boston daily balance book would not be practicable in all places.

In this bank the accounts of depositors or dealers are divided into four classes, and are kept by eight individual bookkeepers—

four of whom are on depositors' ledgers and four on the balance ledgers, thus:

Names from A to D,
E to K,
L to R,
S to Z.

The accounts of correspondents or other banks are arranged under two divisions: A to L,
M to Z.

Thus twelve individual bookkeepers are employed, eight on depositors' accounts, and four on accounts of other banks. The balance books are extended before the hour for opening next morning, and the footings made so as to compare with the general ledger before the close of the next day.

THE PRINCIPAL BOOKS.

The number and character of the books of a bank which make up the general set varies according to the volume of business transacted. The routine practiced is also dependent upon the extent of the transactions. For the purpose of illustration, we shall give in these pages a description of the books and routine best adapted to the needs of a bank of a moderate type.

Commencing with the organization of the Lunar National Bank, we will follow the transactions of a period sufficient to embrace a history of the general routine. The preliminaries for organizing a banking corporation have been fully described under Chapter V. We will presume, therefore, that all the preliminary arrangements have been perfected. The bank is organized with a capital of $250,000. This amount is paid in by the shareholders. For the original entries of what has transpired, we look to the minutes of the shareholders' meetings and the book of stock subscriptions.

The opening entry in the books of account is made in the general journal, a book with the ordinary journal rulings. The account representing the certificates of stock is debited, and the account of capital stock credited for the amount of the bank's capital. Before any of the certificates have been issued to subscribers, they (the certificates) form the only resources of the corporation. They are the assets against the liability of the corporation for the amount of its capital stock. As the stock is subscribed for, the certificates go out, and the corporation holds the stockholders individually and collectively for the amounts thus issued. This operation is recorded by charging in the books to the account of "Stockholders" the amount subscribed for, and crediting the account of stock certificates. When the shareholders pay in their subscriptions, the general account of "Cash" is debited, and the account of stockholders credited with the payment. Thus far the records of these transactions are the same in all joint-stock companies.

In the General Ledger the account of "Stockholders" represents these several accounts collectively. A book called a "Stock Ledger" is kept for the purpose of keeping the accounts of these persons separately. The Stock Ledger is an auxiliary to the general set.

The capital having been fully paid in, a purchase is made of $220,000 in United States bonds, on which a premium is paid of $30,000. The bonds are deposited with the Treasurer of the United States at Washington, and in return the bank receives its National bank notes to the amount of $198,000, less $9,900, the five-per-cent. fund for the redemption of circulation by the United States Treasurer.

The premium on bonds, ten-per-cent. fund to secure circulation, and five-per-cent. fund to secure redemption, together may be treated under one general title, they forming a reserve growing out of the bank's circulation. The title we have chosen is "Circulation Reserve." This is not arbitrary. The account represents an asset which, in the example used here, is $61,900. The premium paid in on the bonds forms nearly one-half of this reserve. But so long as the present rate of interest holds, this resource is as substantial as so much money locked up where it cannot be used until the bank withdraws its circulation. The three items which, combined, make the reserve fund, or circulating reserve, could, if it were desired, be treated each under an independent title. It would, however, only encumber the books and serve no practical purpose in the end.

The first three entries in the journal could, in a case of the kind used as an illustration, be condensed under one journal entry. But, suppose, instead of all the stock being subscribed for at once, only a part had been taken. Then, too, presuming that the amount subscribed for had been only paid in part. It will be seen that each of the entries given would have been necessary for recording the operations, step by step as they transpired.

For all that has been done up to this time, it was not necessary that the company should have a place of business of its own. It may have had one, however, and got fairly under way before its circulating notes had been sent on from the Treasury Department. But, presuming that our records represent the transactions in the order of their occurrence, we now find the new corporation ready to rent or buy a place to conduct its business, open its doors and receive deposits. Let us proceed to examine the history of what takes place, and record the various operations in the books of account.

ITEMS FOR ILLUSTRATING THE DEBIT AND CREDIT JOURNALS.

(1.) Rec'd notice from First National of Cleveland that Brown & Bacon's d'ft on Hardin had been paid, and the amount, $842.25, placed to our credit. Brown & Bacon deposited, cash, $500. (See Credit Journal, deposits column, $1,342.25; also Depositors' Ledger, acc't of B. & B. For charge to First Nat., Cleveland, see Debit Journal.)

(2.) Bo't 100 U. S. 4s@123 ($12,300), paying by draft on Fourth Nat., New York. (See Credit J., general col. for credit to Fourth Nat., and also Debit J., general col. for credit to Government stocks.

(3.) Rec'd notice from Second Nat., St. Louis, that John Adams's d'ft on Beeten for $500 had been paid and placed to our credit. (See C. J., deposit col., and D. J., general col.; also Depositors' Ledger.)

(4.) Paid bill, stationery and printing, $47.50. (See D. J., general col.)

Note.—This is entered to the account of "Expense." In some banks the general expenses are divided under various headings, such as "Salaries," "Stationery and Postage," "Rent," "Fuel and Gas," etc. The "Expense Account" in such instances would embody only items of contingencies not provided for by special classification. Classifying the items is a matter of taste. As a rule, it is well to adopt such a practice.

FORM OF CREDIT JOURNAL.

Washington, January 2, 1885.

L. F.	Title of Account.	Items and Notation. Col. & Ex.	Deposits.	General.
	Brown & Bacon......	500 Col. 842.25	1,342 25	
	Fourth National, N.Y.	U. S. 4's @ 123....		12,300
	John Adams..........	Col...............	500	
	Henry Smith........	"	250	
	C. C. Brown.........	"	1,250	
	National Park, N. Y..	C. Goodnough..... 10		4,000
		J. Peters........... 4		1,600
		F. Brokaw......... 3 14		1,256
		R. Albert.......... 80		320
	P. Fisher............	Disct..............	3,979	
	Amos Smith.........	"	2,953 50	
	F. Hill..............	"	2,467 50	
	Interest.............	Disct. Register....	6 25	93 75
	Col. & Exchange..	....	24 19	24 19
	Deposits...........	....	12,742 25	12,742 25
	Cash, Dr.........	....		32,336 19

Form of Debit Journal.

Washington, *January 2, 1885.*

L. F.	Title of account.	Items and Notations.	Col. & Ex.	Deposits.	General.
	First Nat., Cleveland..	B. & B. Col.......			842 25
	Governments.........	4's pr. dft. 4th Nat.			12,300
	Second Nat., St. Louis.	J. Adams, Col.....			500
	Expense..............	Stationery, Print'g.			47 50
	Fourth National, N.Y.	Remittance........			1,000
	Second Nat., Phila....	C. C. Brown's, K.. Goodnow, 4,010.. Peters, 1,000..			5,010
	F. Brokaw............	1,259 14...........		1,259 14	
	T. Swift..............	120, 145 50, 200....		465 50	
	L. Loveland..........	18 10, 14 60, 105 30.		128	
	H. Smith.............	300, 12 50.........		312 50	
	John Adams..........	105, 318 10........		423 10	
	Bills Discounted......	D. R..............			4,000
	Dom. Exchange......	D. R..............			5,500
	Deposits, Dr......	Checks paid.......		2,588 24	2,588 24
	Cash, Cr..........	Disbursements....			31,787 99

Discount.

When Discounted.	No.	Drawer or End.	Drawee or Mkr.	Where Pay.	Date.	Time.
Jan. 2......	1	P. Fisher.......	J. C. Vermont..	Washingt'n.	Jan. 2	60
2......	2	Amos Smith....	T. Wilder......	N. Y.......	Jan. 2	90
2......	3	C. Stevens......	Brown & Bacon.	Chicago....	Jan. 2	60

(5.) Sold drafts on Nat. Park, New York, as follows: C. Goodnow, $4,000, exch. $10; J. Peters, $1,600, exch. $4; F. Brokaw, $1,256, exch. $3.14; R. Albert, $320, exch. 80c. (See C. J.) Rec'd in payment, Goodnow's c'k on Second Wash'n, $4,010; Peters' c'k on do., $1,000, balance cash; F. Brokaw's c'k on us, $1,259.14. (See D. J. and Depositors' Ledger, d'ft to Albert paid in cash.)

(6.) Discounted notes for P. Fisher, $4,000; Amos Smith, $3,000; F. Hill, $2,500. Total, $9,500. (See D. J., general col. from Discount Register; also C. J. deposits, and col. and exch. from Discount Register.)

Note.—The original entries of these transactions would be those in the Discount Register. The transactions then find their way to the Ledger through the Debit and Credit Journals.

(7.) Paid checks of Swift, Loveland, Smith and Adams. (See Debit Journal, deposits col.)

THE DISCOUNT REGISTER.

The purposes served by the Discount Register are what, in a mercantile business, would be found in the use of a Bill-book. The formular arrangement of the Register is somewhat more extensive than that of the Bill-book, as the information desired by a bank covers a broader field than that sought by a commercial house. In this book are recorded, in the order of discount, the notes which become the property of the bank. The names of the drawer or endorser appear first, and then come those of drawee or maker. Following these are columns for information as to where the note is payable, the time specified on its face, date when due, and time it is to run for which discount is charged. The amount of

REGISTER.

W'n Due.	To Run.	Bills Dis.	Dom.Ex.	Int.	Col.& Ex.	Proceeds.	Credited To	C'k.
March 6..	63	4,000		21		3,979	P. Fisher....	✓
April 5 .	93		3,000	46 50		2,953 50	Amos Smith.	✓
March 6..	63		2,500	26 25	6 25	2,467 50	F. Hill......	✓
		4,000	5,500	93 75	6 25	9,400 00		

the note is sometimes classified under two headings, as seen in the illustration, viz., "Bills discounted" and "Domestic exchange," and sometimes it is entered under one heading, as "Amount" or "Face." When the two columns are used, the first embraces the notes payable at home, or in the place where the bank is located, and the latter those payable at other places. A column is provided for "Interest," another for "Collection and Exchange," and one also for "Proceeds." Finally the name appears to whom the proceeds are credited, and a narrow column is added for the "check" which is made as the items are posted.

There are many forms of this book in use, some less and some more elaborate than the one we have given. Some banks treat all notes discounted under the one general title of "Bills Receivable," and use as a record only the simplest form of a bill-book. In many banks a large number of books are used which the experience and skill of progressive accountants have demonstrated are not really essential. There is a growing tendency among bank accountants to dispense with every book not absolutely necessary, and to abridge the bookkeeping in every way possible. This is a commendable spirit of reform, but care should be taken that the abridgement is not carried to excess, lest grave inaccuracies creep in through the lack of proper checks and proofs.

THE OFFERING-BOOK.

Chapter VIII. is devoted chiefly to the subject of discounting paper. The information there given is so explicit that nothing remains to be said here more than to explain some special functions of the Offering-book, and give an idea of its place in a system of bank accounts. On page 62, in the chapter referred to, reference is made to the formula arrangement of the Offering-book. There is no prescribed rule for the form to be employed. Any arrangement that will best meet the requirements may be adopted. But little difference in the style is to be noticed among the many in use. We submit a form that seems to fill the requirements. The form may be improved upon for some institutions. Some Offering-books have a column headed "Average Balances." This is to give the information contained in the Average-book, for a description of which see page 59. Where an Average-book is kept, the addition of the average balance column is not essential, and if it tends to make the book cumbersome, should be omitted. The Offering-book is commonly termed a memorandum or auxiliary to the regular set. It, however, acts as the book of original entry for the class of transactions which originate therein. From the Offering-book the record is carried to the Discount Register, through which it enters the ledgers. A record of the discounted paper must also be carried to the Domestic Ticklers, if payable at home, or to the Domestic-exchange Book, if sent away for collection.

Many banks have dispensed with the Offering-Book. The information given in Chapter VIII. explains why the book may in many cases be unnecessary.

OFFERING–BOOK.

No.	Date.	Offered by	Guarantee.	Payable at	Amount	To Run.	Ac- cepted	De- clined	Re- marks
1	July 18	Joseph Arnold.	H. Coulter......	Our bank......	1,000	60 ds.	1,000		
2	17	W. T. Bartlett	U. P. Bds $3,200.	Arctic, N.Y....	2,500	60 ds.	2,500		
3	18	H. Coulter....	O. B. Arnold....	Our bank	3,500	90 ds.	3,500		
4	16	D. Robb.....	J Hurd.........	do.	750	60 ds.		750	
5	17	J. H. Watt....	G. A. Lewis,. ..	Chemical, N.Y.	2,780	30 ds.	2,780		
6	18	C. T. Wood...	J. Green........	Our bank,.....	1,800	60 ds.		1,800	
7	17	P. Young.....	T. W. Bush.....	do.	500	30 ds.		500	
8	18	F. Zahn.......	R. Ladd........	do.	3,400	60 ds.	3,400		

HISTORY OF TRANSACTIONS.

July 1.—Concluded purchase of property known as Treasury Hall, for bank building, paying for same $27,500. Recording deed, $2.50.
12th.—Bill of carpenter for fitting up bank building, $562, paid.
13th.—Bought furniture and fixtures, for which bill amounted to $375.
15th.—Paid for books and other stationery, including express charges, $155.
16th.—Bought postage stamps, $12. Bill for printing, paid, $75.10.
Correspondence with Arctic Nat. Bank established by depositing in current funds $50,000. Paid expenses of President, trip to New York, $55.
18th.—Received following deposits: H. M. Lutz, 585.30; Theo. Kitchen, 1,624.90; G. A. Lewis, 1,210.40; E. P. Graham, 482.60; W. H. Webb, 1,540.82.

Among deposits were following checks and bills:
First Nat., 513.80, 75.50, 12.40. 1,210.40.
East River, N. Y., 1,105.82.
Hanover, N. Y., 269.95.
Stebbins, F., & Co., Lawrence, Dak., 71.50.
Exchange, Pike, Ill., 25.30.
Discounted paper as follows:
For Joseph Arnold, H. Coulter's note, 60 days, 1,000.00.
For W. T. Bartlett, his note, 60 ds., for 2,500.00; secured by U. S. bonds.
For H. Coulter, O. B. Arnold's note, 90 ds., 3,500.00.
For J. H. Watt, G. A. Lewis's note, 30 ds., 2,780.00.
For F. Zahn, R. Ladd's note, 60 ds., 3,400.00.

Bought following bills on New York, and sent same for credit to Arctic Nat. Bank :
Theo. Kitchen's dft. on Imp. and Tdrs.', endorsed by W. T. Bartlett, 7,000.00; premium, 7.00. H. C. Rider's dft. on C. S. Hough, payable at Nat. Park, 4,000.00; premium, 3.50.

122   PRACTICAL BANKING.

Sold exchange on Arctic Nat. as follows:
H. M. Lutz, 2,500.00; prem., 3.25.
F. Zahn, 1,800.00; prem., 2.50.
W. H. Webb, 250.00; prem. 50 cts.
Paid the following checks:
W. H. Webb, 250.50, 13.25.
Theo. Kitchen, 270.50, 18.42, 5.10.

19th.—Received the following deposits:
G. A. Lewis, 516.80; W. H. Webb, 275.10; G. A. Linton, 1,255.00; H. M. Lutz, 346.10; John Rapson, 1,842.70; J. D. Brown, 540.15; J. W. Torrey, 178.40.

Among the deposits were the following checks:
First Nat., Hartford, Conn., 175.80.
Chemical, New York, 255.10.
Fourth Nat., New York, 156.50.
Merch. Nat., New York, 127.40.
All of which were remitted Arctic Nat. for credit.

Paid checks as follows:
W. H. Webb, 75.80, 37.50, 42.60.
G. A. Lewis, 13.15, 27.50, 105.85, 10.10.
Theo. Kitchen, 8.75, 75.80, 327.40, 8.25.
H. M. Lutz, 107.10, 46.60, 3.27.
G. A. Linton, 36.40, 27.85.
J. D. Brown, 8.40, 10.75, 41.85.

Received for collection the following bills:
No. 1—John Rapson, on Brown Bros., Chicago, 246.80; No. 2—J. W. Torrey, on Smith & Wood New York, 47.25; No. 3—W. H. Webb, on Drexel, Morgan & Co., 1,247.50; No. 4—E. P. Graham, on Prince & Whitely, 385.10; No. 5—J. D. Brown, on John H. Davis & Co., 470.50.

GENERAL JOURNAL.

Lunar City, July, 18........

Stock Certificates.....................	250,000	
To Capital Stock...............		250,000
Stockholders.........................	250,000	
To Stock Certificates............		250,000
Cash................................	250,000	
To Stockholders.................		250,000
United States Bonds..................	220,000	
Circulation Reserve, (Premium).......	30,000	
To Cash........................		250,000
Bank Circulation.....................	198,000	
Circulation Reserve, (Ten p. c. fund)..	22,000	
To United States Bonds.........		220,000
Tellers' Circulation..................	188,100	
Circulation Reserve, (Five p. c. fund).	9,900	
To Bank Circulation............		198,000

Paying Teller's Cash-Book and Journal.

Journal	Exch'ge	Dis. & Prem.	July.	L.F.	Deposits	Exch'ge	Dis. Paper	Exp. Items	Journal
188,100			On hand..............						26,502 50
									937
									155
			Real Estate..........						30,000
		5 62	Furniture and Fix.....						
		3 75	Books and Stationery..						
		12	Postage and Printing..					87 10	
		75 10	Arctic National Bank...						
			Contingent Exp........					55	
		10 50	No. 1 Coulter.........				1,000		
		26 25	No. 2 Bartlett........				2,500		
		54 25	No. 3 Arnold..........				3,500		
		15 29	No. 4 Lewis...........				2,780		
		35 70	No. 5 Ladd............				3,400		
		7 00	Kitchen...............			7,000			
		3 50	Rider.................			4,000			
		3 25	Lutz..................						
		2 25	Zahn..................						
		50	Webb.................. 250 50, 13 25		263 75				
	2,500		W. H. Webb........... 270 50, 18 43		294 02				
	1,800		I. Kitchen............ 5 10						
	250								
		137 49	D. & P. Cr. Depositor's Dr.		557 77				557 77
137 49	4,550		Cr. Arctic Nat'l Bank. Dr.			11,000			11,000
4,450			Rec. Teller Cr. Dis. Paper..				13,180		13,180
1,889			Expense Items.........					142 10	142 10
104,676 49			Balance...............						91,202 12
91,202 12									94,676 49

PRACTICAL BANKING.

Receiving Teller's Check-Book.

Depositor.	Cash.	Dom. Ex.	For. Ex.	Total.
July 18.				
Lutz	413 00	75 30	96 80	585 10
Kitchen	841 00	513 80	269 95	1,624 75
Lewis		1,210 40		1,210 40
Graham	200 00	12 40	270 10	482 50
Webb	435 00		1,105 82	1,540 82
By Paying Teller	1,889 00			
" Dom. Collections		1,811 90		
" For. Collections			1,742 67	
" Dep. Ledger				5,443 57
July 19.				
Lewis	300 00	41 00	175 80	516 80
Webb	20 00		255 10	275 10
Linton	1,200 00	55 00		1,255 00
Lutz	300 00		46 10	346 10
Rapson	1,500 00	300 00	42 70	1,842 70
Brown, J. D.	240 00	5 05	295 10	540 15
Torrey	150 00	28 40		178 40
By Paying Teller	3,710 00			
" Dom. Collections		429 45		
" For. Collections			814 80	
" Dep. Ledger				4,954 25

Collection

Date Left.	No.	Drawer or Endorser.	Drawee or Maker.	Where Payable.	Date.
July 19	1	John Rapson	Brown Bros.	Chicago	Jul. 1
19	2	A. Cranberry	Smith & Wood.	N. Y.	10
19	3	W. H. Webb	Drexel, M. & Co.	"	15
19	4	A. Apple	Prince & W.	"	19
19	5	J. D. Brown	J. H. Davis & Co.	"	19

Domestic Tickler.

August.

Date.	No.	Payer.	Amount.	Collected for.	Remarks.
July 18....	4	G. A. Lewis.........	2,780 00	Dis.	

September.

July 18....	1	H. Coulter..........	1,000 00	Dis.	
18....	2	W. T. Bartlett......	2,500 00	Dis.	
18....	5	R. Ladd............	3,400 00	Dis.	

October.

July 18....	3	O. B. Arnolds.......	3,500 00	Dis.	–

Register.

Time.	Due.	Amount.	Collected for.	Sent to.	C'k.
30 ds.	Aug. 2	246 80	John Rapson.......	First Nat...........	✓
60 ds.	Sep. 11	47 25	J. W. Torrey.......	Arctic.............	✓
30 ds.	Aug. 17	1,247 50	W. H. Webb.......	Arctic.............	✓
30 ds.	Aug. 21	385 10	E. P. Graham......	Arctic.............	✓
30 ds.	Aug. 21	470 50	J. D. Brown.......	Arctic.............	✓

Depositors' Balance Ledger, July, 18.....

Depositors.	18		19		20	21
H. M. Lutz........	270 50 18 42 5 10	585 10	107 10 46 60 3 77	585 10 346 10	774 23 910 53	
Theo. Kitchen.....		1,624 75	8 75 75 80 327 40 8 35	1,330 73		
G. A. Lewis.......		1,210 40	13 15 27 50 105 86 10 10	1,210 40 516 80	1,570 60	
E. P. Graham......		482 50		482 50	482 50	
W. H. Webb........	250 50 13 25	1,540 82	75 80 37 50 42 60	1,277 07 275 10	1,396 27	
G. A. Linton......			36 40 27 85	1,255	1,190 75	
John Rapson.......				1,842 70	1,842 70	
J. D. Brown.......			8 40 10 75 41 85	540 15	479 15	
J. W. Torrey......				178 40	178 40	
	557 77	5,443 57	1,014 92	4,885 80 4,954 25	8,825 13	

THE DEPOSIT JOURNAL.

The Deposit Journal is not as universally used as the General Ledger, the Tickler or Discount Register. It is used in many country banks, and helps to simplify and abridge the entries in the General Journal. One side of the book shows the work of the paying teller, and the other that of the receiving teller, coupled with the records of certificates of deposit issued. Certificates of deposit are sometimes issued by one official and sometimes by another. In some country banks the cashier is also paying-teller and receiving teller, *i. e.*, he performs the duties of both, and may be also the book-keeper, note teller and discount clerk. We do not refer to the functions of the various departments of service with the idea that the various duties must be performed by one and the same person. If the one person acts as both paying and receiving tellers the Deposit Journal becomes a mere cash-book for recording a special line of transactions.

THE DEPOSIT-JOURNAL.

Debits, *Monday, Jan. 5, 1885.*   Credits, *Monday, Jan. 5, 1885.*

L.F.	Names.	Checks.	Ctf's Dep.	L.F.	Names.	Deposits.	Ctf's Dep.
	C. H. Pine........	210 40			Alex. Hawley......	750	
	Jos. Arnold........	1,406 10			W. B. Hincks.....		1,000
	F. N. Benham.....	75 50			F. W. Marsh......	150 40	
	H. B. Drew, 1510..		500		C. H. Pine........	75 50	
	T. L. Bartholomew.	405			J. P. Wood........	535	
					Total Deposits....	1,510 90	1,510 90
	Wm. E. Seeley....		175		Total Ctf's issued.		1,000
	I. B. Prindle.......	57 10					
	E. E. Post.........	146 60					
	Total C'ks Pd......	2,300 70	2,300 70				
	Total Ctf's Pd.....		675				
	Paying Teller's *Credits.*		2,975 70		Receiving Teller *Chg'd*....		2,510 90

Besides the books described, there may also be named several records or registers, such as the Certificate of Deposit Register and Draft Register. These are simple forms, and require no special explanation upon their formular arrangement nor instruction upon their use. The former is a mere record of the certificates of deposit: when issued, to whom, the amount, and when paid. The latter furnishes information as to the drafts or bills drawn on corresponding banks, date, in whose favor, on whom drawn, and amount.

NOTE.—For explanation of "Depositors' Balance Ledger," see pages 112, 113. Figures in italics represent balances, which are carried forward in pencil.

CHAPTER XV.

THE RUNNER AND PORTER.

He is a young man, and occupies the lowest position in the bank. He is simply a messenger to collect drafts and notes. Boys are hired who are eighteen to twenty years old, are paid a small salary, and are quickly trained to go around the city with notes and drafts for collection. Their instructions are simple and definite, They must not take anything beside a certified check or good money, unless instructed by the Note Teller to do otherwise. He has charge of the runners, who are promoted whenever vacancies occur. Many bank clerks and not a few cashiers and presidents began as runners.

In London a bank messenger or runner is called an out teller, or collecting clerk. His duties are quite the same, though his methods differ in some respects. When he starts out from the bank, on what is there termed his "walk," he leaves behind him a record of the route he is to travel, and of the collecting, notifying, and presenting he is to do, in a book called the WALK BOOK. In this way the bank is kept informed of the whereabouts of their absent messenger, a bit of information that must be highly appreciated. In our banks and offices the inquiry, "Where is that messenger?" has become as familiar as the question, "Where are the police?" The London collecting clerk, or out teller, invariably has his wallet strapped to his body with chain and belt, a practice which has in some cases been copied here, and ought to be here more widely in vogue. The drafts which he takes upon his route for presentation, for acceptance, are always left with the drawees, who have twenty-four hours in which to return them to the bank.

The porter is the janitor. His duty in some banks is to appear when the watchman leaves at six o'clock in the morning. He puts the bank in order, and stays until the clerks come, then takes all the books out of the vault and puts them in their proper places. It is now probably about half-past nine. At night, after the clerks go away, he puts the books back, locks the vault and stays in the bank until the watchman appears at eight o'clock. After the clerks are gone, the janitor, porter or watchman is always present. In some banks the porter is a special messenger during the day. After doing his work in the morning he retires, and, having arranged his dress, appears again, and is thus engaged during the day. When thus employed, if a bank has any coin to transport, he generally attends to it.

CHAPTER XVI.

DEALINGS IN EXCHANGE.

A bill of exchange is a familiar instrument, for it is one of the oldest used in commerce. It may be defined as an order by a person on another living in a different place, directing him to pay a sum of money to a third person. Worcester's definition of exchange is: "the method of adjusting accounts or paying debts, when the debtor and creditor are distant from each other, by means of an order or draft called a bill of exchange, so as to avoid the transmission of either money or goods." The person who writes the bill is called the drawer, the person to whom it is addressed is called the drawee, and the person who is to receive the money is called the payee. When the drawee has accepted the bill he is called the acceptor. This is done by writing his name and the word "accepted" across the face of the bill, and also the date if the bill is payable after sight. In accepting a bill, the acceptor cannot vary the terms of it; for example, if it be drawn on a person living in New York, and payable there, he cannot accept it payable in Boston. He must follow the direction in the bill.

The phrase "bill of exchange" is often abbreviated and called simply exchange. In newspaper quotations the one word is generally used. Thus "exchange on New Orleans," or "exchange on London," is quoted at a certain figure. The term is somewhat ambiguous, however, sometimes meaning the rate of exchange and sometimes the instrument. But the term is employed in such relations to other words that persons have no difficulty in understanding what is meant.

What is the use of these instruments, and what purpose do they serve? Suppose that Jones, who lives in New York, owes Williams, of St. Louis, $10,000. Exchange on New York being almost always at a premium, Jones will either send his certified check on his New York bank for the amount he owes in St. Louis, or he will deposit the money in his New York bank, and take the bank's certificate of deposit for the amount, payable to the order of his debtor, Williams, in St. Louis. Williams will have no difficulty in negotiating this certified check, or the certificate of the New York bank, because, as already stated, New York exchange is almost everywhere acceptable. But if, on the other hand, Williams, of St.

Louis, desires to pay $10,000 to Jones, of New York, he will either draw a draft on some party in New York who is indebted to him, and send the draft to Jones, or he will go to his bank in St. Louis and buy, at the current rate, exchange on New York, *i. e.*, the bank's draft on its New York correspondent, payable to the order of Jones. If bills of exchange did not exist, Williams would be obliged to ship the money from St. Louis to New York. This would cost expressage, besides the danger of loss by robbery or other accident, and the loss of interest during the period of transmission.

Many bills are drawn payable at sight, and in certain States these must be paid when presented. In other States, however, the drawees are entitled on sight drafts to three days' grace. To render bills payable at once when presented the words "at sight" are omitted, and the drafts are then payable on demand.

The business of buying and selling exchange is a very large one, especially that of foreign exchange. The buying of exchange comes about in this way. Suppose Williams, of St. Louis, having sold a bill of goods to Jones, of New York, has drawn a bill of exchange on Jones for the amount payable to his (Williams') own order. Williams wants the money at once, perhaps to pay for purchases. He goes to a bank and asks the cashier if he will buy the bill. The cashier looks at it; he knows that the drawee is perfectly good, and that in the event of his failure to pay he can hold the drawer responsible. He buys the bill and pays Williams the money therefor. Transactions of this kind are occurring daily among the banks. Enormous quantities of cotton, wool, breadstuffs, provisions of all kinds and other commodities are bought and paid for by means of bills of exchange. The bank charges the agreed rate of exchange and interest to reimburse itself for the use of the money until the draft or bill can be collected. The bill is then forwarded for collection to the correspondent of the bank in the place where the draft is payable.

It is a very common thing for the western merchant to make advances to the farmer or planter to enable him to grow his crops. He may advance him cash or furnish him with the necessaries of life, usually·in either case taking as security a chattel mortgage on his stock and a lien upon the growing crops. Suppose the product to be cotton. When gathered the cotton is shipped to the merchant, who proceeds to sell it for account of the planter, and to reimburse himself for the advances made. When sold the cotton is shipped East, and the transportation company's bill of lading for so many bales is attached to the merchant's draft on the consignee for the value of the cotton; or the merchant may forward the goods to a commission merchant East for sale. He then attaches his draft for the approximate value of the goods, and goes to his local banker and sells his bill of exchange with documents, the latter being endorsed so as to convey the title to the cotton to the owner of the draft.

Merchants in St. Louis, Chicago and the other Western and Southern points are constantly buying merchandise, groceries, dry goods, etc., from merchants in New York and the East. For this merchandise the West and South is indebted to New York and the East. On the other hand, the products of the West and South, cotton, grain, beef, pork, etc., are constantly being shipped North and East.

The transactions in cotton, for example, exceed three hundred millions a year, a large portion of which is consigned to houses in the North, who make advances on the security of these instruments. Formerly the method of doing business was different. Then the banks in New York and other places would not advance on bills of lading and warehouse receipts, and if the broker or merchant did so he had the money from which the advance was made. In those days cotton was sold on sixty days' time. As soon as it was purchased in the North the planter drew on the receiver, and after the bill was accepted the local bank cashed the paper. But now the Southern banks have not enough money to do this business, and cannot take the paper when offered, and consequently the planter consigns the cotton and draws for three-quarters or more, of its value. By the present method, it may be added, the receivers must have more capital than formerly, as then they had two months in which to sell and get money before their acceptances became due.

Several years ago a quantity of wheat was sent from Chicago on a bill of lading to order. The bank in that city advanced on it, and the grain was forwarded, under the direction of the bank, to a certain storehouse, with instructions to keep it until the drafts that represented the advance were paid. As these had several months to run, the storekeeper, who was a speculator, thought it would be a fine thing to use the grain, intending to put other grain, similar in quality and quantity, in its place before the drafts matured. Accordingly, he forwarded it to a house in New York for sale. The consignee was a careful, cautious man. He examined the bill of lading, found that it was genuine, examined the wheat also, and found that it answered the description required, and made a large advance at the request of the consignor on the same. The grain was sold, and the balance, after deducting the charges, etc., was paid over to the storekeeper.

It is needless to add that his speculation turned out disastrously, and consequently he could not replace the wheat. Then the bank in Chicago found out that their wheat was not where they supposed it to be. They traced the wheat into the hands of the consignee of New York, and though he had obtained it in a perfectly honest way, yet, inasmuch as the storekeeper had no title to it, he could convey no title to the consignee, and consequently the latter was held liable. This doctrine has made the business of advancing money on the security of bills of lading more perilous than is agreeable to bankers and commission merchants, and the question arises whether it is not possible to grant greater protection to them than they now receive. Ought not common carriers to be held responsible for the acts of their agents in issuing bills of lading? A bill embodying this obligation was introduced into Congress at the last session. It substantially declares that bills of lading, issued by an agent authorized to issue such instruments, should be conclusive evidence against the carrier in the hands of a *bona-fide* holder for value, that the freight was actually received as in the bill of lading stated, and that the agent issuing the same had full authority to do so. To prevent this rule from becoming too severe in its practical application as against the carriers, the proposed law contained a further provision that the carrier should not be responsible under the provisions of the same on any bill of lading on which he stamped the words "not negotiable," nor for any statement of fact in such a bill of lading caused wholly by the fraud of the shipper of the merchandise therein named, the holder of the bill, or the person under whom he claimed.

It was hoped that this measure would meet the necessities of the case, for while it is true that much may be said upon the propriety of making principals responsible for the acts of their agents, it is also true that that doctrine may be carried to such an extent as to work positive injustice. To make carriers responsible to an unlimited amount upon bills of lading issued at remote and unimportant stations by agents, of whose actions, owing to the circumstances, carriers have but little actual knowledge or control, is perhaps to increase the risks of the transportation business beyond its legitimate limits.

The practical effect of the bill would be, if enacted, that railroad companies would issue to their agents generally non-negotiable bills of lading, which could not be made negotiable by any erasure or alteration; they would provide their trusted agents at the largest receiving depots with negotiable bills of lading, which would be issued as required.

There is another kind of bill which may be described. A firm in New York sends an agent to Chicago to buy grain. Mr. Snooks, the agent, buys a considerable quantity, and in order to make payment draws on his principal or consignor for the full amount of his engagement. He takes this bill to a bank and asks them to advance the money, as in the case just mentioned. The bank, if having funds, is usually willing to grant the advance requested.

The bank forwards the draft to its corresponding bank in New York, which presents it to the drawee in due time. He accepts it, and pays according to its tenor. In this case, as the wheat is purchased for the consignee, of course he is liable for the amount, and the bill is drawn for the full sum that is due for it.

When a draft is offered for sale, how much will a bank pay for it? To answer this question clearly a brief explanation is necessary. If the business men in New York are selling about as many goods to the merchants in St. Louis as they, on the other hand, are selling to New Yorkers, then the bills of exchange drawn in both cities will be at par—in other words, they will be transferred from one person to another for just the amount expressed on their face. There may be a very slight difference, enough to pay the banks for the trouble of buying and selling them; but, for the moment, we will leave that fact out of sight. But now, suppose that the merchants of St. Louis are selling the New Yorkers three times as many goods as the former are buying in New York, then the merchants of New York would owe those of St. Louis three times as much money. The reader will perceive that there will be three times as many bills drawn by the merchants of St. Louis as by the New Yorkers, and if all the St. Louis merchants should wish to sell their bills they could not get par for them, because the buyers could not sell them at a profit, for the simple reason that there would be occasion for using only one-third of them in settling the debts due by the St. Louis merchants to the New Yorkers. On the other hand, if all the New Yorkers should desire to sell their bills they could get more than par for them, because the entire amount would settle only one-third of their indebtedness to the St. Louis merchants. The bills, therefore, which the New York merchants would draw on those in St. Louis would command a premium, while the bills drawn by the St. Louis merchants on the New York ones would be at a discount. It may be added here, in passing, that the bills drawn by the New York merchants on those in St. Louis would be called St. Louis exchange, and the bills drawn by the St. Louis merchants on those in New York, New York exchange. When the New York merchants cannot get St. Louis exchange at par, but must pay a premium therefor, the rate of exchange as between the two cities is said to be against New York; if the St. Louis merchants should owe a balance to those in New York, then they would be obliged to pay a premium to get New York exchange with which to settle their indebtedness, and the rate of exchange would be in favor of New York. In other words, the rate of exchange is always against the place that owes the most money, and in favor of the place that owes the least. But the rate of exchange does not exceed the cost of transporting specie, and the cost of doing this between many places is small; for this reason the rate of exchange between Boston and New York is very little. Although a great many bills are drawn on these two cities, yet the rate is very low, because they are so near together, and the modes of communication are so perfect that money may be readily sent from one city to the other to discharge any indebtedness which may exist between them which cannot be easily settled with the medium of bills of exchange. Further on we have given quotations of bills of exchange drawn on New York by other places. It will be seen that the rate is only five cents on $1,000 in Boston —a sum too insignificant to be considered. But between New York and other places farther away the rate is higher.

One thing further ought to be said in this connection. At certain seasons of the year a large amount of grain is shipped from the West to the East, also pork, beef, lard, and other provisions; enormous quantities of cotton are shipped from the South, too, and many other articles which need not be mentioned. At the same time, Western merchants are making large purchases in the East, New York, Philadelphia, Boston, and elsewhere. But the purchases made in the East are not so heavy as those made by the Eastern men of the West. The consequence is, there are not enough bills of exchange made in the East to pay all of the indebtedness to the West; in other words, the rate of exchange during those seasons of the year is pretty steadily against the Eastern cities. When the balance becomes large and the rate of exchange considerable, it is absolutely necessary to remit currency to the West to restore the balance of trade. There is no other way of restoring it. Years ago, when money was less plentiful in the West than it is at the present time, there was a more urgent need of transmitting money to effect these settlements. Even now, large quantities go at certain seasons of the year.

The banks buy bills of exchange in order to sell them again; this is a part of their regular business. They buy at one rate and sell at a higher rate. When the exchange is said to be at par between two cities it is not strictly so, inasmuch as a bank will not give quite as much for a bill of exchange as it asks for one when selling it. Of course, if it bought and sold at the same price no profit would be made in the business, and there would be no reason for undertaking it; hence, the buying and selling rate is never the same. Thus, in an ordinary newspaper report we find the following, which is extracted from the New York *Journal of Commerce* of August 1st:

The following are the rates of exchange on New York:
Savannah, buying ⅛; selling ¼ premium.
Charleston, buying par@⅛; selling 3-16@¼ premium.
New Orleans commercial, $1.50 per $1,000 premium; bank, $2.50 per $1,000 premium.

St. Louis. 50c. per $1,000 premium.
Chicago, 75c. per $1,000 premium.
Boston, par@5c. per $1,000 discount.

When a Charleston bank, for example, buys exchange on New York, it expects to sell it again to persons who have payments to make in the latter city. It does not sell the same bills that it buys; it could do so, however, if any persons desired them. What the bank actually does is to forward the bills purchased to the bank with which it corresponds in New York for collection; that bank presents them to the drawee at the proper time and they are paid, and the amount is credited to the Charleston Bank. When a man enters the Charleston Bank desirous of buying a bill of exchange on New York, it simply draws a bill on its corresponding bank in that city and sells it to the party desiring the same, charging him therefor whatever the prevailing rate may be at that time. Just now, as will be seen from the above quotation from the newspaper, the rate is one-quarter of one per cent.

Banks do not always charge their customers for a bill of exchange, either when selling or collecting it. The custom, however, of charging generally prevails among banks; nevertheless, the fact that exceptions are sometimes made is worth noting. In the exceptional cases the dealer's account may be a very profitable one, and this favor is shown to him as a kind of reward or gratuity or premium to make him feel better satisfied with the bank. But a gratuity of this kind granted to a dealer is rather an outside matter, and does not pertain strictly to the banking business.

It may be stated in this connection that some depositors, instead of going to their bank and buying a bill of exchange when they wish to pay a debt due in another city, send their check to the person whom they owe; he receives it and deposits it in his bank which afterwards sends it for collection to the bank on which it is drawn. It will be seen that the depositor by doing this cuts off his bank from selling him a bill of exchange, and his real object of doing this is to save money by the operation. This has become a subject of considerable complaint among bankers. The question has been raised whether some method cannot be devised for collecting these checks, and thereby effecting a considerable saving among all the parties concerned. In that part of this work relating to the Clearing-house, a chapter will be found pertaining to this subject.

In regard to foreign bills, what we have already said applies in most respects to them. The rate of exchange does not exceed the cost of shipping gold from the debtor to the creditor. As between Great Britain and our own country this rate does not exceed cents to the pound sterling.

There are occasions though when the exchanges sink and rise much below the specie point, which is not accounted for by the single fact of a balance of indebtedness, either for or against a given country. Such an occasion occurred early in 1861, when war was impending between the North and South. Fluctuations in the American rates of exchange extended far below the specie point. The balance of trade was in favor of the United States, and a large sum was due from Great Britain. Yet, exporters sacrificed three or four per cent. on their bills in order to get their money immediately. The exporter had two courses open to him—either to sell his bills for what they would fetch, or to transmit them to Europe with instructions to his correspondents to demand payment and remit the amount in bullion. The former course was pursued, consequently the bills were sold at a large sacrifice.

The items determining the question whether to send specie or buy a bill of exchange are the following: cost of sending specie, insurance thereon, and the loss of interest on the specie during shipment from one country to the other.

Suppose that Jones owes a bill in London; he goes to a house in Wall Street which deals in foreign bills. The par of exchange between the two countries is $4.86\frac{65}{100}$; that is the legal value here of a pound sterling. The question in Jones' mind when he goes into this house is, whether he shall buy a bill and send that to London in discharge of his debt, or whether he shall transmit specie for the same purpose. Of course, he will do the thing which is cheapest. Remembering that the par of exchange between the two countries is $4.86\frac{65}{100}$, and that the cost of shipment is two cents in the pound, if he can buy a bill at less than $4.88\frac{65}{100}$ of course it would be cheaper for him to buy the bill than to send the specie. On the other hand, if he were obliged to pay more than $4.88\frac{65}{100}$ for the bill, then it will be cheaper to send the specie.

Suppose an Englishman has a debtor in New York who owes him £10,000, payable in that city, shall he send over there and get the money and import it into his own country, or shall he draw on his debtor for the amount and sell the bill? Remembering that the par of exchange is $4.86\frac{65}{100}$, and that it will cost him two cents in the pound to transport his specie, it is clear that any sum which he can get for his debt exceeding $4.84\frac{65}{100}$ is a saving on the importation of gold. On the other hand, if he cannot sell the bill for $4.84\frac{65}{100}$, but only for a sum considerably less than that figure, his more profitable course is to import specie.

When bills are payable on time, say 30, 60 or 90 days, they command a lower price than when they are payable at sight. The reason is, the buyer pays cash; he sends the bill to Great Britain to pay his debt, but it is not paid, say, for 60 days, and as he is out of the money during the interval the bill is bought at a reduced rate.

The sum paid for a time-bill, therefore, will depend on the length of time it has to run and the rate of interest in the country where the bill is payable. A bill drawn payable in London three months after date is bought by a banker at a price which is equal to a bill payable on demand, less three months' interest at the rate at that time prevailing in London, for the purchaser must discount the bill there at the ruling rate before he can make it equally available with a draft on demand. It may be added, that when foreign bills are bought as an investment, a thing often done, it is for the purpose of earning the higher rate of a foreign country, in the place of the lower rate ruling at home.

It may be well to note that when bills are quoted at $4.84 the quotation does not mean that they are two per cent. less than par, but simply that they can be bought for two cents and $\frac{85}{100}$ less than the regular value of a pound sterling. If, for example, a bill of exchange were drawn for £1,000, the amount would be equivalent to $4,866.50; if it were quoted at $4.85, this quotation would mean that the bill could be bought for $4,850.00, or $16.50 less than the par of exchange.

Within a few years the practice has arisen of transferring money by telegraph, or, as it is termed by the newspapers, "cable transfer." By this method a merchant who desires to ship wheat to London can complete the transaction in a few hours. He can ship the wheat, telegraph the fact to the consignee at London, obtain particulars concerning the conditions of the market, and, if he think best, have the wheat sold at once, "to arrive," and to remit the proceeds through a London banker. A bill does not appear at all in the transaction. The amount of business done in this manner has materially reduced the volume of bills in some places. In the Eastern trade with London, in which competition is exceedingly keen and the margin of profit consequently small, the telegraphic transfer system has been in use for several years. The amount of cable transfers between this country and European countries is constantly increasing.

CHAPTER XVII.

PRIVATE BANKS.

Although of less relative importance than formerly they were, private banks continue to maintain a good standing, and prove well adapted to some phases of the business of banking. According to the last report of the Comptroller of the Currency (December, 1883) the private banks hold about fifteen per cent. of the totals of capital and deposits, excluding those of Savings banks. The capital employed by a private bank is apt to be variable in amount, not a fixed sum represented by stock certificates, so that the returns, which are made the basis of a tax, probably represent the minimum of capital employed.

In addition to this, it may be said that many of the State banks, while running as such, are in reality private institutions, the capital stock being held by one or two owners, and the directorship being nominal. This use of bank organizations is facilitated by the ease with which they can be formed in most of the States, and is resorted to from various reasons. In some cases it is to have the benefit, when starting a new concern, of the prestige and credit which the title of "bank" is supposed to give; in others, and more frequently, to secure the immunity of limited liability; in others, again, to retain the name and clientage of a long-established business. One of the largest State banks in the West, with a deposit line of millions, and a very large volume of business, reports a capital of $100,000, but in this instance the owner advertises that "the stockholders are individually responsible, without limit, for all the liabilities of this bank."

In view of these facts it is probable that private banking occupies a rather more important place than the returns published by the Comptroller would indicate.

His figures, however, furnish the only trustworthy basis of comparison to be had, and from them some interesting results are to be obtained.

The following table, taken from the last published volume of the Comptroller of the Currency, shows the geographical distribution of bank capital and deposits, excluding Savings banks:

PRACTICAL BANKING.

Geographical Division.	National Banks.		State Banks and Trust Companies.		Private Banks.	
	No.	Capital. Deposits.	No.	Capital. Deposits.	No.	Capital. Deposits.
		Millions. Millions.		Millions. Millions.		Millions. Millions.
New Eng. States.	560	166.23 193.15	40	8.30 31.64	94	6.22 6.57
Middle States...	691	173.19 556.55	210	40.60 244.02	967	62.42 112.69
Southern States.	214	34.8 68.84	248	25.34 45.94	289	6.33 20.68
W. States & Ter.	843	110.66 301.28	563	48.90 168.40	2062	30.31 149.02
Totals........	2308	484.88 1,119.82	1061	123.14 490.00	3412	105.28 288.96

The average capital and deposits in the three classes of banks are as follows:

	Capital.	Deposits.
National banks.................	$210,100	$485,200
State banks......................	116,000	461,800
Private banks...................	30,800	84,700

The ratio of capital to deposits is, in the National banks........ .433
" " " " State banks............ .251
" " " " Private banks......... .364
" " " " All classes............. .376

The proportions of the totals of capital and deposits as held by each class in the several geographical divisions are given below:

For the Three Classes.	Per Cent. of Total.	
	Capital.	Deposits.
New England States....................	.254	.122
Middle States..........................	.387	.481
Southern States........................	.093	.071
Western States and Territories........	.266	.326

For the National Banks.	Per Cent. of Total.	
	Capital.	Deposits.
New England States....................	.343	.173
Middle States..........................	.357	.497
Southern States........................	.072	.061
Western States and Territories........	.228	.269

For State Banks and Trust Companies.	Per Cent. of Total.	
	Capital.	Deposits.
New England States....................	.067	.064
Middle States..........................	.330	.498
Southern States........................	.206	.094
Western States and Territories........	.397	.344

For Private Banks.	Per Cent. of Total.	
	Capital.	Deposits.
New England States....................	.059	.023
Middle States..........................	.593	.390
Southern States........................	.060	.071
Western States and Territories........	.288	.516

These figures show, among other things, that the average of capital and deposits is, as might be expected, lowest in the private banks, and highest in the National banks. About midway between the two, in respect to average capital, come the State banks, while the average deposits of the latter nearly equal those of the National banks. As the profits of banking come chiefly from loaning deposits, it would seem that in the greater ratio of deposits to capital is to be found a source of gain to offset that which comes from circulation, especially when, as at present, the margin of profit from this source is reduced to so thin a shaving. The high ratio of capital shown by the National banks is due, in part at least, to the provision of the National Bank Act, which fixes the minimum limit of capital for banks organized thereunder, scaling them proportionately, in some degree, to the population of the towns and cities in which they are located. The ratio of capital to deposits of the private banks closely approximates to that shown by three classes taken as a whole.

This analysis of the Comptroller's table furnishes other interesting and instructive comparisons, which, however, cannot be dwelt upon here, as they do not bear upon the subject of this chapter.

The general character and function of the private banks is shown by their small averages, and also by their geographical distributions. Nearly two-thirds of their number, and over fifty per cent. of their deposits, are reported from the Western States and Territories. It is in that region of new and small communities where active enterprise and industry abound, along with a plentiful lack of capital, that the conditions are found most favorable to their establishment and maintenance. A town too small to establish or support a National bank, with a capital of fifty thousand dollars, may yet feel the need of banking facilities, and this need becomes more and more pressing until a leading merchant, or some man who has been in the way of buying notes or making small loans at remunerative rates, either assumes or gradually has forced upon him the functions of a banker and puts out his sign. His capital may be, and usually is, small at the outset, but in a rural community every man is known to his neighbors. His "means" are closely estimated, his integrity and ability are pretty correctly gauged, his habits and manner of life are known. In respect to these he is subjected, not to periodical and perfunctory examinations by National or State officials, but to continuous and rigid watchfulness by self-constituted examiners who are very apt to reach correct results, although they are not permitted to count his cash or scrutinize his bills discounted and his ledger. If he passes this investigation successfully he will win the confidence of his townsmen and his business will prosper. Such has been the origin of many of the largest and most respectable private institutions now in existence.

Private bankers, so far as they command public confidence, do so upon their reputation for wealth and their character for honesty and ability, and these are applied directly to the management of the business confided to them. Under these circumstances there must be, other things being equal, a greater concentration of responsibility, a stronger sense of direct, personal liability than is felt by either the directors or officers of incorporated institutions, so that this form of banking offers to the dealer, equally with any other system, that which must after all be his chiefest and best guaranty, namely, faith in the integrity and capacity of the management.

Private banks, however, lack one important quality, that of permanency. Especially is this the case in the United States, and as, from various causes, they may be wound up, they are little likely, in the great cities and larger towns, to be replaced by similar institutions. Gradually, with the growth and development of the country, the function which they are best fitted to fill diminishes, and their business is merged into or usurped by National and State banks; and this tendency will continue.

As to the details of their management, little need be said. These should in no wise differ from those of well-conducted National and State banks, and for the most part they are so managed. In rare instances private banks have adopted the practice of making public reports of their condition, and publishing them along with those furnished periodically by their National and State competitors. It would be well if in some way this could be made a universal custom.

Occasionally there is to be found a banker who affects to despise theory and red tape, names by which he designates the restrictions which it is the intention of National and State statutes to impose, but it will generally prove that, if successful, he adheres to their substance if not to their form. The advantages which are sometimes claimed to be found in an immunity from these salutary requirements are questionable. So far as such so-called advantages are embraced, their tendency is to allure men from the safe paths of correct banking; the prudent and successful bankers, under any system, are those who hold themselves strictly amenable to the rules and principles which experience has proved ought to govern.

A few words should be said about the large banking houses that are only to be found in great commercial centers like New York. Many of them were originally founded with a view to conducting a regular banking business, of receiving deposits and discounting commercial bills, and numbers of them continue to do a large business of this kind, especially for out of town correspondents.

But they have, for the most part, gone largely into the business of placing corporate loans, of acting as agents for States and municipalities, and of dealing in foreign exchange. Along with their growth in this direction there has been a decline in that which may be more strictly termed banking, until many of them have come to resemble the great financial firms of London, who style themselves merchants, not bankers.

A description of these and of their methods hardly falls within the scope of this book. It is true that dealing in exchange, foreign as well as inland, is a perfectly legitimate if not a necessary branch of banking; but it is also true that the larger transactions in foreign exchange are conducted by private firms, many of whom receive no deposits. Several of the larger banks in New York have from time to time sought to enlarge their dealings in this direction, but never with any marked degree of success.

The causes of this are not far to seek. A busy banker engrossed in the management of a large line of deposits and discounts cannot scan with sufficient care the wide field of foreign exchanges. The conditions of supply and demand, the different standards of money, the changing rates of interest in the various financial centers, and the numerous other influences, ordinary and extraordinary, which affect the business of exchanges, demand nothing less than constant study by the man who would master them, and their perfect mastery is necessary. It is probable, too, that the foreign agencies which are available for a bank to employ do not render the effective service that is requisite; that the London and Continental branches, having common interests, which form a part of the organization of all the large houses dealing in exchange, are essential to success. This segregation of the exchange business from that of banking is, however, but an illustration of the inevitable tendency to specialization which marks commercial progress.

CHAPTER XVIII.

COUNTRY BANKING.

General principles of banking apply alike to banks irrespective of location. Details in conducting the business may be materially influenced by the bank's position in the country. The routine of large banks in commercial centers is usually the outgrowth of long experience, careful experiment and constant thought of improvement. The bank president in a country town, though he may have carved his way to position, through gradual advancement from runner or sweeping-boy, would, if placed at the head of one of the large banks of a metropolitan city, be found unable to manage its affairs. He may be a better financier and possess greater executive ability than many city bank presidents, but he would lack in that particular knowledge which comes only from experience. What we say of bank presidents will apply as well and possibly with more strength to other officers and to the clerical force. And in selecting the president in our illustration we do not refer to that class who are presidents only in name. We mean presidents who are in every sense entitled to the position. And, thanks to the progress of the times, figurehead presidents are not so numerous now as a few years ago. Sharp competition has lifted banking to a science. It has brought capable heads almost without exception into president's chairs. This is true of country as well as of city bank presidents.

However true the above, it furnishes no evidence that less capability, thoroughness, or good financiering is required in the country than in the city bank. Especially good judgment, careful calculation, and a close watch over the finances are requisite in conducting a country bank. Opportunities to loan money are not often as favorable in the country as in large business centers. The securities offered, too, are of a different kind. The country banker's customers are more frequently personal acquaintances and friends. He is called upon oftener to lay aside personal and friendly considerations in loans and discounts. He must know his customers better because he trusts them more on personal obligations. Loans in large cities are made largely on collateral securities. In country banks such securities are seldom received. The personal responsibility of the borrowers or of their endorsers is more usually the thing to be considered.

The routine of bank work varies according to the volume of business transacted. The methods employed in a bank where the average balances due depositors reach half a million dollars would, in a bank where such balances did not exceed one hundred or two hundred thousand dollars, prove cumbersome and complicated. On the other hand a system which meets every requirement in the medium-size institution would, if introduced in the large city bank, be found wholly inadequate. The clerical force of a bank, too, has much to do with the method that may be introduced to the best advantage. In the larger city banks it is not unusual to see employed as the clerical force twenty to forty persons. Many banks in small cities and towns find that two or three persons will do the work comfortably. We could name many banks of respectable size where the average deposits reach one hundred thousand to two hundred thousand dollars, in which not more than two clerks are employed, and some where one clerk and the cashier get through with the work. The cashier in such case is also paying teller, receiving teller, discount clerk, note teller, and general bookkeeper. The work is often divided up between the two or three persons without any special reference to the functions of individual members in a fully organized force.

The books used in a country bank do not differ materially in number or formular arrangement from those used in metropolitan places. The following are those in most common use: general ledger, general journal, deposit journal or teller's cash, deposit ledger, sometimes called individual ledger and sometimes customers' ledger, collection register, discount register, tickler, sometimes two ticklers, foreign and domestic; certificate of deposit register, draft register, deposit ledger balance book, or as some term it depositors' balance ledger, and offering book, the latter being sometimes dispensed with. Then there are also used in some banks a discount ledger and daily general balance book. A monthly statement book is kept by National and also by many private or State banks.

An experienced country bank bookkeeper gives the following description of his daily routine:

"I enter in the journal all remittances in detail; total amount of loans and notes discounted each day, the latter I get from the discount register; notes and loans paid, which come from the tickler, these being entered separately in the journal with the total only extended into the money column. Collections paid, if belonging to our correspondents, go in the journal; if they do not belong to correspondents, they are remitted for direct; the draft register, in these transactions, completes the entry which opens in the collection register. Drafts drawn on our correspondents are journalized and other transactions such as exchange, interest, expense, etc. In closing the journal for the day, the footings of the deposit journal, which with us are the total amount of checks paid and the total amount of deposits received, are entered. In one respect my journal represents a cash book. I bring forward each day the balance of cash on hand. This enables me to prove my cash by my journal by balancing it the same as a cash book. The journalizing is done at the close of banking hours and the entries are posted to the ledger during the first hours of the next day. As the posting is done, the new balances are entered in the daily balance book which is lying conveniently on the desk. Opposite the accounts not affected the previous day's balances are extended. When the posting is finished the daily balance book is footed, which furnishes a proof of the work.

"On the debit side of the deposit journal appear all checks and certificates of deposit paid; on the credit side are deposits received and certificates of deposit issued. The footings only of this book are journalized. The footings are made direct to the depositors' ledger. The account in the general ledger of "Deposits" is charged and credited from the journal.

"Our ledgers are provided with balance columns, the general ledger having one account to a page, the deposit ledger two. In the general ledger there are four money columns, two for items and two for balances. In the deposit ledger there are but three columns, Dr., Cr., and balance. In the balance column over-drafts are distinguished from credit balances by being entered in red ink.

"We use only one collection register. It is made to serve a double purpose, viz.: it is a record of bills, etc., brought in by our customers to be sent out for collection, and also of collections received from our correspondents and others, excepting sight drafts. After the record is made in the collection register, it is entered in the tickler under the day on which it falls due. When the collection is paid we make the proper notation in the tickler and either credit our correspondent or remit direct to the sender according to directions. In case the collection is not paid and is protested, immediate notice is given. Of sight drafts received for collection we make no book record. The letter accompanying the collection is the original and only entry we have. After presenting the draft for payment we note on the accompanying letter how it was disposed of—whether paid or returned. If paid and belonging to a correspondent it is properly credited. If it does not come from a correspondent we remit for it immediately, so noting on the letter. The letter is then filed as a history of the transaction. Our letter-copying book furnishes a history of all collections passing through our hands."

The cashier of a well regulated and carefully managed country bank says:

"Three persons do all the work in our bank. The president attends to the correspondence and takes charge of the loans and discounts. I perform the work of paying and receiving tellers and general bookkeeper, besides the ordinary duties of cashier. An assistant keeps the customer's ledger and helps me in some of the details about the other books. Our loans and discounts range from one hundred and fifty thousand to two hundred thousand dollars. The depositors' balances are in the aggregate usually not far from the loans and discounts. We hold readily convertible stocks and bonds to the amount of forty thousand to sixty thousand dollars. Our capital is two hundred thousand and circulation one hundred and sixty-two thousand. Cash on hand seldom gets below twenty thousand dollars, and our surplus is fifty thousand. The net profits enable us to pay the stockholders seven per cent., and we generally carry two or three per cent. to the surplus. A dull season occasionally cuts our dividends down to half the usual amount. We have run so close that no dividends were declared for a year.

"My aim in the routine work is to avoid all unnecessary labor. I use as few books as possible. A few years ago I thought a huge journal was indispensable, but I have so systematized the work that I now have no use for it. In fact I have not used a journal at all for more than a year. The bookkeeping is done in such a manner that I can make up a verified statement of our condition within an hour any day after we close. Besides the general ledger I keep only the ordinary balance ledger for depositors' accounts. In this I also keep the accounts of banks and bankers. The accounts in the balance ledger are arranged alphabetically, and this book is kept so closely posted that the last check paid and last deposit made are entered up within a few minutes after the bank is closed for the day. We have only a few depositors who draw more than four or five checks in a day on an average. For these special cases I provide by giving their account a double space in the balance ledger. In posting the checks and deposits my assistant makes his entry direct from the checks and deposit slips. As the entry is made he marks the page by leaving projecting at the top of the book a narrow strip of colored paper. This enables him to turn at once to the pages on which changes have been made during the day. These pages are footed, and the footings compared with the columns in my cash book, headed "depositors' debits" and "depositors' credits." The comparison furnishes a proof that all checks and deposits for the day have been posted. An additional test comes when the balances of all the accounts are extended for the next day and the footings compared with the general ledger account of "depositors" after the totals of the various books have been posted. I do not enter in my cash the names, but merely the amounts of debits and credits belonging to the depositors' accounts. After the work has been proven I take the balance ledger and have my assistant read over the checks and I compare his postings to satisfy myself that the postings are all properly made. When this is done I run over the general ledger, the postings to that having been made, and carry the balances to the daily balance sheet. This proves the entire work of the day."

The Daily Balance Sheet is a device for proving the work of the bank bookkeeper and for preserving, in a concise and regular form, daily statements of the bank's condition. The new balances are arrived at daily through debit and credit differences. The illustration given in this chapter, though not a complete showing of all the accounts upon the specimen pages furnished for the purpose, will serve to demonstrate the principles of the work. For example in explanation see the first account, viz.: Loans and Discounts. The balance on the evening of August 15 was 167,150.73. The following day there were payments in excess of new loans and discounts to amount of 311.44. This credit difference is subtracted from the debit balance, leaving the new debit balance 166,839.29. Again; the balance against the First National of Philadelphia on the evening of August 15 is 40,737.31. On the following day the remittance to that bank in excess of credits given it were 23,513.10. The debtor difference is added to the debit balance, and the new balance is 64,250.41. The first or upper line of footings represent the total balances of banks and bankers' accounts, the lower line of footings are the proofs or trial balance. All the entries in this book may be made in either ink or pencil as may be desired. Ink is, of course, preferable, but as they form only an auxiliary proof and leave a record for future reference, if desired, there is no special objection to pencilings.

GENERAL LEDGER ACCOUNTS NOT APPEARING ON ILLUSTRATION OF DAILY BALANCE SHEET. (*See Appendix.*)

Circulating Notes Received.
Unpaid Dividends.
Certificates of Deposit.
Cashier's Checks.
Remittances.

Cash
    Notes of this Bank.
    Notes of other National Banks.
    U. S. Legal Tenders.
    Gold Coin.
    Silver $ Nickels $

Treasurer of United States.
Comptroller of the Currency.
Suspense Account.

PART II.

SAVINGS BANKS.

CHAPTER I.

UTILITY OF SAVINGS BANKS.

This class differs from State or National banks in that they have no special capital owned by a few or by many individuals, but their capital is the deposited money of a great many saving people. They are mutual. That is, every one who puts money in is practically an owner in the bank, and the profit made by the bank, after paying taxes and expenses, and putting aside a proper reserve, is paid to the parties whose money earns the profit. The people, in their dimes and dollars and tens and hundreds, own the Savings banks. Hence it is that these institutions are very rigorously guarded by the laws of our States. It is not the idea of a Savings bank to pay a large percentage of interest. Safety is the first thing, and in order to be safe, only choice and high-priced investments can be purchased by the managers.

Savings banks are voluntary trusteeships, undertaken by a few persons in a particular locality, either self-appointed, renewing their own number as vacancies occur, or chosen by the depositors. The corporate body thus formed receives deposits or funds, small in amount, and from the poorer classes of society. It undertakes to invest them with due diligence in the safest practicable way, and to divide all the income, after paying necessary expenses, among the depositors, at stated and convenient times. None of the profit on these investments belongs to the corporation itself. All of it belongs to the depositors. If a surplus is created, it is only for a safeguard against occasional losses or emergencies. In every respect, the corporation is nothing but the agent or trustee of the whole body of depositors, and works for their account and benefit, not for its own.

"The principal reason for the creation of a Savings bank is to offer to the poor and to those of small incomes a means of keeping safe their occasional savings. A secondary reason is to enable such persons, by combining these small sums, to invest them, so as to earn some interest. Such persons do not ordinarily draw out their deposits, except on an emergency. The deposits are made to meet emergencies in the private life of the depositors, and are not subject to the daily calls of business. It thus appears that, as such emergencies usually result from sickness or lack of employment, the drafts will be gradual, not sudden, and are not subject to sudden increase by reason of commercial revulsions, unless in the exceptional case of panic. Large deposits, which do not come from savings, but which are the capital of persons who have acquired wealth, should be rejected.* They can invest their own funds, and they are likely to withdraw their deposits suddenly and in large sums."

In the introductory chapter of this part of our work we shall briefly set forth the utility of Savings banks. This, however, has been well done by another, Henry L. Lamb, and we cannot improve on what he has said concerning the utility of these institutions. His paper was read at an annual meeting of the American Bankers' Association in 1879, when he was acting as superintendent of the banking department of the State of New York.

First.—The savings institution is founded to help men and women.

Some one has said that they are meant "to help men to help themselves." It is not in simple human nature to save and to put by a store for the ever possible rainy day. The savage and the child go on in reckless improvidence. Some one must take care of the improvident, as society is organized now in the enlightened nations. There are saving people and spending people. There are people who create property and people who waste it. There are people who earn money and keep it, and people, too, who earn money and squander it. This is inevitable. By and by the spend-

---

* "Certainly, the use of these institutions should be confined to the class for whose benefit they were devised, and only that class who have not the time, opportunity, or ability to investigate and determine for themselves a proper investment or adequate means to enable them to pay for the information through private sources, should be permitted to become depositors.

In case of temporary embarrassment, the largest deposits, those belonging to what may be properly termed a capitalist class, would be soonest withdrawn, and whenever private investment promises better returns these funds leave the banks. Whenever money is cheap and hard to place, this class solves the difficulties of investment by placing their moneys in our Savings banks. Instead of supporting the banks, they make of them a convenience, and prey upon their resources; instead of being an element of strength, they are a constant menace.

Most States recognize this principle, and have fixed limitations designed to exclude this class of depositors. Instance: Connecticut limits amounts receivable in any one year from a single individual to $1,000. Vermont limits the aggregate to $2,000. New York limits the aggregate to $3,000. Massachusetts limits deposits to $1,000 from each individual, and allows it, by accumulation of interest, to reach $1,600, but allows no dividend upon any sum exceeding $1,600. Each of these States makes varying exceptions as to trust funds, &c.

Recently, while examining a discount bank, I found twelve pass books from several different banks, and in four different names, but all belonging to the same individual, calling for sums aggregating $28,000, put up as collaterals for a loan. While this shows that any law is liable to evasion, it emphasizes the necessity for specific regulations as to the reception of deposits —*Extract from address of A. B. Hepburn, Bank Superintendent of New York, at the American Bankers' Association in* 1882.

thrift has run his life, and comes in poverty and need to his brother and asks for support. Misfortune may follow the prudent and bring them, by unexpected reverses, to want. In the artificial conditions which our civilization creates, the demands of the needy are greater than they were in primitive conditions of living. Such demands as these meet the intensely practical mind to-day, just as they do that of the philanthropic. So they did a hundred years ago.

When a great want is felt in the world a host of men begin to try to solve the problem to satisfy the want. Great inventions then seem to be contemporaneously made by different men. This very question of dealing with simple men and women, of taking care of the humble who had no estates, of taking care of the poor who come to want by improvidence or by misfortune, appears to have received the studious notice of the economist and philanthropist at the same time. While Jeremy Bentham and Malthus enforced the benefits of providence and savings in the interests of the great body of the people as well as of those who saved, about the opening of this century an English clergyman and a Scotch minister, each in his own parish, set in operation a plan for his parishioners to save money, which embodies in substance the fundamental principle of the savings institution. Contemporaneously, a woman, Mrs. Priscilla Wakefield, established such an organization in England. Similar ideas also were advanced at the same period by a London magistrate, Patrick Colquhoun, who wrote upon the question of popular indigence and measures for its relief as early as 1806.

In America, in 1816 and 1817, the needs and the claims of the poor awakened attention at Boston and New York, and thought was immediately directed towards the savings institution, because it was deemed most helpful. At Boston, in 1816, it was proposed "to form an institution for the security and improvement of the savings of persons in humble life until required by their wants and desires."

The first Savings bank in the State of New York seems to be the direct result of a meeting of citizens at the New York Hospital on December 16, 1817, to take into consideration the subject of pauperism. A society was there formed for the prevention of pauperism. A committee was then appointed to report on the prevailing causes of poverty. The report recites, among other causes, that "Prodigality is comparative among the poor; it prevails to a great extent in inattention to those small but frequent savings when labor is plentiful which may go to meet privation in unfavorable seasons." When the constitution of this society was drafted it declared that one prime purpose of the organization should be "to hold out inducements to those people to economy and saving from the fruits of their own industry in seasons of great abundance." The earnestness of the men who were members of this organization is proved in the passage of an act, upon their petitition, by the Legislature of 1819, for the incorporation of the Bank for Savings. In each of the two years thereafter a Savings bank was incorporated in this State.

Second.—The savings institution is not organized to make money. Right here it is wholly different from the discount bank in motive and aim. The Savings bank receives money chiefly to keep it securely for the benefit of the depositors. The ordinary bank performs some service for such as need it in business, and justly is paid for such service. The aim of the bank is profit—gain upon the capital which is employed in the work. The savings institution seeks to serve those who are not fitted by knowledge and habit for safely keeping and investing their money when saved. The discount bank is equipped with money, with skill in business, with acquaintance with monetary affairs, and offers to the busy managers of commerce and trade its aid in making exchanges and in all their operations which require its assistance. The savings bank opens its doors to savers; it receives and permanently invests money. The bank opens its doors to borrowers and users of money, for pay. One serves by receiving and keeping, the other serves by lending. One aims at profit, the other never makes profit an end; the Savings institution is a receiving reservoir from little springs; the bank is a distributing reservoir of accumulated capital.

There ought to be, therefore, no antagonism between the Savings bank and the bank. If the Savings bank is kept to its original idea, as it should be, it will not encroach on the domain of the bank, and the last will by no means come in conflict with the Savings bank. The time has been when men had the idea that the best way to get on in the world was to rob each other. Juster ideas than that now prevail. The Savings institution is a conception which demonstrates this truth. It is the reverse of the communistic notion recently prevalent. The communist proposes the division of capital, the drone to share with the worker in the accumulation of his production. The Savings institution aims at making all men producers and savers too. It offers the aid of the strong, who can manage well, to the weak, to receive their small gains and hold them securely against that time when need or desire may require the store for prudent use. The Savings institution enlarges the number of capitalists; it reduces the army of possible prodigals, paupers and tramps. The communist is the enemy of capital, for he proposes to rob the man who has money. The Savings-bank depositor is himself an owner of money. He belongs to the conservatives by the logical tendency of his position. In this land, where there is such room for growth, such demand for money, such room for men of the right stamp, the Savings institution is an educator, is the friend of capital, of order and stability, both political and social. Whoever earns and saves, lengthens continuously his arms for service. Whoever earns and spends as he goes does not lengthen his arms, but shortens his legs for running his race in life. While the Savings bank is not organized to make money it is most profitable in several ways. It accumulates money; it inspires and trains men to get money and to the wise use of it; it spares those who have capital from charges upon it for the support of those who might otherwise become poor; it makes better men and families and better citizens; it adds to the sum of National resources in money, and adds to the means for advancement in material improvement. It is thus a many-sided benefaction —to those out of it, as well as to those in it.

Third.—The Savings institution does not hoard money.

Some men object to the Savings institution because it withholds money from circulation. This is an obvious fallacy. If the depositors in such institutions were to save an amount of money as large as they deposit, a great part of it would be hoarded. All who have acquaintance with Savings banks know this. If a panic comes upon the depositors in one institution, or in several, and money is drawn in large sums, much of it is hoarded and much of it is squandered. After the fright is over the identical money that was withdrawn and kept is often returned for deposit months after withdrawal. This demonstration of the disposition of saving men to hoard is always made under these conditions. The Savings bank encourages the habit of saving. Many of you, I have no doubt, were born and bred as boys on farms. You may still recollect the eager hunt for hens' nests in the hay mows, bays and scaffolds of the old weather-stained barns; you will recollect, too, perhaps, that the nests require the invitation of a "nest egg" to coax the fecund fowl to make her diurnal deposit in it. I think that men need such solicitation, too. The man who is profligate while he has nothing to "lay to," will often become stingily saving when he has a "nest egg" to win him from other temptations. Those who can do this, and would otherwise lay their gains in stockings, prefer the Savings bank, for money there makes money, which this class of men are quick to see.

The Savings bank invests its money. Its managers are, in theory, intelligent men, competent to make safe investments in solid securities. The genuine Savings bank is conservative, and does not encourage speculation, ballooning, and failure with disaster. It puts money into circulation, and does not withhold it. It adds substantially to the sum of active capital in the country, which is not less useful because it is permanently invested. These little savings, when gathered into masses and discreetly invested, serve great purposes. As the tiny streams which trickle from hidden springs upon remote hill sides flow together and make the willing power to turn mill wheels, or to furnish the water for the thirsty people of a great city, so these savings of humble people and of small owners, when aggregated, become available to build the mills, or to buy the wheels for the mills, or to lay the pipes to convey the water to the thirsty town, or to help the thrifty saver to rear his own house, or to aid the State itself when its financial burdens are too great to be discharged at once.

Fourth.—Why should any man become the manager of a Savings bank?

I have been asked this question often. The trustee cannot be paid. Why should a man do anything that will not pay him? I hope I have given some reasons why a Savings bank does pay the community in which it is placed. No man with capital can turn a deaf ear to the promise to save that capital from the moth and rust of taxation. You know that now. A host of Savings-bank depositors is a better class of citizens than an army of tramps. The self-sustaining person, who is self-respecting, too, is a safer neighbor than the vicious drone or the indolent beggar. The Savings bank is not a pauperizing charity. But it is a school, teaching the sound lessons of self-denial, of economy, and of sober industry.

> Ill fares the land, to hastening ills a prey,
> Where wealth accumulates and men decay,

says the poet.

But if wealth accumulates, and men and women grow stronger by its possession, and better in character and aspiration by the habits of saving, happy is the land where they dwell. There is no man who has capital, who is acquiring capital, that has not, in fact, an interest in the success of Savings banks, though he may not have seen this or felt it. You, gentlemen, give freely to support churches; you pay taxes to maintain schools, to watch criminals, to punish the bad. These things cost you money, and a good round sum, too. Have not you, has not every man who can do it, an interest in these institutions, which are saving in many senses?

Their great success will spare your own pockets; their great success will add to the total of the resources which can find profitable employment in this land; their great success will breed a class of people of moderate means, who will look up in the world, and not down. Why should not any man, every man, indeed, who has the capacity for the work, lend something of his time, something of his judgment and knowledge, to the people that need them? He shall lend not chiefly for the sake of the borrower of such services, but for his own sake. I put it upon the last ground that the wisest self-interest of every man of substance will dictate his support of Savings banks in which he is a shareholder just so long as he has any relations with other men and is a citizen bearing the tax burdens of a citizen.

Fifth.—The Savings bank is one of the best safeguards of property. Trustee service is more agreeable than jury duty. Personal attention in a Savings bank is more economical than constables, police, poormasters, hospitals, prisons.

It is sure that the three-quarters of a million of depositors in Savings banks in this imperial State are arrayed as a solid phalanx against communism, rioting and disorder. The facts are too significant to be disregarded by intelligent men. Ireland, Germany and Russia to-day should admonish the American citizen, who has property, and who is a leader in business and in politics, that security and progress will be found in the diffusion of property among the great body of people, by training them to its acquisition and maintenance. The Savings bank is a fortress which resists the dangerous classes. It is garrisoned by men who stand actually for their altars and their fires on their own hearthstones. Who of you has not a personal interest in this army, which is perfectly loyal always, and which is not the consumer of your goods, but is itself a constant producer and saver, as well as guardian?

The real Savings bank in our country has done great good. It can come nearer in practice to the ideal. It contains infinite possibilities to this teeming land for future beneficence as respects depositors, and safety and advantage in respect to other men with capital. To bring these institutions, which save money and save men, at once, up to a higher standard of excellence in administration and to a higher degree of utility and results and influence, only demands the moderate attention and service of thoroughly practical men. The Savings institution is benevolent on one side, but it is a business enterprise at bottom, and must be conducted on business principles. When it is so conducted it is one of the most profitable investments that can be established. It does not pay the honest manager in dividends and salaries, but it saves him a vast deal now, and will save his children after him a vast deal more, and will pay for all the service which he can give it.

CHAPTER II.

JANITOR.

In order to give the reader as clear an idea as possible of the interior workings of the modern Savings bank, we will describe the functions and the daily routine of each person connected with one of these institutions. We will begin with the janitor.

Since seven o'clock, when he relieved the night watchman, this humble, but important functionary has been preparing the bank for the business of the day. He has swept and dusted the banking room, seen that the ink, pens and other appliances were provided, and has stamped with the proper date the books and documents representing the business of the previous day. The tickets, when made out by the clerks, are purposely left undated; when made out by the depositors there are sometimes errors or discrepancies in the date, therefore this stamping gives the official date of their passing through the books.

At the opening of the bank at nine o'clock, the next duty of the janitor will be to arrange the many account books in their proper places for the business of the day. During the active business hours he sees that persons wishing to do business are directed to the proper department of the bank, he attends to any calls or messages between those departments or outside of the bank, he carries the deposits to the deposit banks, he copies letters or places them in the files, sees that the doors are opened and closed at the proper hours. These hours are from ten to three daily, but on Mondays and Saturdays the closing hour is seven P. M.

Between nine and half-past the members of the executive staff of the bank begin to arrive. The treasurer, the secretary, the paying teller, the receiving teller and the bookkeepers. The duties of these officials will be described in order, but first, we will consider the person for whose benefit and on whose behalf they are acting in every official transaction of the day, namely, the depositor.

CHAPTER III.

THE DEPOSITOR.

As a convenient, though perhaps unfamiliar name, we will call our typical depositor John Smith. John Smith arrives at the bank soon after its opening on the day in question, having in his possession $1, which, contrary to the usual desires of mankind, he is anxious to part with. He proposes to relinquish the possession of this dollar for an indefinite time and to place it in the custody of the bank. Now, what are John Smith's motives in this eccentric conduct?

First.—He thinks that the dollar out of his hands will be less likely to be uselessly spent than in his hands, which is incontestable.

Second.—He thinks that the dollar out of his hands will be less likely to be lost or destroyed than if in his possession.

Third.—He believes that, aggregated with a great many thousand other dollars belonging to other depositors, this dollar of his will possess an earning power which, in his pocket, it would entirely lack. These homely thoughts of John Smith represent or convey the Savings banks' reason for existence. Their object is three-fold. To prevent waste, to prevent loss, to give profit..

Again, taking up the practical operations of John Smith's case, we will suppose that this is his first attempt at saving. As he comes into the bank, if intelligent, he will look about him, and see a very plainly expressed printed notice, headed, "how to open an account." If unintelligent, or uneducated, he will probably apply to the janitor as a guide, philosopher and friend, who shall give him the necessary information for becoming a member of the numerous partnership, which owns the handsome building in which he stands, and all its contents. Following the directions of the notice referred to, he goes to one of the tables or desks on which are writing materials and all the necessary blank forms, takes a deposit ticket, which is printed on green paper to make it easily distinguishable, and writes,

First, the amount of his proposed investment; second, his name; third, his address, and lastly, the date.

It is not usual in Savings banks, in general, that the tickets, either for drawing or depositing, should be made out by the depositor. This bank finds it in every respect preferable so to do. The average style of writing is better than would probably be the case if made out by a clerk working rapidly, because each depositor naturally takes pains with his own ticket. There is the further great advantage that we have his evidence as to the amount and circumstances in case of future dispute. It is too much the practice in Savings banks to assume that the depositor is uneducated and ignorant. The writer once mentioned this idea of tickets made out by the depositors themselves in the largest of our Savings banks, and was answered, "well one out of every three of our depositors is unable to write." He inquired whether this proportion was obtained by actual count or by guess. On being informed that it was merely a guess, he, suggested that a count be made of a few pages of the signature book, and it was found that the proportion was one in nineteen; that is, eighteen able to write, to one who is obliged to make a cross. In our bank the proportion is about one to twenty. It is found also that the depositors, when once accustomed to this more dignified way of doing business, far prefer it. They feel as if they were treated with more respect, not as inferiors or subjects of charity, and finally there is a great saving of time and error for the receiving teller.

This he carries to the window occupied by the receiving teller. He hands the ticket and the dollar to that official, and also names the amount aloud, "one dollar," or if English be not his native language, he is perfectly at liberty to say "ein thaler," "un dollard," "uno scudo," "un peso," or whatever equivalent expression in his own vernacular may signify his intent. Now the functions of the receiving teller begin, and Smith is only informed that he must next step to the signature desk. Here lies a large book on a revolving desk, and, like a guest in a hotel, he is requested to write his name and address, or if unable to write, his name is written for him, and he makes his mark, but instead of getting the number of his room, the number of his pass book is printed opposite the line on which he writes. The clerk, whom he now sees, obtains from him, besides his name and address, the following information: Where do you live? What is your age? Are you married, single, or a widower? Are you colored? What is, or was, your father's name? Mother's name? Wife's name? Occupation?

The particular points of information obtained from the depositor vary in different banks. The place of nativity is taken by some, and this would seem an excellent test of identity. The color of the eye, as being the one bodily characteristic which is unchangeable, is also taken by some institutions. Perhaps in the future photography may come to our aid, and instantaneous photographs of small size be taken on the occasion of the first deposit.

The entries in the signature book having been made, the clerk again asks Mr. Smith "how much money did you deposit?" and on being answered correctly hands him the pass book.

This pass book has stamped upon it, both on the outside and inside, the same number which stands opposite the depositor's name in the signature book, and this number will hereafter be the key to all the dealings of Mr. Smith with the bank. It is written on the deposit ticket, it is written opposite the first entry in the books of the bank, it stands at the head of his ledger account.

* * * These consecutive numbers are printed wherever they possibly can be, to avoid mistakes, but as Smith will very probably forget the number of his book, especially if he is a careless person, and loses the book, it is necessary somewhere to be able to find him by name. Therefore, the signature clerk has one more duty to perform in connection with Smith's account. Lying opposite him is a pile of cards about one inch by three. On the top one of these, which contains Smith's number, the signature clerk writes very plainly John Smith. This, as will be seen afterwards, serves as an entry in the alphabetical index.

When next Mr. Smith has any sum of money to deposit, he will make out and sign his deposit ticket as before, except that he now knows the number of his book, and will insert that in the proper place. Perhaps he will find several other customers awaiting their turn at the receiving teller's window. In this case, he must fall in at the end of the line in proper order. But Smith will not go on depositing forever. His deposit of savings has only half performed its mission while it is lying in bank. Ultimately it is to be used. When Smith has become sufficient of a capitalist to invest his money at his own discretion, then he will wish to withdraw his accumulations. But frequently before that time he wearies of well doing, or he miscalculates the amount which he can spare from his current expenditure, and it is necessary for him to withdraw a portion, or the whole; or this necessity may be caused by removal, by calamity, by sickness, or by death. In this case he finds his way to the paying teller's window, having first filled out a ticket of another form, the draft ticket. This he presents with his book, and again names the sum to be withdrawn. After proper scrutiny, which will be described under the paying teller's duties, his book is handed to him again, and between its leaves, instead of the draft ticket, is the money desired. If this exhausts his account, the form called a closing draft is used. In this case, the pass-book is surrendered, and is filed away according to its numerical order. But, if Mr. Smith continues his deposits for a sufficient length of time, he will be entitled to his share of the earnings. Any amount over $5, participates in the profits of the concern. It is considered that the use of any sum less than that does not more than pay for stationery and labor. Semi-annually, a few days after the first of January, and a few days after the first of July, the book may be presented for the purpose of entering therein the dividends to which he is entitled, In the majority of cases, Smith takes it for granted that the calculation of this dividend is correct, though occasionally, he scrutinizes it very carefully.

The conditions of this dividend in many institutions, are these:— Deposits begin to participate in the dividend on the first day of each quarter, but they only are entitled to it if they remain till the end of the half year; thus, money which is in bank on the first day of January, provided it remains until the first day of July, receives a half year's dividend, but if withdrawn, even during June, receives nothing. If in bank on the first of April, and remaining until the first of July untouched, it draws a quarter's dividend. Furthermore, the first few days of each quarter, may be allowed to the depositor as a sort of grace, the limit being 10 days, at the half-year, and three days at the quarter.

The dividend is now usually spoken of as *interest*. As the rate in the State of New York is not promised in advance, but depends upon the profits of the half year, the term dividend, is considered more proper, but considering that it depends on the time, it is in that respect, strictly speaking, interest. The word *interest-dividend* would seem to be the most exact.

A few banks in New York allow interest to begin on the first day of each month, instead of the first day of each quarter, but with the same provision as to forfeiture in case of withdrawal before the end of the half year. In Pennsylvania, in some parts of New England, and in Great Britain, money bears interest for every full calendar month during which it has remained undisturbed, and is credited only once a year, unless the account is closed.

The current rate at present (1884) is wavering between four per cent. and three per cent. Ten years ago, the current rate for Savings deposits was six per cent., but the general investment rate has greatly lowered. Some banks make a distinction in rate for different amounts. For example, four per cent. on amounts not exceeding $1000, and three per cent. on any excess over $1000. Or on another plan, less than $500 receives four per cent., but if the whole deposit exceed $500, only three per cent. is paid on the whole. On this manifestly unjust plan, a depositor whose book has amounted to $501, receives absolutely less of the profits, than he whose aggregate is only $499. It would be better to preserve rigorously a limit as to the maximum which any depositor shall accumulate, or which he shall deposit in a given period, and then divide the profits *pro rata*, on all sums.

If interest is not withdrawn, it will itself draw interest as a deposit. The more ignorant depositors, however, frequently desire to draw their interest, even if they immediately re-deposit it, forfeiting thereby a quarter's interest on it. Their intellect in money matters has not yet been sufficiently developed for them to grasp the idea that there can be an increase of money value, without a visible amount or representative having touched their hands.

Besides the individual deposit which John Smith or Mary Smith may have made in their own names, there are various other forms. Frequently, money is deposited "John Smith, in trust for William Jones," or "John Smith, Trustee for William Jones." Often this trust is to some extent a fiction, the legal effect of which is that, upon the death of Smith, Jones will receive the deposit without the formalities and expense of administration. Frequently, also, it is intended as an evasion of that rule which makes a different rate of interest for higher sums. The thrifty John Smith will have the maximum amount in his own name, and scattered through the books of the bank you will again meet him as trustee for his wife, trustee for each of his children, trustee for his son-in-law, etc. Accounts may be opened in two names jointly, as John Smith *or* Mary Smith. Sometimes John Smith *and* Mary Smith. In the former case the book is marked "To be drawn by either signature." In the latter case, "To be drawn by both signatures only." The money of benevolent and other associations is frequently accepted by the Savings banks on deposit, generally with special regulations as to the officials who shall have control of the funds. A special signature book is provided for societies, in which is allowed, not a single line, but an entire page, so as to provide for changes in officers.

Smith occasionally loses his book, and it is then his duty to report it to a clerk in charge of that department. It is usually required that he advertise its loss for a certain number of times in one of the daily papers. The reason of this precaution is that he may have assigned his claim to the moneys in the book to an innocent holder, and be thus endeavoring to obtain payment twice. If the book is not then returned he is required to execute a bond of indemnity, with a surety, making the bank good against any loss from adverse claims, and to make an affidavit as to the circumstances of the loss.

When Smith has gone over to the great majority of Smiths his legal representatives will ultimately appear at the bank, presenting letters testamentary, or letters of administration from the Surrogate of the County. Generally, upon these being admitted as correct, the money is transferred, without loss of interest, to a new book in the name of the executors or administrators, or paid to them in cash. Sometimes their names are simply added at the head of the original pass book, but in the bank which we are describing, it is a rule that *no* change in the heading of an account shall be made, except by transfer to a new book, lest unauthorized changes should be made, or alleged to have been made, by the employees. Such changes are sometimes desirable, for example, in case of a woman who has changed her name by marriage, but in this case she may continue to be recognized as a depositor by her former name.

The depositors of our bank are of all ages, occupations, religions, nationalities, colors and social grades, the children, from ten years upwards, are quite as exact and business-like in their transactions as their seniors, and the habit of carrying on a Savings bank account is quite prevalent among the children of all classes.

As the official with whom the depositor comes first and chiefly in contact, we will describe the duties of the receiving teller.

CHAPTER IV.

RECEIVING TELLER.

After the doors of the vault have been opened in the morning he takes out the large tin box containing his cash, and closed by his own combination lock. Placing the bills in the compartments of his drawer according to denominations, so as to be able to give change, if necessary, and arranging his tray of silver conveniently, he is ready for operation. As has already been said, the depositor hands in his pass book, between the leaves of which is the money, accompanied by a deposit ticket. The first duty of the teller is to count the money. To facilitate this, depositors are requested to have their bills neatly laid out facing in one direction, and the same denominations together. The teller usually counts the amount twice. He then sees that the amount as stated on the ticket is correct. He next sees that the depositor has correctly stated the number of the account; then he proceeds to make the entry in the pass book on the next vacant line, writing the date, the amount in words, and extending the amount in figures into the column headed "deposit." Then, with another glance at the ticket, he sticks the latter on a spindle, and hands the book to the depositor, again repeating the amount.

This process is very brief, and detains the depositor less than any other, but in many banks it is thought that further entries should be made before the depositor leaves the bank. In many, a different clerk enters the amounts from the pass book into the deposit book, which will soon be described, and then hands out the book. In others, the pass book is taken direct to the ledger, and the amount posted there directly from it. The object of these precautions is, first, to insure accuracy, and, second, to check embezzlement on the part of the receiving teller. It is always more difficult to prevent embezzlement on the part of a receiving agent than of a disbursing agent, because the latter is compelled to produce vouchers for all his expenditures, but unless guarded in some way the receiver may withhold or destroy the evidence of his having received. There are two classes of methods employed to prevent this in moneyed institutions; one is that which makes another employee cognizant of his doings; and another, that which makes that known to the public. It is manifest that there is no absolute security in the former method. If you multiply the number of hands through which a transaction passes, you somewhat diminish the probability of fraud, but there is always the possibility of collusion; but collusion with the chance public, whose interests are directly opposite, is impossible. Therefore, the writer considers that the only security against embezzlement lies in making the acts of a receiving agent to some extent public, as the bell punch does on the horse-car lines. There may yet be invented a method by which the teller will, by pressing certain keys, cause the number and amount to be legibly written in a book which shall face directly from him and directly towards the depositor, who will be requested by a sign to observe whether the correct amount is entered upon it.

Only black ink is used or kept at the receiving teller's desk. The reason for this will be seen when speaking of the paying teller. It is the duty of the receiving teller to explain the regulations of the bank, and give all information to persons inquiring with reference to opening accounts; to explain the system of deposit tickets to those who are not acquainted with it, and, in case of illiterate persons, to assist them, or to perform it for them. As the first impressions of depositors will be formed from their intercourse with him, it is essential that he should be perfectly courteous and of even temper. He will frequently meet with depositors who will endeavor to defraud him—who will pass in $99, for example, and a ticket made out for $100, and when told of the error, will pull the other $1 bill out of their pockets, saying very innocently, "Is that so? I must have counted wrong," hoping that once in a thousand times the teller may make the same mistake.

The receiving teller should be an excellent judge of money, an accomplishment which is not so needful for the paying teller. In fact, although in business banks the paying teller is the higher officer, it would seem as though, in the Savings bank, the receiving teller's position were the most important. During the day the receiving teller may be called upon to supply funds to other departments of the bank. The paying teller regularly keeps his cash filled from that of the receiving teller. He draws this in even amounts, making requisition for so many thousand dollars in such denominations; therefore, when not otherwise occupied, the receiving teller should package up his bills with paper strips properly marked. An excellent rule for this is always to put 50 pieces in one package, so that a package of $2 bills is known to contain $100, and a package of $5 bills $250, etc. If the receipts are largely exceeding the expenditures, or, as it is frequently expressed, "the bank is running ahead," the Treasurer may make requisition in a similar manner for a part of the receiving teller's funds to deposit in bank. Checks, drafts, money orders, and similar documents are by this bank freely taken on deposit and credited as cash, but with a particular mark which indicates the nature of the funds, and nothing is ever paid against such deposits until they have been actually collected. Some of the more conservative banks, probably from force of habit, rather than otherwise, refuse altogether to receive checks on deposit, but as the irresistible tendency of the age is to make all payments of any moment through the agency of banks, the rule will ultimately prevail that checks are *prima facie* cash. Towards the close of the business day, or whenever he has leisure, the receiving teller gets ready the tickets representing the transactions of the day, in order to have them written up in his book called the "Deposit Book." This book simply contains number of account and amount of deposit. . . . . . . As we have remarked, it may very properly be written up from the pass books before they leave the bank, especially if the business is sufficiently voluminous to give the receiving teller an assistant who can attend to this and also to the signature book.

For convenience, the tickets are frequently assorted, proximately into numerical order, before writing them up. The only advantage in this is that it facilitates searching for error, if any, in the next day's "Bookkeeper's proof." There are, on the other hand, some advantages in entering the tickets in the exact order in which they were received, because, sometimes, in the case of dispute, this enables us to find the names of the depositors who were standing near at the time the questioned deposit was made, and also enables us to ascertain, proximately, the hour of the day when said transaction took place. The receiving teller is required, by an inflexible rule, to turn over to the Treasurer, before three o'clock, all checks, drafts, or other cash items, not actually money or currency, so that the cash balance carried over night by the teller is *bona fide* cash, and available for payments. The liberty of holding checks over night, or memoranda, in place of cash, may very easily lead to a fictitious balance covering a real shortage. The checks received are entered in a special book, which gives the name of the bank, the name of the maker, the name of the depositor from whom received, and the amount. Shortly before three o'clock the janitor goes to the desks of the various tellers, and asks them for their checks and check lists. He counts the items received from each one, and brings them, with their contents, to the Treasurer, who receipts in the margin of the check-list book. Now the day's work is over, and it is the teller's duty to "balance his cash." His deposit book is fully written up and footed. His transactions with other departments of the bank have been noted by him as they occurred, and are vouched for by receipts taken and given. He therefore has all the elements of a balance, except the verification of the amount on hand. He counts, first, his packages of bills, assuming the contents of the packages in themselves to be correct; next his loose bills, and last his coin. He is now prepared to make up and prove his report to the Secretary. This contains three columns—"debits," "credits," and "cash on hand."

In the debit column is entered, first, the amount in his hands at the beginning of the day; second the amount received from depositors, being the total of the deposit book. He also states, as a matter of statistics, the number of depositors, and also the number of accounts opened.

Then follow receipts from other sources, either from the treasurer or from the other tellers, but this is exceptional, for the receiving teller, as such, is constantly parting with his money inside of the bank, and has no occasion to receive from others. It might have been mentioned, that in our bank, more as a matter of convenience than otherwise, expense vouchers, unless paid by check, are paid by the receiving teller from his cash, after receiving the approval of the treasurer or secretary. It is considered that there is an economy of labor in thus relieving the receiving teller of part of his money, making so much less for the paying teller to recount.

On the credit side of the teller's report is, first, "amounts paid to depositors," but unless he has acted during the day as paying teller, the receiving teller will have nothing to record here. Next come amounts paid to the treasurer. This will embrace the checks turned over by him, the currency turned over to be deposited, expense vouchers paid on the approval of the treasurer or secretary. In the two former cases, he has a receipt on the margin of his check list. In the latter case, he holds the authorization on the voucher. Next come payments to other tellers. This is normally, of course, to the paying teller. The last item of credit, which is balance on hand, is not inserted until the cash has been counted. The results of the count are written in the last column under the heads "Packaged bills," "loose bills," "coin." Then the aggregate of these is placed opposite the words "actual cash on hand." Now this may not be the correct amount which should be on hand. If in excess, the cash is said to be "over," if deficient, it is said to be "short."

A line is provided for each of these contingencies, and if, after thorough search, the cash is "short," the amount of deficiency is entered on the proper line, and added to the actual cash on hand, the result being carried into the credit column, last line. If the cash be "over," the amount of excess is similarly entered, but subtracted. The amounts of the debit and credit columns should now be equal. This report, signed by the teller, is handed to the secretary, who extracts from it the information necessary for his books, which he will hereafter test, and marks it "examined and entered, ———secretary," and places it on file. The teller begins his report for the following morning, with the balance on hand, as corrected. During the following day, unless he succeeds in finding the error, he is required, in case of an "over," to charge himself by ticket, approved by the secretary, with the amount, placing it to the credit of an account called "excess account," from which it may ultimately be transferred to the credit of the rightful owner when ascertained. In case of a "short," he is charged in an account called his "deficiency account," and has ultimately to refund the amount to the bank.

Besides the daily report of all transactions, the teller makes a monthly report of his transactions with depositors alone, for more convenient examination by the auditing committee.

CHAPTER V.

THE PAYING TELLER.

It has already been explained, in connection with the receiving teller, that the moneys received by him are the principal sources of supply to the paying teller, but if the payments at any particular time are running heavier than the receipts, recourse must be had to depository banks for funds. In this case requisition is made on the treasurer, who draws the amount from the nearest bank, and takes the paying teller's receipt on the stub of the check book. The bank accounts are drawn upon for payments to depositors, also, in another way. A depositor frequently prefers to receive his payment in a check on some commercial bank, rather than in money, thus lessening the risk of loss, and in many cases creating additional evidence of his transaction. In this case the paying teller sends the depositor, after verifying his draft, to the secretary's window, and himself hands the draft to the secretary, who gives the check to the depositor. On the return of the draft, the paying teller receipts, as before, in the margin of the check book. Thus, the receipts of the paying teller are, first, from the receiving teller; second, from the treasurer in money drawn from the banks; and, thirdly, in checks which are immediately issued. His payments are almost exclusively to depositors. When, as has already been said, the depositor presents himself at his window with a request for a certain sum of money, the paying teller has to make the following inquiries:

First.—Is the pass book presented?

Second.—Is there sufficient money on the account to pay the draft? In order to ascertain this he requests the bookkeeper, by mentioning the number of the account, to inform him of the present balance, or, if there be sufficient time, examines it himself.

Third.—Is there a properly made out draft for the amount? If not, the teller usually makes it out himself.

Fourth.—Is the signature genuine? To ascertain this, he turns to the signature book (the entire series being near him), and, finding the number of the account, compares the signature of the draft held in his hand with that originally written in the book. It is very frequently the case that there will be some slight disparity, far more frequently than in case of a commercial bank. The last withdrawal was perhaps many years ago, and very naturally some change may have taken place in the character of the handwriting. Any substantial variation, such as writing initials instead of full names, or abbreviations instead of initials, he causes to be corrected by a re-writing of the name on the back, if the depositor is present in person. It is not his duty to refuse payment where the signature is not absolutely identical. He must, using the best of his judgment and discretion, form his opinion as to whether the signature is genuine. A by-law of the bank, which has been sustained as reasonable by the courts of the State, declares that any payment made to any person producing the genuine pass book shall be considered valid, and shall discharge the bank. A payment without the pass book is very exceptional, and is never made without the approval of one of the officers of the bank, noted on the draft itself. In this case, of course, a perfectly incontestable signature must be presented. In the case of persons who did not write, but made a mark on the opening of their account, the mark is now made in the presence of the teller, and the person is asked the various test questions which were asked at that time. If answered correctly, and the appearance of the person sufficiently answers the description, this, with the presentation of the pass book, is considered sufficient evidence to pay on.

In some of the older Savings banks the signature of the depositor, when coming in person to draw, is not taken. They rely, not on comparison of signatures, but on the asking of the so-called test questions. This seems to us a very improper way of transacting business, of which the only advantage has been, in past years, the saving of two cents for an internal revenue stamp, now abolished. The bank retains no voucher for the payment. It is perfectly easy, especially in our crowded tenement houses, for a person who has abstracted a pass book, to obtain such information as the names of parents, etc., and the writer has no doubt that many cases of fraud have occurred in this way, which even the depositors have not been aware of. The identification by questions should only be employed as a last resort, where comparison of signatures cannot be made.

Fifth.—To whom is the amount payable? Instead of coming in person, the depositor frequently gives his draft to another. The printed forms given by the bank read "pay to myself, or bearer," and in the forms given in the pass book, the word "bearer," is always recommended to be inserted. Occasionally, a draft is presented, payable to order. In this case, of course, identification is necessary, as in a business bank. The bank claims the right to decline any such draft, as it is no part of its business to verify endorsements, but frequently the difficulty is overcome by paying in check to the order of the payee named. Some drafts are presented through the medium of business banks, having been deposited for collection. These are also usually paid by check. The bank has the right, in case of a financial panic, or similar emergency, to demand sixty days' notice before making any payments whatever. In this case, it is the duty of the paying teller to accept such written notices.

The paying teller keeps a draft book, precisely corresponding to the deposit book already described. His daily report is precisely similar to that of the receiving teller, the footing of his draft book being entered as a credit, and the statistics of the number of drafts, and number of books closed, taking the place of number of deposits and number of accounts opened. When an account is closed, the pass book is always retained by the bank; therefore, at the close of the day, the paying teller should have a pass book for each account which has been closed, and his report of the number closed is made by counting these pass books. The following morning this account is verified by a report from the bookkeepers of the number of accounts actually ruled off on the ledger. In case of a lost book, an envelope, of the size of the pass book, and marked with the number, date, &c., is put in as a substitute or dummy. It is the paying teller's business to keep himself supplied with funds, and to give timely notice to the treasurer, or to the receiving teller, that they may have money ready for him in the morning hours when he has leisure to count it.

CHAPTER VI.

THE BOOKKEEPER.

The bookkeeping department of the Savings bank has charge, solely, of the accounts with depositors. The general accounts of investments, income and expenditure, are a separate system under the direct charge of the secretary. The province of the bookkeeping department is to keep a classified record of the tellers' transactions, which shall, at any moment, indicate the standing of any given depositor with the bank and the balance to his credit, at the same time corroborating the accuracy of the tellers' figures. The transactions with the depositor are: first, deposits; second, interest; third, drafts; fourth, transfers. The tickets already described as deposit tickets and draft tickets form the basis of all the bookkeeping operations. The transfer, which consists in withdrawing from one account and crediting the same sum to another, is effected by a double ticket. Half of this is of the size and form of a draft ticket, and the other half of that of a deposit ticket, and any clerk is authorized to make a transfer, being responsible for all the parts of it. He makes the entry in both pass books, writes up a description of the transaction in a third book, called the transfer book, giving the number of the account from which, the number of the account to which the transfer is made, and its amount, and also the date from which it bears interest. The double ticket is placed upon a special spindle kept near the transfer book. The bookkeeping work of one day is always done on the following day. The result of the day's business is an accumulation of tickets of the three kinds, as already described, and these are stamped with the official date, the transfers being divided into their component parts. We then have two series, one of debits against depositors, and the other of credits in their favor. The first duty of the head bookkeeper is to take each series and to divide it according to the numbers belonging to the different ledgers. The ledgers of the bank contain 5,000 numbers each, in consecutive order, but when the majority of the accounts have been closed, several of these are consolidated and kept in one volume. Each bookkeeper has certain ledgers assigned to him, for the accuracy of which he is responsible. One bookkeeper, whose share of the work is the twenty-fifth and

twenty-seventh ledgers, receives the tickets, debit and credit, belonging to accounts contained within those limits. He next makes a further arrangement, so as to bring them into exact numerical order, which greatly facilitates posting.* It may be briefly described as follows: The ledger consists of three columns besides the date: debits, credits and balance. After each transaction, and in the same line with it appears the resulting balance or amount to the credit of the depositor. The posting is done entirely from the tickets in the first instance, but only consists in rewriting the balance, plus the deposit, or minus the draft, as the case may be. Thus, if the bookkeeper has a deposit ticket on John Smith's account for $29.32, he turns to the proper page of the ledger, as indicated by the number on the ticket, and there he finds that the present balance is...$270 44
Adding mentally, figure by figure, he writes on the next line 299 76 which is the new balance produced by the transaction. He also writes the date, but does *not* make any entry in the column devoted to deposits. Each ledger has a book corresponding to it, called the "Journal," which might more properly be termed a "Proof Book" of that ledger. It is a transcript of all the postings each day to accounts in that ledger. In writing up the tickets in this book, which is done as soon as the posting is finished, the amounts are omitted, only numbers and names being copied. Now comes the process of verification. Turning to Mr. Smith's account, the verifying bookkeeper (not the one who posted it) infers from the two balances that the transaction must have been a deposit of $29.32. He therefore writes that amount in the credit column of Smith's account, and copies the same into the credit column of the Journal. Now it is evident that if there were a mistake either in the amount of the entry, or in subtracting instead of adding, or in computing the balance as changed, the aggregate of the entries on this ledger, and the aggregate of the entries of the entire day will be incorrect. This aggregate is carried to two forms, called respectively, the "Daily Proof of Deposits," and the "Daily Proof of Drafts." Opposite "Ledger twenty-five" and "Ledger twenty-seven," the bookkeeper enters the amount posted to each side, as shown by the journal. When the daily proofs have been completed by filling up every line, their total is compared with the total aggregates derived from the teller's reports, and if there is any discrepancy, it indicates some error, either in the teller's accounts, or in the balancing of some depositor's account, or in the transaction on some depositor's account, or in addition. It is the duty of the clerk who last made an error which threw the daily proof out of balance to search for the error now existing. When

---

*The process employed in posting is fully explained in an article, entitled "Balance Posting," in *The Bookkeeper*, No 51.

he has found the present error, and fixed the responsibility for it upon one of his colleagues, the latter holds the unenviable appointment of searcher, until he again relieves himself of it by detecting some other offender.

A "Monthly Proof" is also made, which involves the total transactions for the month, and the aggregate balance of each ledger, being a summary trial balance; and there are intermediate "Saturday Proofs," which are not obligatory, but made by the bookkeepers for their own convenience.

We have described one of the most advanced methods for keeping accurate accounts with depositors, and one by which it would seem almost impossible that any error should escape detection. It involves two principles which seem to us vital in insuring accuracy. First, that where there is a great volume of work to be gone over, it should be cut up into such small portions, each separately proved, that the area of search for errors is narrowed. Second, that the process of verification should be totally different from the process verified. A familiar illustration of the latter principle is in the process of addition, where, having added upwards, we then add downwards, lest the same error occur in the same combination of figures. We will now describe one of the primitive methods which are still in use in some institutions and which violate these principles.

The ledger contains columns for drafts only and deposits, none for the balance. The posting is done, not from tickets but from the tellers' deposit and draft-books. The verification is merely a going over the items in the same order, affixing a check-mark if the original book and the ledger agree. There is no division of the transactions and balances of different ledgers or sections. The only thorough proof is in the semi-annual trial-balance, and it is an almost hopeless task to find an error in this, if there is a discrepancy, as usually happens. Experience has shown that this method neither prevents nor detects with certainty, errors in posting.

The interest, or dividend, is computed semi-annually, and its calculation devolves upon the bookkeepers, each for his own ledger. The calculations are gone through twice. The first operation is entered in a book called "Interest and Balance Book, Ledger ———." This contains, on the left hand side, the numbers of all the open accounts in succession, followed by columns for the amount of interest at each half-yearly period, separated by other columns for the balance, which will hereafter be explained. The so-called "balance column" of the deposit ledgers, greatly facilitates the calculation of interest. Making the calculation mentally, figures are put down in the "Interest and Balance Book," opposite the principal, in pencil. When the ledger has been finished in this way, the "Interest and Balance Book" is laid aside entirely and the calculations again made, the result being noted in pencil on the margin of the account. Thus there are two independent calculations of dividend, and if, upon comparing these two, they are found to be identical, it is assumed that the calculation is correct. As this work is commenced before the end of the interest period, there are changes during its progress, caused by the withdrawal of money. These are corrected each day. After the first of January, or of July, the amounts penciled on the margin are written with red ink in the body of the account, and the resulting balance carried out, also in red. The "Interest and Balance Book" is added up by pages and aggregated by ledgers, so as finally to show the total amount of the dividend. It is the duty of the bookkeeper to enter in the depositor's pass book, whenever required by him, all dividends standing to his credit up to date. This is also done in red ink, and it is the invariable rule to foot up and balance his pass book at that time, compare its balance with that shown by the ledger account, and check off the latter, if correct. The book is also similarly balanced whenever the page is full; thus the daily and monthly reports of the bookkeepers verify and control the daily and monthly reports of the tellers, the cash department and the accounting department each reporting to the secretary, who balances one against the other.

In connection with the signature book the index cards are described and exemplified. These are kept in a chest of drawers which will contain about 10,000. They are arranged in alphabetical order, the index cards of each day being inserted in their appropriate places, and the cards representing closed accounts being each day extracted and filed in a separate series, so that the regular series contains only the open current accounts.

Many forms of index books have been and are used—simply alphabetical, alphabetical with vowel divisions, and alphabetized according to the first three letters. In none of these can the arrangement ever remain absolutely alphabetical, and there is always a considerable space to be gone over to find a certain name, and a great chance of missing it. In the card method a certain name can occupy but one place, as in a directory, and the dead accounts do not have to be gone over in order to find the open ones.

Little zinc cards indicate the divisions between letters, and between combinations of letters, so as to facilitate search.

We have now considered the principal functions of all the clerks of the bank, and have next to describe the duties of its executive officers. These are, in the bank under consideration, the president, treasurer and secretary. The treasurer and secretary perform, to a certain extent, co-ordinate duties. That is, they assist each other, and relieve each other when absent. We will describe first the duties of

CHAPTER VII.

THE TREASURER.

This officer is elected by the board of trustees, and holds office at their pleasure. He may or may not be a member of the board, but it is customary that he should be. His department is the custody and management of the investments of the bank, but, as the senior officer present, he exercises a general direction over all departments. The cash deposited in banks is principally under his control. He, or the secretary acting for him, directs the deposits to be made in different banks. Checks on the banks are signed by him and by the secretary, and countersigned by the president. He is the proper officer to collect interest or rent due the institution, to receive payment for obligations which mature, to receive applications from borrowers, and to lay before the board of trustees all matters pertaining to investments which may require their action. The principal investments of the bank, as permitted by law, are—1st, loans on pledge of stocks; 2d, stock investments; 3d, mortgage loans.

The kinds and amount of these various classes of investments are guarded by law, which differs in the various States. In the New England States loans may be made upon bills receivable as security, which is not the case in this State. In some States loans may be made upon bank stocks or railroad stocks.

The *First* of these classes, loans on pledge of stocks, are considered as a temporary investment. The loan cannot exceed par, and there must also be a margin of ten per cent. These loans are made upon the sole discretion of the Treasurer, as it would be impracticable, in case of a loan from day to day, to await the action of the board at its monthly meeting. The borrower deposits the securities, the treasurer is responsible for seeing that they are genuine and that they are sufficient, and for their custody. He takes from the borrower a voucher, and also a note, which are at first embodied in one document, afterwards separated.

The raising and lowering of the rate on such loans is also at his discretion, and if the loan should not be paid, principal or interest, when due and demanded, it is his duty to sell the stocks pledged as collateral security, as prescribed in the note, and to account properly for the proceeds. It is also his duty, in case of the depreciation of the security below the legal margin, to make a call for a sufficient part of the loan to bring it within the margin.

Second.—Stock investments. These are usually voted by the board, but the practical business of buying and selling is effected by the treasurer. The board usually authorizes a purchase at not exceeding a certain price, or a sale at not below a certain price, and it is the duty of the treasurer, of course, to obtain the most advantageous terms possible for the bank, and his contract, even if it should be contrary to the vote of the board, would bind the institution. These securities are frequently of the class known as coupon bonds, where each maturing amount of interest is represented by a small promissory note attached to the margin of the bond. These bonds and their coupons being payable to bearer, there is greater danger in case of theft than from registered securities. The treasurer is, therefore, usually instructed to convert any coupon bonds, which may be purchased, into registered. As an expert in the money market, the treasurer is expected to submit to the board at its meetings all desired information as to what appear to be the most profitable investments. When the interest on the stock investment matures, the treasurer attends to its collection through the regular channels, referring to the register of interest due, kept by the secretary.

The law of the State of New York permits Savings banks to invest only in the following stocks and bonds: 1, United States bonds, including District of Columbia 3.65's; 2, New York State bonds; 3, bonds of any State in the Union which has not during ten previous years defaulted on principal or interest; 4, bonds (if issued in pursuance of a State law) of any city, county, town or village in the State; 5, any interest-bearing obligations of the city or county in which the bank is situated. In loaning on collateral security, the banks are restricted to the same classes of bonds.

Third.—Mortgages. A person desiring to borrow from the bank upon his mortgage on real estate, fills out the application, which contains spaces for a full description of the property and other information concerning the proposed loan. This is, in the first instance, investigated by the treasurer, and in a great many cases declined by him at once. He is understood, by custom, to have a veto upon such applications as seem *out of the question. If the loan appears advantageous, and within the limits prescribed by law, the treasurer submits it, with others, in a list at the next meeting of the board; a printed copy of the list, giving a brief description of the security in each case, being laid before each member. If the loan is accepted, and the application forwarded to the attorney to whom the applicant is then referred, and the title is, by the latter, pronounced good, the treasurer draws the bank's check in favor of the attorney for the amount of the loan. He will receive from the attorney the application, with the receipt of the borrower endorsed thereon. Also the bond, the insurance policy, the mortgage, when it has returned from the office of public record, and the abstract of title when it has been copied. It is his duty to examine each of these documents, to see that the correct amount has been paid upon the voucher, to see that the bond is in accordance with the vote of the board, that the insurance policy is in one of the companies selected by the bank, and made payable to the bank as mortgagee, that the mortgage describes the property correctly, and that the abstract is properly certified to by the attorney. He furthermore sees that the documents are appropriately filed under the serial number of the mortgage.

All the documents, except the application and abstract, are kept in a single envelope, headed with the number of the loan, and they retain this number so long as they are the property of the bank. The application is filed as a cash voucher, and the abstracts, which are somewhat bulky, are kept in a separate series. Semi-annually, on the first days of May and November, it is the duty of the treasurer to collect from the mortgagors the interest on their mortgages. He sends to each mortgagor, about twenty days previous to those dates, a statement of the amount of interest due, the computations for which are made and verified by the secretary. This statement is so arranged as to constitute, when signed and returned by the mortgagor, a letter of transmission accompanying the payment to the treasurer. These statements are required to be signed, even when the party pays in person, as evidence of the correctness of the amount paid. In return, the treasurer gives a receipt. In the majority of cases the payment of interest on mortgages is made by check on some bank in favor of the institution. If it is made in money, a statement is handed with the money to one of the tellers, who receipts therefor by writing his initials after the words "Received by," and returns the statement.

The secretary debits the teller and credits the treasurer. It is the theory of the bank that every document representing the payment of money in either direction should be doubly signed, by the party or bank official giving, and also by the one receiving it.

Interest on loans, it might have been stated, is collected in a precisely similar manner. If a mortgage becomes in default of interest or principal, it is the duty of the treasurer, after applying all other means, to place the mortgage in the hands of the attorney for foreclosure, and upon the conclusion of the action, to collect and account for the proceeds. He also receives money in partial payment of mortgages, usually where the same are over-due, and running by mutual consent. In this case, he requires a statement of the general form, and gives a receipt.

Besides these classes of regular current investments, the bank may, in certain cases, invest in real estate. These cases are the following:

1st. A building for its own use; but, as it would be unprofitable to confine the building to the single story required for bank use, it is allowed to add portions thereto for the purpose of deriving revenue from renting. 2d. Where mortgages are foreclosed, it is frequently necessary for the bank to bid at the sale in order to protect itself, and in this manner it may become the buyer. When the fee of a piece of real estate has been thus acquired by the institution, it then becomes the duty of the treasurer to act as the bank's agent in managing the property, to sell it whenever that can advantageously be done, and to derive the best possible revenue from it, so long as it is held. The collection of rents, both from the rented portions of the bank's premises, and from foreclosed real estate, is effected in a manner analogous to the collection of interest. A statement is sent out as a notice, returned as a voucher, and exchanged for a receipt. As to the sale of real estate held by the bank, the board usually instructs the treasurer as to a limit, above which he is authorized to dispose of it. When a bargain is made, he and the purchaser sign in duplicate a contract of sale, and the amount paid in hand at the signing of this contract is considered as a liability, and credited to the account "contracts of sale."

The expenditures of the institution are under the supervision of the treasurer. In every case, whether the payment be as an investment, or as the expense of managing any of its departments, he takes from the payee a voucher, and if the actual payment is made by a teller, it is countersigned by the latter.

CHAPTER VIII.

THE SECRETARY.

The secretary is supposed to be the accounting officer of the bank. It is his duty to know, from its books and records, the state of the institution in every department, at any time. In practice, he performs a large share of the duties just described as belonging properly to the treasurer, he being constituted by the by-laws, a vice-treasurer; but his duties will be described as they exist in theory, for the secretary alone. His duties may be divided into three branches: as correspondent of the bank, as recorder of the board of trustees, and as accountant of the bank. All letters should be received by him, and answered by him, either immediately, or upon reference to the appropriate department. It is the rule of the bank that every letter received, however unimportant, be filed in its alphabetical place, and that every letter sent, however apparently unimportant, be copied in the impression book. This refers to all correspondence not of a personal character, or all which is signed officially. There can be no such thing as an unimportant letter, because the fact of every letter being copied enables us to say positively, "I did'nt write a letter to so and so on such a day, because if I had, it would appear in the copying book." This being able to swear to a negative, which can only be done by the aid of a rule without exceptions, is, of itself, worth all the labor attending the copying of letters. Official letters of the bank are written upon its letter sheet, the heading of which, printed in copying ink, contains the clauses, "referring to your letter of ———," and "subject———," which enables a correspondence on a given subject to be traced through the letter book. Special forms of letters often required, are printed, as letter of transmission to attorneys, with check for the mortgage; letter to depositor, with remittance on his account; request to depositor to present pass book (for the tracing of errors, &c.); circular, explaining to persons at a distance how to deposit without coming in person, called the "remittance circular." Circular with rules as to interest on mortgage, &c. This is used to "stir up" delinquents by under-scoring the part against which they have transgressed. Notices of meeting of board of trustees.

Second.—As recording officer of the board of trustees, the secretary performs the ordinary duties of keeping the journal or minutes, and filing and preserving documents. He submits to the board at each meeting a report which is confined to the dealings of the bank with its depositors, giving all the statistics as to number and amount of receipts and payments and averages.

Third.—The chief duties of the secretary, or those which occupy the most of his time, are those which he performs as accountant to the bank. Strictly, he has no custody of any values whatever, but all records of transfers of values are directly or indirectly made by him. Thus, he is an auditor of every department of the bank, all of which contribute to him through reports. He keeps personally, or through assistance, all the general books of the bank, that is to say, all the books of the bank except those containing the accounts with depositors. His daily cash book classifies transactions in two ways: 1st, as they affect the general standing of the bank in its relation with the outside world; and, 2d, as they affect merely the increase and diminution of some one of the departments of its cash. These departments are:—

1st. Money in the hands of tellers.

2d. Funds in the vault in the direct custody of the treasurer.

3d. Deposits in banks subject to check signed by the president, treasurer and secretary.

These together constitute the total cash account, and the possible transactions may be of the following kinds:

1st. Money received from the public and paid to one of these departments, or, in other words, an increase of the total cash with an increase in a department.

2d. Money paid to the public, and drawn for that purpose from one of the departments, or, in other words, decrease of total cash, and decrease of department cash.

3d. A transfer from one department of cash to another, or increase of one department and decrease of another.

By means of the inner columns of the cash book, which represent transactions with the public, and which, alone, find their way to the monthly cash, and the outer columns, which represent the various departments spoken of, all the records for a single day are made upon a single page. The possible transactions of a single day will be shown by an example, in which a page of the daily cash book will be shown, together with the reports, documents and vouchers which form its basis. It will be seen that every figure appearing in the columns of the daily cash has its counterpart in two different documents or reports, and that these bear upon and corroborate each other. The only exceptions, or apparent exceptions, to this, are caused by a transfer of the funds, which are entirely in the direct custody of the treasurer.

For example, a transfer from one bank to another, or a transfer from the vault to one of the banks. Here there will be no voucher on the one side, because the treasurer cannot give a receipt to himself, and this is not necessary, being similar to the case where a teller merely exchanges money of one denomination for that of another, not affecting his total balance. The lines of our specimen page of the daily cash book will be numbered, and each document relating to it will be lettered, and in our explanation the two supporting vouchers of each line will be given in succession.

The intermediate transfers or interchanges between departments of the bank, which occupy so large an amount of the space of the daily cash book, do not, as a rule, go beyond its pages. The inner columns which we have spoken of as representing the relations of the institution to the public, contain all that enters into the general books of the bank, and, with the exception of the entries "deposits received," and "drafts paid," every item in these inner columns is supported by a voucher. These form two series, called the "general vouchers for receipts" and the "general vouchers for payments." Each series is numbered consecutively, but the vouchers for payments form two series. For the sake of convenience, vouchers relating to expense, either of management or of the banking premises, are numbered from 1 to 1,000, repeating these numbers when the thousand has been reached. The remaining vouchers for payment are numbered from 1,000 upward. Upon reaching No. 2,000, the numbers re-commence at 1,001. The reason for this is that the series with smaller numbers or expense vouchers are subjected to a special analysis in a book called the "Expense Book," and it is therefore preferable to keep them together. These two series of general vouchers for receipts and payments are the basis of all further records. No entries are made from book to book, but always from the voucher to the book, the fact of such record taking place being noted on the back of the voucher. Thus, a voucher for expenditures on real estate other than the banking house is recorded in the daily cash book, in the monthly cash book, under the heading "real estate," in the real estate ledger, under the head of the particular property, and in the general ledger, under the account of "real estate." These four entries are made each direct from the voucher. The letter "D" on the back of the voucher indicates that it has been transcribed in the daily cash book; the letter "M" that it has been entered in the monthly cash book; and the folio of the real estate ledger and of the general ledger are also noted on the back. These four entries must correspond, and any discrepancy between them will be detected by the operation of the trial balance.

The practice of requiring signed vouchers for payments of money has long been an established rule of mercantile practice, but, strange to say, where value of some other kind is paid or given, and money received, it has not usually been customary to insist upon a voucher. In this bank the principle is rigorously carried out that in every transaction involving an interchange of values, there shall be a corresponding interchange of documentary evidence between the parties.*

As the entire accountability of the bank rests upon these documents, so their arrangement in convenient form for examination and reference is of importance. The vouchers for each month are arranged in two series—the receipts and the payments, and each of these has a list, the form of which is printed on strong manilla paper. The inside of the list of vouchers for cash payments contains, first, a certificate from the auditing committee that they have examined all the vouchers mentioned in the list below, amounting to $, and have passed the same as correct. The committee not only signs this, but one of its members marks, with his initial or otherwise, each particular voucher, in order to prevent its being again presented. When the examination is completed, this list serves as a wrapper or jacket, within which the vouchers themselves are tied up. On the outside of the wrapper is a printed form, giving the amount as classified for posting aggregates to the general ledger. The total of this outside list will be the same figures as the total of the numerical list verified by the committee, but it gives simply the aggregate to be charged to each ledger account. For example, the list inside may contain a number of vouchers for money loaned on mortgage. The classified list will simply state—" Mortgages, $." These lists, on the outside of the bundles of vouchers constitute what might be called a grand voucher, which authorizes the secretary to record the transactions in bulk.

An examiner would not, for the great mass of transactions, require any books in order to ascertain the past history of the institution since this method has been in practice. He would simply be handed a number of bundles of vouchers—two for each month—with the authenticated list on the inside of the wrapper and the classified list on the outside, and from these he could himself make up an authenticated history of all the substantial transactions of the bank during the period covered. These are the real records of the bank. All the books are simply transcripts in various convenient and ingenious forms, in which the order of the vouchers is changed for obtaining special results. The vouchers are the history—the books are philosophical combinations of, and deductions from, the facts.

The primary vouchers of the deposit department, as already mentioned, are the deposit tickets and draft tickets, but it would be in-

* See Lecture on Documents as Related to Accounts, published in *The Bookkeeper*, No. 58.

convenient, from the number of these, to file them with the general vouchers. Each teller's daily report is a substitute or grand voucher for those of the day in his department, and these might be filed in that relation; but as they are stated in the form of an account, they would have to be made in duplicate, and therefore, for convenience, the monthly return is required from each teller as to his deposits and as to his drafts.

The secretary makes up at the end of the month two combined vouchers from these monthly returns. He brings together the total amount, and he certifies to its agreement with the aggregate reports given independently from the bookkeeper's department, so that these two vouchers contain the ultimate condensation of the thousands of drafts and deposits which accrue each month. This might be called a cumulative voucher of the fourth degree. The primary voucher being that signed by the depositor, the secondary voucher being the teller's daily report, and the tertiary being the teller's monthly report. As corroborated by the accounting branch of the deposit department, it consists of even more steps.

The business of the bank has three different units of time—the day, the month, and the half-year—and each of these has its historical record, its counterbalancing proofs, and its final statement of results or balance sheet. The daily transactions are brought to a focus upon the page of the daily cash book, and are also repeated in various forms in special ledgers, namely, the deposit ledger, mortgage ledger, loan ledger, stocks ledger, real estate ledger, rent ledger. For information, there is also kept in the daily cash book, below the cash entries, a daily statement of profit and loss and a daily balance sheet, so that at the close of each day the exact status of the bank, as near as can be ascertained, is recorded.

An accurate account is kept, in this book only, of the interest, to the nearest fraction of a cent which is earned on each class of investment, and this is added to the accrued interest account daily, and also credited the income account. Similarly the accretion of rents and any other profits is recorded. On the other hand, the exact daily amount is apportioned for payment of salaries, of taxes, of dividend as estimated, of general expenses, and for the extinction of the premium on bonds as they approach maturity.

Each of these elements produces its effect on the profit and loss or surplus account, and equally on some branch of the resources or liabilities, actual or estimated, so that the business of the day results in a balance sheet, the cash transactions appearing above, being, of course, taken into consideration.

The balance of each department of the cash, and also of the cash as a whole, is also verified daily. The monthly work consists in the aggregation, by the means already explained, of all the events of the month into two sets of columns, which give the general condition. These totals, when posted to the general ledger, form the basis of its trial balance. The trial balance of the general ledger is not precisely identical with the balance sheet contained in the daily cash under the last day of the month, for this reason: The general ledger, in its current or normal state, is kept on the basis of cost. No profit or loss, by depreciation or appreciation, is recognized until realized by the actual disposition of the proceeds. Hence, the trial balance of the general ledger is a balance sheet on the cost basis, while the daily balance sheet is on the basis of present market values.

The secretary completes his monthly work by making up, from the figures thus obtained, the reports to be submitted to the next following meeting of the board of trustees. At the monthly meetings in June and December, being the last months of the half years, it is required by law that the dividends be fixed according to the profits earned. It is therefore necessary for an estimate of the earnings and expenditures of the half year to be submitted, as a basis of this dividend. This can very readily be done, as five-sixths, or nearly eleven-twelfths of the period have elapsed. At this meeting, therefore, the secretary submits such an estimate, showing, as its result, the rate of dividend which can be allowed, usually leaving a margin to be added to the surplus. The board then votes upon the dividend, and the secretary issues orders to the bookkeepers to make the calculations at the prescribed rate. At the same meeting the examining committee is appointed, and this is the first step in the preparation of the semi-annual official reports. It is necessary that every facility be provided for this committee to examine in detail, as far as advisable, the exact condition of the bank. The secretary prepares a balance sheet in blank, containing headings and spaces for all the departments, of resources, of liabilities, and the surplus, with their several values. He also prepares numerous blank schedules, each referring to one of these departments, and giving the individual units which make it up. Thus, under the head of stock investments, Schedule C, for instance, would be given the following information: Title of stock and by whom issued; rate of interest; year of maturity; amount at par; cost; present market rate; present market value; interest paid to what date; amount of interest earned but uncollected.

As the last day of the month approaches, at the close of which it is the duty of this committee to make its examination, the secretary begins to fill in the figures of these schedules, first, of course, in those departments in which there is the least chance of a change occurring. Thus, if it is not probable that there will be any further purchase or sales of stocks and bonds, the stock schedule can be filled up as to all the particulars, except "market rate" and 'market value." In order to ascertain the market rate of such securities, recourse must be had, where possible, to published quotations or to the opinions of experts. The secretary usually sends, a few days beforehand, to several firms of respectable brokers who make a specialty of dealing in public investment stocks, a list of the kinds of securities held by the bank, giving the title, date of maturity and the rate of interest, and requesting a reply in the margin to the question, "What would be a fair market value for each of these classes of securities at the close of business on the last day of——?" These are filled up and returned by the brokers on the last day, for the information of the committee. Other departments of resources also require corroborative evidence, which it is the duty of the secretary to procure. As to balances deposited in banks, he requests the cashier of each depository bank to certify the balance on deposit at the close of the month to the chairman of the committee direct. In case the amount thus certified differs from the amount appearing on the check book, it is the duty of the secretary to explain and to furnish evidence of the disparity, which usually arises from checks issued but not yet presented, and the committee should, during the following month, or whenever it can be done, make a re-examination of the checks which were outstanding. If there be any papers in the mortgage department which the committee is entitled to see, and which are in the hands of the attorney for the purpose of foreclosure or otherwise, a certificate of their contents must be furnished by the attorney. As to real estate owned by the bank, if necessary, a disinterested appraiser, experienced in real estate values, should be employed to make a survey and report; and this should also be done in the case of mortgaged property, if there has been such depreciation as to make the margin precarious. All of these preparations, although part of the committee's work, are, in practice, attended to by the secretary in order to lessen the burden of labor for the committee. Besides the report of the committee to the board of trustees, there is an official report to the superintendent of the bank department, which is required by law to be made semi-annually at the dates mentioned. The body of this report, or balance sheet, is verified by the oath of the examining committee, and is identical with the balance sheet contained in their report to the board of trustees. The report however, is submitted and sworn to in its entirety by the president and secretary, and is prepared by the secretary from his books. The main report or balance sheet, just described, contains, in the blank form furnished by the State department, a column headed "resources," and another headed "liabilities."

Besides the main report above given there is a summary of cash transactions for the half year, or in the December report for the whole year, and schedules, marked from A to I.

The table of cash transactions begins with the balance on hand

and in banks at the commencement of the period, to which are added the receipts, classified according to their sources. Then follow, on the other side, the payments similarly classified, concluding with the balance on hand and in banks at the close of the period. Under our system, these aggregates are readily obtained from the bundles of cash vouchers for receipts and payments, respectively, being in most cases simply an adding together of the six monthly totals. In some of the particulars a little analysis is necessary from the wording of the blank, some items not exactly coinciding with either of the accounts kept in the General Ledger of the bank. It is, however, a principle in this institution, that every official report must have its figures, in some shape, derived from the books of the bank. It is too frequently the custom, in institutions of this kind, and perhaps of other kinds, that the sworn reports are made independently of the books, and that there is no way of directly tracing the connection between the two. As duplicate blanks are furnished by the department, in order that the bank may retain a copy of its official report, it is the practice in some banks to make references, by book and page, on the face of the copy retained, which will show precisely how the figures are obtained from the books. These schedules are given in the appendix.

Schedule A, No. 1, contains a list of mortgages taken during the period covered, with the valuation of the property mortgaged as security, and serves as a general mortgage account, corroborating item 1 of the resources.

Schedule A, No. 2, contains a list of mortgages paid off, in whole or in part, during the period covered.

The theory of these two reports is to enable the department to ascertain the amount out on mortgage, and the security therefor; but to make up such a statement from the schedules of many years, would be a very laborious process. It would seem preferable, that occasionally, say once in three or five years, a special report should be called for, giving a full list of the mortgages as they then existed, with the location of property, and an appraisal, which the department could verify at its leisure.

Schedule A No. 3, is a special list of those mortgages, the interest on which is more than six months in arrears. By the law, in the State of New York, any mortgages, on which the interest is not more than six months in arrears, are to be taken at their full value, and the superintendent has a right, in case of the mortgages comprised in Schedule A, No. 3, to affix a value. It is not known that he has in any case made such a valuation. In a prosperous bank, in ordinary times, this schedule should be blank.

Schedule B is a list of the bonds or stock investments of the institution, and its arrangement is commendable. In the case of stocks and bonds, a different plan is pursued from the one adopted in reference to mortgages. In mortgages, the increase and decrease during the period are alone considered. In stocks, the increase and decrease are entirely disregarded, and only the final status given. This would seem a defect, as there is far more opportunity for covering up frauds by exchange, barter, purchase and re-sale of securities, than mortgages. Every purchase, and every sale of stock securities during the period, should be reported, with dates and prices.

Schedule B is recapitulated on a smaller blank for the convenience of the department.

Schedule C is headed "stocks upon which loans are made in accordance with section 261," a rather inverted title, as the primary object is to give the amount loaned upon stocks.

Schedule D gives the details of cash; first, as to that deposited in banks and trust companies, not only is the amount on deposit stated, but also the capital and surplus of the depositary bank, as shown by its last official statement. The reason for demanding this information is, that a Savings bank is prohibited from depositing in any bank or trust company more than a certain proportion (twenty-five per cent.) of the capital and surplus of the latter.

Schedule E, No. 1, is intended for those investments which are contrary to the present law governing Savings banks. Only in case the bank has had such investments before the change of the law, which it has not been able to dispose of, can there be anything to enter in this schedule.

Schedule E, No. 2, is devoted to assets other than those enumerated, and would be very appropriate for miscellaneous and abnormal resources, but the bank department has included in it also, interest earned but uncollected, which is not an abnormal resource, but one which must exist in every Savings bank. There must always be interest which is earned and not collected, and it would therefore have seemed more appropriate to provide a separate schedule, under the head of income earned but uncollected, for interest and rents. Interest is divided into accrued and due, and the interest overdue is divided into that which is overdue less than six months and more than six months, and, finally the total is divided into collectable and uncollectable, and the collectable portion is extended into the principal money column. The remainder of the blank is for miscellaneous assets, other than income.

Schedule F contains a classified account of the current expenses of the bank for the period, such as salary, taxes, insurance, repairs, stationery, advertising, &c. The numbering of the schedules, which, previous to this point, was regular, now becomes arbitrary, as different schedules have been inserted according to the views of different officials.

Schedule G contains payments of all kinds not otherwise stated. It is difficult to see why there should not have been a similar schedule of receipts of all kinds not otherwise stated, or a schedule of both.

In Schedule H we again return to resources. This contains a description of all real estate owned by the bank, whether for banking purposes or purchased under foreclosure sale, giving the location, how acquired, when acquired, original cost, present appraised value, amount of income derived during the period, amount of expenditures on it during the period. Only one of these columns demands special remark—the one giving the cost. There is a difference of opinion as to what constitutes the cost of a piece of property bought in at foreclosure sale for less than the face of the mortgage, and other charges.

First.—It is the usual way to consider that the entire amount of the mortgage, interest, taxes, legal costs—that is to say, the entire cost of the mortgage investment is also the cost of the real estate. For example,

The face of the mortgage is	$10,000.
The interest is	600.
The bank has paid taxes	230.
Insurance	42.
And cost of suit	325.
	$11,197.

Now, under the present view, this $11,197 would be considered the cost of the real estate bid in, regardless of what the bidding price was, and regardless of what it was really worth. But, suppose the property is offered at public sale, and the bank bids $9,000, no one offering more, then,

Second.—I hold to the opinion that the cost or purchase price of this piece of real estate is not $11,197, but $9,000. It is true that the entire investment was $11,197, but what have we done? We have taken, in part satisfaction of our claim, a house worth $9,000, and for which no one else has bid more. The remaining $2,197 is not wiped out. We have a deficiency judgment for it against the bondsman. If this proves worthless, of course we lose the $2,197; but that is not to be assumed *prima facie*. Suppose another person had bid $9,000, and we, thinking that the full price, had let it go, would he, the purchaser, consider the property worth any more than $9,000? He does not know of our claim; $9,000 represents to him the entire cost. We, on the other hand would have still the deficiency judgment for $2,197. Possibly this is worthless. If so, it is our loss; but the loss is on the bond, not on the real estate. When we buy in the property we happen accidentally to be the purchaser and, at the same time, the judgment creditor; but this should not merge in one two entirely different transactions. Suppose, after buying the property for $9,000, we sell it for $10,000. This gain of $1,000 does not lessen our claim on the deficiency judgment. If the debtor should be, or should become, solvent, we can still collect of him the full amount. The rise of $1,000 is our gain. But how can it be a gain if the cost was $11,197? I am aware that in this opinion I am nearly single-handed against all parties and current opinion, but believe that my view is strictly correct.

Schedule I is a miscellaneous one, and very crudely constructed. Before the statement of cash transactions was precribed, Schedule I contained questions eliciting much of the information which is now contained in that statement. Therefore, its present contents are, to some extent, a repetition of what has already been given in the statement of cash transactions, and to some extent contains matter which more properly belonged there. All statistics which relate to financial values should be grouped either under the resources or the liabilities, or the receipts, or the payments, not in a miscellaneous schedule which contains such items as the number of trustees and the number who have attended each meeting. In this schedule occurs the question, "Date of taking last abstract of balances due depositors as shown by depositors' ledgers," and "What was the amount of the discrepancy, if any, between the aggregate of such balances and the amount shown by the general ledger due to depositors at the same date?"

The law requires, what a prudent bank would of its own accord prescribe, that an accurate list or balance of amounts due depositors shall be taken at least once in six months, and that the discrepancies, if any, found on that occasion be reported to the superintendent. The process of this balance might have been described under the bookkeeper's department. It has there been stated that the balance due each depositor is proved whenever there is a change, so that, substantially, the ledgers are always in a state of proved accuracy as to individual balances. We have also seen that each month the aggregate amount due the depositors of each ledger is ascertained, and that by aggregating these the grand total, as shown by the general ledger, is corroborated. These processes continue during the half year, and the results of monthly reports are entered in a book kept by the secretary called Ledger Balances. At the end of six months there is an additional column for dividend, and, including this, the balance due depositors is again ascertained, and this is the basis of the semi-annual trial balance required by law. Each of the ledgers, from one to thirty, ought to show a certain amount of aggregate balances, and this list, added together in the book called Ledger Balances, equals the amount reported to the bank department as due depositors on the 1st day of January or

July. Each bookkeeper transcribes into the book already mentioned under the name of "interest and balance book," opposite the proper number, the amount owing to each depositor. Having done this, and carefully compared it, he adds the entire amount together, and, if perfectly correct in every respect, the sum total should equal the corresponding line in the ledger balances. If it does not so equal, there is probably an error, either in transcribing some amount, or in adding up some page, or in adding the interest to the previous balance. It might be mentioned that the work is facilitated by writing in red ink, in the balance column, the result produced by crediting the dividend. It has been found by experience that any partial method of examination, in order to find the reason of any discrepancy, is ineffectual. Such methods we call "stabbing." We have an exhaustive method, which we call "taking off drafts and deposits." It consists in taking the original tickets of all the transactions of six months, and assorting them in a mass, numerically, so that, for example, in ledger 27, the transactions of six months will be represented by two series of tickets, the deposit tickets beginning with the deposits on account No. 135,001, and ending with the deposits on account No. 140,000. The draft tickets form a separate series, beginning and ending in the same way. When this assorting is completed, we copy off each of these series of tickets by amounts only, but we do this in sections. Suppose the first page of the interest and balance book comprises Nos. 135,001 to 135,050, then we write down all the deposits in the same compass, and take their total. We write down all the drafts in the same compass, and take their total. Then we form an equation thus: Old balance + deposits + dividend=drafts + new balance. Or, in another form: Old balance + deposits + interest—drafts=new balance. If this equation holds good, the first page is considered correct, or proved. Then we go on to the second page, and so on. Probably we discover by this process the whole or a part of the discrepancy by the time we reach the end. If not, we put together the totals; that is, we arrange the page footings in tabular form in five columns, so that by footing these columns we obtain of the entire ledger the same equation: Old balance + deposits + interest=drafts + new balance. This ought to prove. If it does not, some one of the pages which we believed to be in proof has really been out of balance. Having brought this final equation to an adjustment, our next step is to ascertain in which column the error is. We have an independent statement of every one of these columns, and we make the comparison of each in succession. The old balance we have before us in the same book—the interest likewise, and the new balance. If one of the two former of these is incorrect, the defect is soon remedied, but when these two columns have been corrected, we still have the drafts and the deposits.

To find the total drafts of six months, add together the drafts of January, February, March, April, May, and June successively, and similarly with the deposits. Now, this gives us a test of the second and fourth columns of our final equation. If, at last, we find that the error is in one of these, we first go back, comparing the tickets with our transcription of them. If this fails to discover the error, it may be necessary to re-assort the delinquent tickets, either draft or deposit, by months, and ascertain in which month the error occurs. Having located it in the month, it may be necessary to re-assort that month by days, and locate it by the tickets. But ultimately we must find it. The process is absolutely exhaustive.

The second question propounded by the bank department as to the balance is, what is the amount of the discrepancy? One of the New York banks constantly reports at present, "Old discrepancy prior to April 13, 1874, $2,386.08." For some years this has not varied. The following is its history: Up to the date mentioned there had been no accurate balances of the depositors' ledgers. While the bank was small, the importance of searching out and correcting the minute errors which then existed was not understood. The first trial balance taken was about $50 out of the way. The accounts were only a few hundred in number. It would have been an easy matter to analyze the work up to that point and to have discovered the error, but it was thought near enough. These two words, "near enough," are the most dangerous that can be used in bookkeeping, for an error which is apparently near enough may be the resultant of opposing errors each of large extent, and one of which will threaten danger. Presumably, the labor of finding this first difference was postponed until a more convenient season. As the work increased, this search, which was the business of nobody in particular, became less and less likely to be effected, and the next year rolled around, and it came time for another trial balance. Now the number of depositors had largely increased, and it was said, "Never mind the old error; it will probably turn up this time." Nobody knows whether it turned up or not, because the error this time was over $100 on the opposite side, so out of the mud we had got into the quicksand. Each year the same trial at a balance was made, and with the same lack of success, ending with the same motto which was at first inscribed on our banner, "Near Enough." Near enough one time meant $6,000 until a few months later it was found that a little error of $13,000 in a semi-annual dividend had been made, which brought the "near enough" to $7,000 the other way. Some radical spirit among the bookkeepers became dissatisfied with this erroneous discrepancy, and began to think that it was better to undertake a great deal more labor, and to know at least that the current work of the bank was proceeding correctly; so, on the 13th of April, 1874, they divided the ledgers among themselves, and commenced, in an imperfect way, to keep each ledger in balance as an independent equation, and to actually search out all the errors in each ledger. It is true this was somewhat like the proverbial needle and haystack, but the difference was that the haystack was very much smaller. Gradually the system has been improved in simplicity and effectiveness until the present time, and the old discrepancy of $2,386.08 is the relic of the old errors. This may some time all be found, but the probabilities are that it will not. The present Secretary began, a few years ago, a process of bridging over the period of chaos by beginning to do what was not done twenty years ago, namely, to take an accurate trial balance of the work at the end of each half-year. Three of the years have thus been completed, but the process of going through the remaining fourteen years involves colossal labor. Possibly it may at some time be thought worth while to employ a special corps of clerks to do this. As an illustration of how deceptive the "near enough" principle is, it may be mentioned that at one time our discrepancy was only $700—apparently. The discrepancy account had, by successive finds, worked down to this point, when, by pure accident, it was discovered that the amount in the general ledger, which had been considered as the standard, or norm, was itself $10,000 away from the truth by a single error. This startling discovery was enough to unsettle the minds of the most fanatical adherent of the "near enough" theory. A search was made through the mouldering pass-books, thousands and thousands of which, having been closed and surrendered, were lying in numerical order in the cellar. Luckily they had been preserved. By comparing them with the ledger it was found that about $8,000 of principal stood open on the ledgers of the bank, when, in reality, the accounts had been entirely closed. A dishonest employee might, by discovering these and compromising with the depositor, have abstracted a large amount, especially as the accrued interest on the same amounted to over $6,000. At one stroke, by the closing of these accounts, there was a gain to the surplus of the bank of more than $14,000, and the effect upon the discrepancy account was to bring it to 2,300 and odd dollars. Very little has been found since that time, but it is considered a matter of duty to report the amount every six months to the bank department. It has often been suggested, Why not close this account into profit and loss? The answer is that an error might be discovered the very next day, which would require its re-opening, and that it is better to leave the account open forever if necessary, or until the last cent of discrepancy of those fourteen years has been discovered. This story of error has been related, because history has so often repeated itself on this point. The writer has been surprised to find how many large institutions have had almost the identical experience, and the old, old story of beginning business with a small force, and with a system which was not expansive, and which was soon outgrown. The Bowery Savings Bank, which is the largest in America, perhaps in the world, only subdivided its work and took a new departure with a large discrepancy within five years; and at this moment the Bleecker Street Savings Bank is still operating, on its initial or fundamental balance, for a new system; a balance taken in the air, so to speak, as a point of departure. A clerk in an old Savings bank in Salem, Mass., was relating to the writer only a few weeks ago the history of the bookkeeping of his bank, which was almost word for word like the one given above, even to the disinterring of the old passbooks from the cellar, with this further incident that in the Salem case the pass-books were unclassified and lay in mouldy heaps. This embellishment was lacking in the case cited above.

CHAPTER IX.

THE PRESIDENT.

In many Savings banks the duties which have been described as shared between the treasurer and secretary, are divided between the president and treasurer, or the president and secretary. The president is usually not a salaried officer, and in that case his duties are practically confined to presiding at the monthly meetings. He is rather president of the board of trustees than president of the bank. In other institutions he receives a small salary, attends daily, but not during the entire session, and has no routine duties, but superintends and advises in all departments. He is required by the by-laws to execute all deeds, releases, satisfactions, or other documents in the nature of a conveyance of real estate, and to countersign all checks. Although it may seem wasteful to employ an officer of a corporation with no stated routine duties, yet where the trust is large the writer thinks emphatically that this should be the case—that the duties of the highest officer should be entirely discretionary with himself, and that he should possess such an intimate and also such a broad knowledge of the business that he himself is the best judge of what department needs his personal attention, and that he himself can be held responsible for everything.

CHAPTER X.

THE BOARD OF TRUSTEES.

This body is the ultimate governing power of the bank. It is the final jurisdiction, from which there is no appeal within the bank, and in fact there is no appeal whatever, for the only remedy in case of wrong-doing is to punish the trustees personally, and to remove them, which, however, would not act as a reversal of their decisions. They are supreme, and responsible only to the people of the State, through their representative, the Superintendent of the Banking Department. The board of trustees consists of not less than fifteen nor more than twenty members. Under the State law, not less than thirteen is requisite. The board elects to fill its own vacancies occurring by death, resignation, or neglect of duty for six months, and its actions in this respect cannot be questioned if the record is clear.

Seven members of the board constitute a quorum, provided the president, or one of the vice-presidents, be among the number. The entire government of the affairs of the bank, from the most minute detail up, is vested in the board of trustees. The powers, which practically are exercised by the executive officers of the bank during the intervals between the sessions of the board, are those delegated to them by the board, as expressed in its by-laws. Some of the duties cannot be delegated. A loan on mortgage can only be made upon vote of the board, based upon the report of the committee. The rate of dividend can only be declared by the board at its annual or semi-annual meeting, and this vote must be recorded by ayes and noes. If a dividend exceeding the accumulated earnings should be declared, it would stand as regards each individual depositor, but the trustees voting for it would be perso1ally liable for the amount of the excess. The election of officers and committees is another duty which must be exercised by the board itself. With these exceptions, the government of the bank is discretionary as to means with the board of trustees, and they may delegate so much of their powers as they desire. It becomes impracticable to do otherwise as regards the routine business of the bank, and the transactions in those investments which are of a less permanent character than upon real estate security. Even the restriction as to loans on mortgage is found a serious inconvenience, and is believed to be systematically disregarded by many banks. Applications are acted upon after examination by a committee, but without previous submission to the board. The more important of the committees usually established in a Savings bank are Finance Committee, the Attending Committee, the Auditing Committee, and the Examining Committee.

The Finance Committee is intermediate between the board of trustees and the treasurer, and considers and acts upon the more important questions which arise in his department.

The Auditing Committee may be regarded as bearing a similar relation to the secretary. It is required by the by-laws to examine and audit the vouchers for all payments. Also to count the cash on hand at least once a month. The process of auditing the vouchers has been described under the secretary's duties. It may be further said, that in so far as the audit is intended as a check upon embezzlement, it should comprise also the cash receipts as well as payments. It should be ascertained whether the receipts have all been fully accounted for. Like all other amateur committees of examination, the proceedings of this committee are almost inevitably perfunctory. They are very seldom thorough—very seldom go to the bottom of the figures which they are supposed to examine. Having ascertained that a certain amount of payment is supported by the proper vouchers, they very seldom even enquire whether this is the entire amount of payment to be accounted for, which simple omission completely destroys all utility of the examination. The officer whose work they are supervising has only to withhold all questionable or improper vouchers from their examination. Such committees seldom take the time necessary for the proper performance of their duties, and seldom possess the ability. They ought, in justice to themselves and to their trust, to employ skilled assistants to point out, at least, the way in which to do their work more thoroughly.

The duty of the Examining Committee is to ascertain the precise condition of the bank at the close of the semi-annual period. An idea of the manner of performance of their duties may be gathered from the description of the schedules furnished them by the secretary as a basis of their examination. One of their number makes up from the figures thus ascertained a report to the board, analyzing the history, results, and prospects of the institution. This committee is also required by law to endorse upon the official report made to the Bank Department their affidavit as to its correctness, so far as the report proper or balance sheet goes.

The Attending Committee. In the infancy of Savings banks, when they were looked upon as charitable institutions, the members of the board of trustees attended in rotation at the bank; but what they did beyond lending a general air of elderly benevolence has never been ascertained. Where this custom is kept up, they almost invariably sign their names in a large book, and this is probably the most important of their functions. Such attendance inevitably degenerates into a farce. In this institution it has been abandoned. All members of the board of trustees are welcome at all times, and even if they were not welcome, it would be their duty to visit the bank, and keep themselves informed. This many of them do, and the more irregular this attendance is in point of time, probably the better it is.

CHAPTER XI.

THE ATTORNEY.

The peculiarity of Anglo-Saxon law with regard to its arbitrary distinctions between real and personal property is well illustrated by the fact that a Savings bank can safely effect investments of millions in securities and valuables with only a layman's knowledge, while it is impracticable or inadvisable to stir in the most unimportant transaction which regards real estate, without a lawyer at one's elbow. Yet the property in the latter case is more readily identified than any other in the world. It is impossible to counterfeit it; it is the most visible, most tangible, most impossible to secrete, and most exposed to the public eye of all property. Nothing but the barbarous state of our laws, borrowed from a form of government whose policy it is, of set purpose, to prevent transfers and diffusion of titles in land, has caused this.

The attorney of a Savings bank is not usually a salaried officer. The greater part of his services consists in the examination of titles to real estate, upon which it is proposed to loan on bond and mortgage. The law prescribes that the charges for such services shall be paid by the borrower. It would in many cases be to the interest of the bank to pay them voluntarily, in order to secure a desirable investment or a greater rate of interest, but the law, as construed by most Savings banks, prevents this.

When an application for loan on bond and mortgage has been accepted by the board of trustees, the fact of this acceptance is endorsed upon it by the secretary and the paper forwarded to the attorney. The proposed borrower is notified to wait upon the attorney with the papers which he may have in support of his title. The amount charged by the attorney for his services in making the examination are on a scale fixed by the customs of the profession, but subject to varying through negotiation. Frequently the borrower, especially of late years, goes to the attorney and says, "I will take this money of your institution provided you do not charge me more than such a sum." Generally the disbursements, that is, amounts paid to public officials for searches, constitute one portion of the charge, and the fee of the attorney for the labor and responsibility of certificate form another portion, and this latter is a fixed or sliding percentage upon the amount of loan. In many cases the labor is very slight, as there may be an abstract giving the chain of title to a very recent date, which has only to be copied. Still there is a responsibility on the part of the attorney for its correctness, and theoretically, at least, he is supposed to be liable for damages in case he has not properly performed his duty. The writer knows of one case in which the attorney assumed the burden of a defect in a case where he was really careful, but where a second person, of the same name as the owner, had personated him. It is proper, in the letter of instructions which accompanies the check sent to the attorney to complete the loan not to direct him to pay to a certain person, but to pay to the owner of such property.

From the amount of this check the attorney deducts the expenses and charges, and pays over the net proceeds to the borrower, taking his receipt, of course, for the full amount, and giving him a receipt for fees. The borrower's receipt is endorsed, as already stated, on the back of the application. When a mortgage is satisfied or assigned, the necessary papers for that purpose are drawn up by the attorney, and he is responsible for their correctness, the officer signing whatever he advises. A payment on account, not being a matter of record, is effected without the assistance of the attorney.

In case of foreclosure, the matter is placed entirely in the hands of the attorney up to the time of the sale. When it comes to the amount to be paid, this is a business matter which is decided by the officers of the bank. If bid in, it is the duty of the attorney to see that the title is perfected in the bank, and the judgment is regularly entered for the deficiency, if any, a transcript of which judgment should be delivered to the bank. It is also his duty, if advisable, to institute supplementary proceedings in order to execute this judgment. If a purchaser be found for the property held by the bank, it is the duty of the attorney to draw up a contract of sale, which generally stipulates that the final delivery of the deed shall be at his office, and here, again, he is responsible for the correctness of the paper.

Very few cases occur in which the bank requires the aid of counsel in regard to its money or deposits. Advice is sometimes requisite as to the construction of the statute law, and there is sometimes litigation arising from adverse claimants to moneys deposited, or from alleged errors on the part of the bank. A certain by-law which has been adopted by most of the Savings banks, and which has in the main been sustained as reasonable by our Court of Appeals, has been a fruitful source of litigation. This by-law is usually to the following effect—that the bank will endeavor to prevent fraud, but any payment made to a person producing the proper pass-book shall be valid. Sometimes the expression is "will use their best endeavors," and this has been construed to require a much higher degree of care than demanded by the other phraseology. What constitutes a proper amount of diligence on the part of the bank is the turning point of many cases, and the question of fact is usually submitted to a jury, who, in the vast majority of cases, find against the corporation. In the cases of trust accounts, of associate accounts, of insolvent depositors, and depositors deceased or supposed to have deceased, there are frequently adverse claims, and the bank is usually secured by having the amount nominally paid into court to abide the result of the action between the other parties; but if paid over to one of the claimants, there is danger of litigation and possibility of loss. This has been the case even where money was paid over on genuine letters of administration granted upon the effects of a person believed to be dead, but who inopportunely appeared and had to be paid a second time.

CHAPTER XII.

STATE SUPERVISION AND REPORTS.

In many, but not all of the States, officers are appointed for the purpose of supervising and regulating Savings and other banks and their affairs. In New York State* no Savings bank can be organized hereafter without the assent of the Superintendent of the Banking Department, and there seems to be no appeal from his decision. During the existence of the Savings bank it is subject to his inspection by means of examinations and reports, as follows:—

A semi-annual report, as already described under the duties of the secretary.

A special report on any subject and at any time required by him.

An examination by himself or by deputies once in two years.

A special examination whenever, in his judgment, it shall be necessary.

The expenses of special examinations are borne by the corporation examined. Those of the regular examinations and other expenses of the department are borne by the corporations in proportion to their size, and, finally, the remedies in the hands of the Superintendent in case of improper action are, first, the publicity effected through his report to the Legislature, and, second, his power to make complaint through the Attorney-General in case of violation of law, or improper exercise of corporate powers; and the remedies which may be applied by the court upon this proceeding are: Removal of the board of trustees or any of their number; appointment of receiver and dissolution of the corporation, or the consolidating of the institution with a similar one which may be willing to accept the transfer. . . . The Superintendent has recently been given supervision over the receivers of failed Savings banks, who are now required to report to him, and he has been made the custodian of any unclaimed balances which the receiver may have on hand in favor of depositors at the termination of his reccivership. Thus, during the existence of a Savings bank the

---

* All institutions of the kind within the State are made subject to its control, and a penalty is imposed for any person receiving or offering to receive Savings deposits in any town where there is an organized Savings bank.

Superintendent has no positive governing power over its acts, but is the head of a bureau of information. He himself has no power to remove trustees, or to annul any of their acts, but the moral power given by his authority for compelling information is probably beneficial.

The problem of State supervision is a very difficult one. A supervising department like the one under consideration usually becomes, after a time, a mere bookkeeping department, and if the reports of the several institutions check off correctly on his summaries, as found by the clerks in his department, the Superintendent goes no further, but devotes his time to the more congenial and dignified pursuits of practical politics. This is without any evil consequences in peaceful times, when there is no financial embarrassment, and everything goes swimmingly, but usually the same let-alone policy is continued from the force of inertia, into a period when the times begin to grow shaky, and generally the superintendent awakes to find that his rose-colored reports, for some time past, have been delusive. Then there will be a reaction from King Log to King Stork, and the state of the most prudently managed institutions will be looked upon with suspicion, and very likely some unnecessary wrecks will be the consequence. This was the case in the period of financial reaction, which followed our Civil War and reconstruction period, and presumably its history will repeat itself.

There is one very important lack in the system of reports as now carried on. There is nothing corresponding to a profit and loss account. There is nothing to show, analytically, whether the dividend which has been paid to depositors has been earned during the period covered, or whether it is subtracted from the previous reserve; whether it is strictly from the income, or whether incidental gains have been relied upon to help it out. Such an account should be required from every Savings institution, and should be most carefully scrutinized. In doing so there is a very important element which may readily prove deceptive. It is the question of premiums on stock investments. Let us suppose that the normal rate of interest on money is about four per cent., and that it does not vary much from that figure on fair security, and let us suppose that a municipality has issued its bonds, bearing ten per cent. interest, and payable in twenty years. Let us again suppose that another municipality has issued its bonds, bearing five per cent. interest, and payable in ten years, that another one has issued three-per-cent. bonds, payable in fifteen years. We are assuming that the security in all these cases is as good as anything human can be. In case of the ten-per-cent. bond running twenty years, it is evident that there is an extra interest of about six per cent., which is to be collected every year above the market rate. Therefore, the longer this thing continues the more valuable is the bond, and we shall indisputably find that it bears a proportionate premium. The value is not expressed by the par $100. It is the present worth of $100 due twenty years from now + the present worth of $10 due one year from now, + the present worth of $10 due two years, + the same at three years, + etc., and in order to be perfectly accurate these present worths must be computed at compound interest, and this computation must be semi-annual or annual, according to the terms of the bond. The five-per-cent. bond would not be worth so much, both because there is a smaller excess of interest over the market rate, and because this excess continues to run for a shorter time. The three-per-cent. bond would be worth still less. In this case there is a deficiency of interest which the buyer should be compensated for now, and the longer it has to run at three per cent. the worse off is the purchaser; therefore, this bond would be worth less than par. Now, it has been claimed that the true measure of the surplus of a Savings bank, as far as its stock investments are concerned, is the nominal or par value of those investments. That is to say, a bank having seven-per-cent. bonds to a certain amount is no better off than one having $3\frac{65}{100}$-per-cent. bonds. A bank whose seven-per-cent. bonds mature next year is no stronger than one where the seven per-cent bonds have twenty-five years to run.

The advocates of this theory consider that they are acting on the safe side. They consider the premium as a loss, once for all; therefore, at a period of buying, they would cut down the dividend to depositors, perhaps to nothing, simply because the institution has been making favorable investments. On the other hand, in subsequent after years, they would treat the entire revenue from these bonds as all profit, and thus the depositors at this time would receive more than would be, on the other theory, the fair earnings of their money.

Another plan is to hold the stocks at the amount they cost. By this means the loss, instead of being thrown upon the year in which they were purchased, is thrown into the year during which they are sold or redeemed, and this is a still more dangerous way of looking at it. In the former plan the stocks, if worth above par, as they usually are, are steadily undervalued, while in this method they are overvalued, in all probability, during most of the time they are held. In one case there is a fallacious calculation of current earnings; in the other case, there is a fallacious estimate of surplus in reserve. The true principle would seem to be that each year or half year an equitable portion of the amount paid for premiums, or conversely, of the amount received for discount, should be wiped out, so that the differences between par and market value would steadily and gradually disappear as the bond approached its maturity. Thus, the ten-per-cent. bond of which we spoke would be considered as earning, each year, the rate to which its cost price would be equivalent when averaged over the term—say four and a-half per cent. The remaining five and a-half per cent, should not be considered as earnings, but as an offset to the depreciation of bond, or a refunding to us of extra premium, which we paid for an abnormally high rate of interest, and while this is true in theory it can be empirically tested by the state of the market. It will be found that, making allowance for the shifting productiveness of money and some other disturbing element, such as public confidence, that the market price of a security will settle in about this manner: That each year there will be a depreciation, amounting approximately to the difference between the current rate of interest on that kind of securities and the revenue actually produced. We would therefore enunciate this formula for ascertaining the true earnings from stock investments. From the cash income (a) received subtract such part (b) of the premium, as will progressively consume the entire premium at the date of maturity. The difference is the current earnings (c).

Again, take the difference between the market value (d) at the beginning of the period, and the market value (e) at the close of the period. The difference between d and e is the gross depreciation (f), or the gross appreciation ($-f$).

Combining b, taken negatively, with f, or $-f$, we have the incidental or speculative loss or gain (p, or $-p$).

$$p = +f - b.$$
$$-p = -f - b.$$

Thus there will be four cases.

First.—A gross depreciation equal to the amount of premium written off. Here there is no loss nor gain.

Second.—A depreciation greater than the amount of premium written off. Here there is an incidental loss to be taken from the surplus.

Third.—A gross depreciation less than the amount of premium written off. In this case there is an incidental gain or a real appreciation.

Fourth.—An appreciation which, together with the premium written off, is always an incidental gain.

Our examination of the functions of a Savings bank brings us to the conclusion that it is simply a money making corporation—an association of small capitalists who combine for the purpose of having their small investments possess an earning power by aggregation. The 'officers and employees of the Savings bank are merely their agents in this. The entire resources of the bank, whether credited to deposits or to surplus, are the absolute property of depositors as an association. The trustees are a body whose constitution is somewhat anomalous, being the unpaid custodians of money not their own, but whose duties are assumed as a public burden and as a distinction. This latter peculiarity, the constitution of a board of trustees, which is independent of the real proprietors of the concern, seems to me the only point which gives a Savings bank, as now organized, a right to be called a benevolent institution. It is benevolent for the trustees to give their time and services without compensation in the management of the money of others. It is not benevolence, however, to invest a man's money and pay him over the proceeds. Although in practice, this plan of organization has worked better than the one where there is a body of stockholders whose capital is substituted for a surplus as guaranteed to depositors, yet it is by no means proved that the advantage would not be on the side of the latter form, which eliminates all pretence of benevolence, and makes the Savings bank what we believe it to be, a pure matter of business. Of the three forms of associated saving, viz., the mutual, which we have described at length, the stock, or business-like form, which we have just touched upon, and the governmental, which, of late years, is becoming the subject of experiment, time alone can decide which will survive as the fittest.

CHAPTER XIII.

HOW INVESTMENTS SHOULD BE MADE.

We shall close this part of our work by giving some rules relating to Savings banks' investments. The Legislatures of the several States have adopted regulations on this subject, thus lightening the responsibility of Savings bank directors. These regulations are the outcome of a conservative spirit, and should be observed. Nevertheless, a wide latitude exists, which cannot be completely traversed by Legislative regulation. To a very important degree the directors must exercise their own wisdom in making investments. The following remarks on this subject were made by Mr. Washington B. Williams at the annual meeting of the American Bankers' Association in 1882. They are worthy the attentive study of those who are entrusted with the duty of investing the funds of these institutions.

Safety is the first consideration, and profit is secondary. Again, Savings banks are not confined to investments which are readily convertible. Here, also, safety comes first; convertibility is of minor importance.

Mortgages on real estate, being less readily convertible than some other securities, bear higher interest. At the same time, no property is more stable in value, and none less likely to depreciate, than real estate. Neither the recent general depression from former inflated values, nor any special instances of loss, affect the truth of this general proposition.

Mortgages on real estate, accordingly, have always been a favorite kind of investment for Savings banks. They have other advantages, in not being readily subject to theft or misappropriation; and the laws of the several States, as well as the general rules by which courts govern and control trustees, declare this mode of investment to be the most desirable.

Taxes are high in this country, are thrown heavily on real estate, and are generally paramount to mortgages. To secure prompt payment of interest and taxes, the property mortgaged ought generally to be improved and productive of rent.

The Savings bank law of New York allows the investment of not over 60 per cent. of the deposits in such mortgages. That of New

Jersey allows 70 per cent., and these serve to indicate the general rule.

By examining the reports as to the Savings banks of the several States it will, however, be found that the Savings banks of New England invest not over 35 per cent. of their trust funds in mortgages, and those of New York City a less proportion.

The best conducted Savings bank in Jersey City, N. J., which has passed safely all the depressions and panics of thirty years, has generally maintained, and still maintains, its mortgage investments at over 65 per cent., of a deposit line of over $5,000,000.

These different usages, though they doubtless result from more than one cause, yet point with sufficient clearness to this important rule: Taxation should be so adjusted as in no wise to deter Savings banks from freely investing on mortgages on real estate. It is a most unwise policy as to the interests of the industrial classes to drive Savings banks out of this mode of investment. It is the mode which is at once solid in basis, understood by and acceptable to the depositors, and beneficial to them and the community where the savings arise, by re-distributing the savings in the form of loans. Such investments ought not to be taxed, even if it should become necessary to accord a special preference in this respect to Savings banks. These institutions represent the industry and frugality of the masses, and every effort should be made to put them on the soundest footing. In my belief, nothing can so surely do this, and so certainly retain confidence, as to encourage, facilitate and require the investment of the savings deposits in mortgages properly secured on the farms, the shops, and the homes of the people. If these are not real values, what are? How can mere promises to pay by the same people, either individually or collectively, be any better?

It is, then, to be regarded as a prime duty of legislators to so regulate taxation as to encourage, not deter, investments by Savings banks in loans on real estate.

A trustee should take no risks that can be avoided. If he acts on this rule, he is discharging his full duty. If he violates it, although from good motives, if he allows his confidence in his own skill in choosing among the many ordinary investments in the market to lead him to transcend it, he would be restrained by injunction by any court having jurisdiction of trusts, even if the particular investment were a successful one. High rates of interest are quite a secondary matter.

In order to avoid, then, as far as possible, all temptation to do more than one's duty, as trustee, or to manifest special financial skill, or to make the earning of interest paramount to absolute safety, we would adopt certain rules.

Large deposits, which do not come from savings, but which are the capital of persons who have acquired wealth, should be rejected. They can invest their own funds, and they are likely to withdraw their deposits suddenly and in large sums.

Bonuses and discounts on buying securities should not be sought or allowed. They tend to drive away the best-secured loans, and to introduce a speculative habit of looking at the immediate apparent gain rather than the ultimate security.

Good mortgages on improved real estate, to about half its value, should be encouraged and granted up to the highest legal limit, without fear. If necessary, the rate of interest on these should be reduced, so as to secure the very best of that class of investments.

Would this be safe in case of a run on the bank?

It would for several reasons:

First.—The remaining 35 per cent. and upwards of convertible securities would be available.

Second.—Such mortgages, though not promptly available at par, are always excellent securities to borrow on temporarily to meet such emergencies.

Third.—The mortgage-investments being to a large extent loans among the same community which affords the depositors, there is a powerful influence at work to sustain confidence in the assets of the bank.

But, as a further means of safety to all, the bank should never hesitate, in case of panic, to enforce its thirty, sixty or ninety day rule, as the case may be, or to close its doors. It is nothing but the common agent or trustee of the depositors, who, as above shown, have a common interest in its funds and investments. It has no financial reputation to keep up as a source of profit to itself or to attract deposits. Its whole duty is summed up in the one word "safety."

A trustee has neither moral nor legal right to sacrifice a part of the common assets in order to give an advantage to those of the common proprietors who first run to his door. A court having jurisdiction of trusts would restrain him by injunction from thus violating his prime duty of taking care of the common property for the common benefit. Some special charters of Savings banks expressly provide for such action. I think the power and duty of the courts plainly arises out of the nature of the trust. But to avoid all question it should be provided for by proper legislation wherever this ordinary class of Savings banks exists.

The salutary effect of such judicial action is at once apparent. The bank stands in this emergency like any other trustee who seeks the direction and protection of the courts.

They will stop any ill-advised suits, hold back every hostile hand, and open the doors again and direct payment by installments if prudence so indicates. This is the best and safest way for real savings depositors, and meets all their actual needs in the supposed case of a panic. In the meantime, the assets are producing their regular income, there are no sacrifices of securities, the ignorant and alarmed depositors are protected against loss, and none gets an advantage over the other, and the bank finally resumes without injury.

Too much unwillingness to adopt this safe and just course, if it becomes necessary, would savor of a desire to do more than the duty of a trustee; a course neither incumbent, nor, indeed, justifiable.

As a corollary to this view, would come the rule of giving all due publicity to the affairs and investments of the bank, at least as to its class and kind of investments and their amounts. Inquiry was recently made of a Savings bank in the City of New York for a statement of this character, such as is made public in many banks, and is required by law once or twice a year in some States. The answer given was, that that bank made no such statements, and that the names of its trustees were sufficient guarantees to the public of its soundness and good management. I need not say that such views are contrary to the true position and office of a Savings Bank.

Investments in expensive buildings should be avoided. In many cases, the whole apparent surplus will be found to be absorbed in an unproductive banking-house.

Government bonds are the safest of convertible investments, and so are generally the bonds of the State in which the bank is situated. They may be guarded against the ordinary chances of fire and theft by well known precautions, such as registry, stamping, &c., but the low rate of interest which they must henceforth produce renders it very desirable to see if the field can be extended without losing sight of our cardinal rules.

It must be conceded that *personal security* of two or more names is not admissible, notwithstanding the custom of many New England Savings banks to accept such security. Not only is this usage entirely opposed to the general law of trusts as established by the experience of two centuries, but it leads to complications and temptations outside of the line of duty which directors of a Savings bank ought to confine themselves to.

Stocks of railway and manufacturing corporations must also be excluded. In fact, railway management, as to treatment of stockholders and value of stock, is now almost synonymous with deception and fraud. If there are exceptions, they serve to establish the general rule.

As to other corporations, the value of their stock depends so much on the changing market, on the course of mechanical invention, on the individual qualities of the managers, that it is too unstable for our present purpose.

Railway bonds, secured by first mortgage on the entire road, would seem a safe class of investment with the exercise of ordinary prudence, and at one time were largely taken by some Savings banks. So vast and so constantly increasing are these great internal improvements, so enormous the flow and reflow of business over them, so immense the probable development of that business in the future, that such mortgages, if they could be had at a proper rate per mile, would be among the safest of investments, assuming reasonable care in selecting those of apparently permanent value. There is difficulty in ascertaining the history, legal position and amount of such mortgages, but not so great as to be insurmountable. The great objection is to the extravagant amount per mile of the bonds issued in many cases, compelling after a while the bondholders to take the road It is always an undesirable thing for a trustee to be compelled to enter into a current business with the trust funds.

Municipal indebtedness has attained large proportions in this country, and has long furnished a field for private and corporate investment. Experience has fully shown that we must strike out from the list of Savings bank investments all municipal bonds issued in aid of any railway undertaking. The Legislatures of several States have recognized this, and after once allowing such investments by Savings banks have very judiciously forbidden them.

Subject to this exception, the public debt of local municipalities within the State where the Savings bank is located, is a sound class of investment, assuming, of course, the exercise of due care in the investigation of the origin and aggregate amount of such debt. You have the savings of many voters in your care. If invested in apparently sound municipal obligations, there is, besides legal remedies, a great force of public opinion to sustain your claim, and to bring about proper provision for payment of interest and principal. Experience shows that such debts, when not disproportionately large, or the result of some arbitrary and unpopular scheme, have been among the safest investments we have had.

It is evident that we must look elsewhere than to Government bonds alone for interest paying securities. The directions to look in are (1) mortgages on productive real estate to a high percentage of the total investments; (2) well selected municipal obligations; (3) selected railway first mortgages.

Those to avoid are (1) real estate of merely speculative value, and unimproved; (2) capital stock of railways or manufacturing corporations; (3) personal security; (4) railway aid bonds, and municipal bonds where the debt is large in proportion to the resources, or is the result of too sanguine speculation on the future.

Call-loans on deposit of collaterals form a large part of the business of some city Savings banks. No doubt, in a large commercial center, these may be safely and quickly made. The objection to them is that they tend to throw the whole management and selection of investments into the hands of some one person. However efficient such management may be for a time, we know that most great disasters have also arisen from this. Other investments, such as mortgage loans, or the purchase of securities, are usually, in well-managed banks, passed upon by a board or committee. This old-fogy method is the safest, and so far as practicable should be followed by institutions whose paramount object is safety.*

Some New England and other Savings banks have loaned funds on mortgage on lands in other States. There is no reason why such loans on suitable and proper security should not be as good and safe in Massachusetts as in New York; but there is a great difficulty in being assured that you are getting proper security. At home your own board or your own investment committee can judge, depositors are more or less familiar with your securities, the risk of acting on other men's judgment, removed from your own responsibility, is avoided, your risk is less, your certainty of protection by the courts is greater. Prudence dictates that even in these days of easy locomotion and of assimilating business and values, you should not extend your reach too far and get beyond the range of your own vision and your own capacity to judge and act. It may be the office of a good judge to enlarge his jurisdiction, but it is not the duty of a prudent trustee.

The same reasons will apply to distant municipal and railway securities. And caution should be exercised in going beyond your own State as to any debt of local municipalities. My own view is that this should be prohibited, except, perhaps, in certain cases, such as well-known large cities whose affairs are conducted on a sound basis, and with the advantage of the best business talent. This is true of Boston, New York, Philadelphia and others, and is not affected by the fact that they have also been now and then attacked by municipal thieves.

* A startling instance of the danger of this call-loan method has recently occurred in the Newark Savings Institution now insolvent.

PART III.

CLEARING-HOUSES.

CHAPTER I.

ORIGIN AND UTILITY OF THE CLEARING-HOUSE.

Closely connected with the general subject of banking is that of the Clearing-house. This is a comparatively modern institution, the Edinburgh bankers claiming the credit of establishing the first one. The earliest of whose transactions we have any record, however, is that of London, founded in 1775, or earlier, and of this little was known to the public until it began to publish regular statements of its transactions, May 1st, 1867. The literature on the subject is almost wholly the creation of the last thirty years. Works on banking and political economy, of an earlier date than this, rarely, if ever, notice the subject at all. For more than three quarters of a century after its establishment the London Clearing-house and that of Edinburgh remained the only organizations of the kind known to exist. The monetary systems of most European States, centering around a single great bank, located at the capital of each, found in this a means of effecting mercantile settlements. Furthermore, the use of bank checks in making payments, which chiefly creates the need of the bankers' Clearing-house, has in recent years attained a development previously unknown. The growth of American banking, decentralized and distributed among many banks, and the increasing use of bank checks as a means of payment, gave birth to the next Clearing-house in the order of time after that of London. The New York Clearing-house was established in 1853, from which date the growth of the Clearing-house system in the United States has been stupendous. Boston followed in 1856; Philadelphia, Baltimore and Cleveland in 1858; Worcester in 1861; Chicago in 1865, all the others are of later date. At present there are thirty-one Clearing-houses known to exist in this country. Each of our prominent commercial cities has one. The United Kingdom has six, Australia one, and they are found in France, Germany, Switzerland and Italy, though checks are so little used on the Continent of Europe that the Clearing-houses of the last four countries have comparatively small transactions. The exchanges of American Clearing-houses were $51,827,000,000, in 1883, and in 1881 reached a maximum of $63,414,000,000, adjusted by the payment of balances not exceeding six per cent. of the amount cleared, the actual cash handled being estimated at about two per cent. of the clearings. From the inauguration of the Clearing-house system in 1853 to December 31, 1883, it had effected settlements amounting to about $880,000,000,000, by paying balances of about $57,000,000, or 6½ per cent. of the clearings. The amount of actual cash handled was very much less than this, as balances are to a great extent paid by means of checks or certificates issued from some common depository, without handling actual cash. The Clearing-house is, therefore, one of the most useful agencies called into being by the wants of modern commerce. It is among the most interesting features of our financial mechanism and well worthy of careful study. Susceptible of almost indefinite expansion, the clearing system in its various forms holds in possibility the solution of problems which have long engaged the attention of thinkers.

A glance at some of the more common banking operations will suffice to show the need of a Clearing-house wherever any considerable number of banks are located in the same vicinity. Mercantile establishments are constantly receiving in the course of business not only specie, but usually, to a much larger extent, bank notes, checks, drafts, or other mercantile paper. To present this paper at the counters of the various banks at which it is payable would take a great deal of time. The dealer, therefore, deposits it in the bank with which he keeps his account, where, either at once, or at latest when collected, the amount is placed to his credit and goes to swell his balance. This is the usual way in which a bank receives the paper payable at other banks. It may also be taken in payment of notes payable at the bank receiving it. Although bank notes, as well as the various kinds of mercantile paper, are so received, yet the great bulk of all such receipts, especially in the large cities, consists of checks. When the paper in question is payable at the bank receiving it, the transaction is closed by the simple delivery in the case of bank notes, and in the case of checks by charging them to the drawer, the result being, in the latter case, a simple transfer on the books of the bank from the account of the drawer to that of the drawee. Where most of the transactions of a community center in a single institution, as formerly in the case of the Bank of England, and at present in the case of the Bank of France, the larger part of the check transactions may be settled in this way. Thus at Paris where the Bank of France performs the functions of a great Clearing-house, its clearings or transfers reached $6,008,243,900 in 1883, as compared with $813,238,000 at the Paris Clearing-house. In 1881, the clearings of the Bank of France reached $8,772,000,000, while those of the Paris Clearing-house were only $908,600,000, the former being nine and three-fourths times the latter. To make provision for this class of business, the Bank of France furnishes special books of red colored checks—so-called, "*bons de virement rouge*"—the object of which is to enable payments to be made by their means to other persons also having an account at the bank without its being possible for any one unlawfully to obtain value for them, since they only operate as orders to the bank to transfer such an amount from the drawer's account to some other account on the books of the bank, and never as vouchers for the withdrawal of funds from the establishment. The Bank of England furnishes no account of its clearing transactions, but they must be a much smaller proportion of the total than those of the Bank of France, banking being less centralized in London than in Paris.

In this country no one bank concentrates in itself the larger portion of the business. Free banking and competition keep the banks more nearly on an equality. The larger part of the checks received by any bank, in the course of business, are likely to be drawn on some other bank, of which they must be collected by the receiving bank. As business increases in any locality, each bank is likely to have a larger number and amount of demands upon most of the other banks in the place, and they eventually become too large and numerous to be conveniently settled between the individual banks. Before the establishment of a Clearing-house in this country this method was pursued in New York long after the inconvenience became so great that it would now be considered quite intolerable. Mr. J. S. Gibbons, in his very interesting and instructive book, *The Banks of New York and the Panic of* 1857, gives the following graphic description of the difficulties attending this mode of settlement:

"During the few years following 1849 the number of banks in New York was increased from twenty-four to sixty. To make the daily exchange, one half of them must necessarily send to the other half. But this plain division of the service was not convenient or economical. It was found better for all of them to do a part of the distribution, and thus the whole sixty porters were in motion at the same time. Each carried a book of entry, and the money for every bank on which he called. The paying teller of the receiving bank took the exchange and entered it on the credit side of the book; then he entered on the debit side the return exchange and gave it with the book to the porter, who hastened to the next bank in his circuit. The porters crossed and recrossed each other's footsteps constantly; they often met in companies of five or six at the same counter, and retarded each other, and they were fortunate to reach their respective banks at the end of one or two hours. This threw the counting of the exchanges into the middle and after part of the day, when the other business of the bank was becoming urgent.

"Instead of attempting a daily adjustment of accounts, which would have consumed several hours and caused much annoyance, it became a tacit agreement that a weekly settlement of balances should be made after the exchange of Friday morning, and that intermediate draft drawing should be suspended. The weaker and more speculative banks took advantage of this by borrowing money on Thursday, which restored their accounts for Friday, and its return on Saturday threw them again into the debit column. In this way the banks distant from Wall Street managed to carry an inflated line of discounts, based on debts due to other institutions. It became an affair of cunning management by some to run a small credit of two or three thousand dollars each with thirty or more banks, making a total of one hundred thousand dollars, on which they discounted bills. Consequently, the Friday settlements proved to be no settlements at all, but a prodigious annoyance. As soon as the paying teller or his assistant completed the exchange balance list the cashier of each bank would draw checks for every debt due to him by other banks, and send out the porters to collect them. A draft on one in favor of another might settle two accounts at once, but there was no understanding that made it possible to secure that small economy; or, if there was, it was disregarded. The sixty porters were out all at once, with an aggregate of two or three hundred bank drafts in their pockets, balking each other, drawing specie at some places and depositing it in others, and the whole process was one of confusion, disputes, and unavoidable blunders, of which no description could give an exact impression.

"After all the draft-drawing was over came the settlement of the Wall Street porters among themselves. A *Porters' Exchange* was held on the steps of one of the Wall Street banks, at which they accounted to each other for what had been done during the day. Thomas had left a bag of specie at John's bank to settle a balance which was due from William's bank to Robert's; but Robert's bank owed twice as much to John's. What had become of *that?* Then Alexander owed Robert also, and William was indebted to Alexander. Peter then said that he had paid Robert by a draft from James, which he, James, had received from Alfred on Alexander's account. That, however, had settled only half the debt. A quarter of the remainder was canceled by a bag of coin which Samuel had handed over to Joseph, and he had transferred to David. It is entirely safe to say that the presidents and cashiers of the banks themselves could not have untangled this medley. Each porter had his tally, and by checking off and liberating first one, whose account was least complicated, and then another, they finally achieved a settlement.

"This scene was re-enacted on every Friday. In consequence of the porters being withdrawn from their regular service in the bank, extra labor was imposed on others, responsibilities became mingled together, and the officers were kept for the whole day in a state of distraction and anxiety. The paying tellers were subject to frequent interruption, as they were obliged to receive and deliver all specie.

"Not the least irritating feature of the case was that a single small draft by any one bank on any other induced a general drawing, and all became involved in commotion and 'war' upon each other. If time were allowed, the debtor banks would finally be obliged to pay the liquidating balance; but three o'clock arrested the process, and the banks where the demand was then in force were obliged to disburse the coin. It was not unusual for a debtor bank to add fifty thousand dollars to its specie at the close of the day, with its debt doubled, while a creditor bank to half a million in the general account, would find itself at three o'clock depleted of one or two hundred thousand dollars in coin."

This, it will be noticed, was when the bank settlements at New York could not have reached to one-sixth of their present amount. It may be safely affirmed that the vastly larger transactions of the present day could not be settled in the old way. It was not until after much deliberation and considerable opposition that a Clearing-house was established at New York, but the success of the experiment soon dispelled all doubts of its utility and necessity, and led to the adoption of the system in other cities.

CHAPTER II.

ORGANIZATION AND MECHANICAL ARRANGEMENTS.

To establish a Clearing-house a number of banks associate themselves together, under certain regulations more or less elaborate, according to circumstances, for the purpose of settling daily, at one time and place, the mutual demands arising between the banks. The officers of such an association are usually a president, or chairman, a secretary, treasurer and manager, with a Clearing-house committee, and such others as the wants of the association require. At New York, in addition to the Clearing-house committee, there are a committee on conference, a nominating committee, a committee on admissions, and an arbitration committee. The manager is sometimes chosen by the association, usually by the Clearing-house committee, which generally has charge of all matters incidental to the operations of the association not otherwise specially provided for. The larger Clearing-houses have also an assistant manager. The salary of the manager is fixed pursuant to the rules of the association, and he gives bonds with approved sureties for the faithful discharge of his duties. At New York the manager gives bonds for $10,000, clerks for $5,000 each. He has, under the control of the Clearing-house committee, immediate charge of all business at the Clearing-house, so far as relates to the manner in which it shall be transacted; and the clerks of the establishment, if any, as well as the settling clerks and porters or messengers of the associated banks, while at the Clearing-house, are under his direction.

At a fixed hour, each day, representatives of the banks meet at a specified place, called a Clearing-house, and exchange the checks or other paper which they hold against one another. The paper which the banks take to the Clearing-house is called the exchange, and the total amount of paper exchanged is called the clearings, or exchanges. Those banks which bring to the Clearing-house a less amount in checks or other paper than they take away—called debtor banks—pay at a later hour on the same day to the banks which bring more than they take away—called creditor banks—a balance, either directly or through the Clearing-house, in cash or its equivalent. The payment of the balances by the debtor banks, and the receipt of these balances by the creditor banks, complete each day's settlements. As the aggregate amount brought is always the same as the amount taken away, so the balances due from the debtor banks must be exactly equal to the amount due to the creditor banks. The clearing system is the application on a large scale of the principle of set-off. "Clearing," says Mr. H. D. Lloyd, in the *Cyclopedia of Political Science, Political Economy, and the Political History of the United States*, "is the settlement of mutual claims by the payment of differences." The saving of time and in the handling of cash is an obvious advantage flowing from the union of banks in a Clearing-house. There are other advantages, not less important, which will appear on further examination.

The mechanical arrangements used by the various Clearing-houses in effecting their settlements differ according to the character and magnitude of the operations carried on. At some of the smaller Clearing-houses there is no permanent place for making the exchanges, the banks taking turns. Where the transactions are of large amount, however, it becomes necessary to have a room specially fitted up for the purpose. The New York Clearing-house, long quartered in the building of the Bank of New York, some years ago secured more commodious quarters in a building which is owned by the Association. Desks, one for each bank, are arranged in three parallel rows, each desk having the name of the bank for which it is designed lettered on a silver plate in front, and being numbered with the bank's number. At Boston, the desks in the Clearing-house are arranged in an oval or elliptical form, facing outward, as they were in the old Clearing-house rooms at New York. The method of doing the business is substantially the same in both. The number of banks in the Clearing-house at Boston, December 31, 1883, was fifty-two, and at New York sixty-four, and the capital and profits represented in the former is $ 50,500,000, against $ 101,930,700 in the latter; yet the clearings at New York are, on an average, nearly eleven times as great as those of Boston, while the balances are only about four times as great.

CHAPTER III.

PREPARATION OF THE EXCHANGE.

The following analysis of Clearing-house transactions is specially applicable to New York and Boston. The peculiarities of other Clearing-houses will be noticed later on. Among the first things done with exchangeable paper when received is its classification according to the banks at which it is payable. The teller into whose hands it comes usually has a pigeon-hole for each bank, numbered with the Clearing-house number of that bank, in which the paper payable thereat is placed. At many of our Clearing-houses it is obligatory, and at all common, to place upon this paper some distinguishing mark, usually the name and number of the bank clearing it, to indicate the channel through which it has passed. In preparing the exchange for the Clearing-house, the *amounts*, merely of the various items making up the demands against each bank, are entered upon a blank called an "Exchange Slip," as follows:

```
        2d Teller.
          No. 1.
        From No. 61.
    FOURTH NATIONAL BANK
    
      2 500 00
        500 00
      1 000 00
        150 00
        800 00
      5 500 00
     10 000 00
     50 000 00
     40 000 00
     85 000 00
    ─────────
    195 450 00
      4 500 00
         50 00
        125 50
     60 000 00
      8 500 00
    ─────────
    268 625 50
```

The figures here given, it will be understood, are presented merely by way of illustration, and not as representing in character or amount the transactions of the Fourth National Bank. The first footing on the Exchange Slip ($195,450 in this case) represents the amount of checks or other items deposited to the close of business on a given day for the clearing of the next day. The addition of the items received the next morning by mail or otherwise in time for the clearing, makes the second footing (in this case, $268,625.50) being the total amount of claims carried to the Clearing-house by the Fourth National Bank against No. 1, the Bank of New York.

There is a different exchange slip for each bank, properly labeled, to show for which bank the exchange is destined. On this slip are entered the amounts merely, of the different checks or other items taken to the Clearing-house. The items on each slip are footed up, and the totals entered, the first footing in the first debit column, and the final footing in the second debit column of another blank called the "Settling Clerk's Statement," ruled as follows, and containing the names and numbers of all the banks, a part of which are omitted to save space:

No. 61, FOURTH NATIONAL BANK.
Settling Clerk's Statement, January 16, 1884.

No.	Banks.	Debit.	Debit.	Credit.	
1	Bank of N. Y. Nat'l Bkg. Ass'n.	195,450 00	268,625 50		1
2	Manhattan Co.	250,000 00	310,000 00		2
3	Merchants' National Bank	50,000 00	71,000 00		3
4	Mechanics' National Bank	175,000 00	200,000 00		4
5	Union National Bank	125,000 00	145,000 00		5
6	Bank of America	90,000 00	125,000 00		6
7	Phenix National Bank	225,000 00	260,000 00		7
	(Other banks omitted.)	1,427,947 78	2,258,772 28		
	Footings	2,538,397 78	3,638,397 78	3,297,323 04	
	Balances	—	—	341,074 74	
				3,638,397 78	

In order to have the exchanges seasonably and carefully prepared, the first debit column is made up and footed at the close of business each day for the next clearing, the entries consisting of the first footings on the various Exchange Slips, as for instance, $195,450 on the one given. The heaviest part of the work is thus done the day before the clearing, leaving for the limited time left in the morning only the work of completing the additions to the exchange slips, and inserting the final totals ($268,625.50 on the Exchange Slip above) in the second debit column, which shows the total exchange sent. The credit column is left blank to be filled up at the Clearing-house with the amounts of the return exchange representing checks or other items payable by the Fourth National Bank.

On the next page is reproduced an actual "Settling Clerk's Statement" of one of the Boston banks, showing an exact transcript of the bank's transactions with the Clearing-house on a certain day. Besides the interest attaching to it as a record of actual transactions, it will serve to make the subject clearer to those not familiar with the details of Clearing-house business.

.... **NATIONAL BANK.**

Settling Clerk's Statement,..........................1883.

No.	Banks.	First Debit.	Total Debit.	Banks Cr.	No.
1	Massachusetts National.....	118 28	6,118 28	50 00	1
2	National Union	75 96	75 96	1,287 50	2
3	Old Boston National........	3,982 02	3,982 02	—	3
4	State National.............	2,009 42	2,122 58	4,500 00	4
5	New England National.....	—	599 25	38 95	5
6	Tremont National..........	1,401 00	1,401 00	405 20	6
7	Columbian National........	—	—	1,000 00	7
8	National Eagle.............	50 00	1,268 57	195 56	8
9	National City..............	—	—	320 69	9
10	Washington National.......	—	—	16 50	10
11	North National.............	159 74	2,971 82	5,410 55	11
12	Atlantic National...........	14 70	14 70	93 15	12
13	Merchants' National........	1,310 88	8,356 05	664 57	13
14	Traders' National	5 70	5 70	—	14
15	Hamilton National	9 00	9 00	34 42	15
16	Market National............	69 91	69 91	—	16
17	Second National............	28 00	1,156 73	3,518 56	17
18	Atlas National..............	10,054 68	10,054 68	648 13	18
19	Shoe and Leather National..	164 14	164 14	112 64	19
20	Shawmut National.........	603 49	2,884 05	1,284 63	20
21	National Exchange.........	869 01	3,251 14	764 10	21
22	National Bank of Commerce.	11 70	311 12	9,175 33	22
23	National Bank of N. America	—	—	—	23
24	Faneuil Hall National......	99 26	2,099 26	164 00	24
25	National Webster...........	46 33	46 33	22 16	25
26	Eliot National..............	7 00	15,376 50	306 00	26
27	Howard National...........	430 83	430 83	332 87	27
28	Suffolk National..	36 93	36 93	1,142 49	28
29	Globe National.............	—	—	—	29
31	Freeman's National........	—	—	203 05	31
32	Boylston National..........	63 36	68 36	1,264 50	32
33	Blackstone National........	1,147 82	1,397 82	145 33	33
34	Boston National	223 55	223 55	334 64	34
35	Maverick National..........	20,748 47	43,400 35	143 89	35
36	National Hide & Leather...	11 59	294 04	294 77	36
37	National Bank Redemption.	5,399 99	105,686 79	32,307 33	37
39	First National..............	49 90	241 41	2,950 36	39
40	National Revere............	40 25	21,173 11	1,222 90	40
41	National Bank of Republic .	—	15,950 00	1,053 80	41
42	Continental National......	162 69	162 69	20,100 00	42
43	Mt. Vernon National........	610 83	610 83	20 75	43
44	Third National.............	70 00	70 00	706 32	44
45	Everett National	—	—	12 19	45
46	National Security...........	110 70	110 70	1,887 86	46
47	Broadway National.........	—	—	213 45	47
48	Nat'l Bank Commonwealth.	355 08	355 08	1,775 97	48
49	Central National..	22 45	505 97	—	49
50	Manufacturers' National....	7 00	7 00	30 00	50
51	Fourth National.............	26 84	17,647 81	54,141 20	51
52	Metropolitan National......	292 26	292 26	65 30	52
53	Merchandise National......	—	—	50 00	53
54	Lincoln National............	228 04	228 04	243 95	54
	Footings................	51,128 80	271,232 36	150,655 56	
	Balance.................	—	—	120,576 80	
				271,232 36	

A study of this statement will make apparent one of the great economies effected by the Clearing-house system, namely, the consolidation into one item of the accounts with all the banks. Thus, in the statement here presented, the forty-five debits are represented by the single total debit of $271,232.36, and the forty-eight credits by the total of $150,655.56, while instead of fifty mutual balances to adjust, the single item of $120,576.80 covers the whole.

The first column represents the first footing on the exchange slip, being the amount of clearing matter received up to the close of bank hours for the next day's clearings. The second column represents the total debit, after adding the checks or other paper received the next morning by mail or otherwise, in season for the day's exchanges. The blank for the Settling Clerk's statement is the same for all the banks. The blank used at Boston contains another column between the two debit columns, designed for "Additions," to show the exchange received each morning in season for the day's clearing. As this column is not needed, and is frequently not used, it is omitted in the form above given. The credit column is filled up at the Clearing-house with the amounts of the return exchange brought by the other banks. When the exchange slips are completed and footed, each slip is attached to the outside of the package of checks and vouchers which it represents, or the amount is marked on the outside of a sealed envelope containing them. The different packages are also arranged in the order in which they are to be delivered at the Clearing-house, and placed in a satchel or other enclosure to be carried thither. The entries in the Settling Clerk's Statement are carefully verified and footed, showing the bank's total *debit* against the other banks, and its *credit*, that is the amount with which it is credited, at the Clearing-house. This total is compared with the paying teller's footings, and if both agree, the correctness of the statement is so far proved. It is rare that an error occurs in the debit figures. The total debit is entered on another blank called a "Credit Ticket," as follows:

New York Clearing-House.		
	No. 61.	NEW YORK CLEARING-HOUSE,
		January 17, 1884.
	Credit **FOURTH NATIONAL BANK**..............$3,638,397.78.	
		J. SMITH, *Settling Clerk*.

The amount of the exchange for each bank is also entered in another blank called a "Check Ticket," as follows:

```
          No. 1.
    BANK OF NEW YORK,
   NATIONAL BANKING ASSOCIATION.
      From No. 61,
      Fourth National Bank.
      $268,265.50.
```

A similar ticket is made up for each of the other banks, and is delivered to its settling clerk at the Clearing-house, by which to "check" the entries in the credit column of his statement, since every debit entry on one statement must, if the figures are correctly transcribed, correspond with a credit entry on some other statement. These check tickets may be made up and delivered by the settling clerks at the Clearing-house while the settlement is in progress.

A copy of the debit columns in the Settling Clerk's statement is made on another partly corresponding blank, with a space on the right for signatures, instead of the credit column. This is called the "Settling Clerk's Receipt," and is taken by the messenger who carries also the packages of checks or vouchers. The settling clerk carries his statement and the credit ticket. At all the larger Clearing-houses each bank is represented by these two clerks, the messenger or porter, and the settling clerk. At New York some of the banks have two settling clerks; the whole force of clerks employed by the sixty-four banks being one hundred and sixty.

CHAPTER IV.

HOW CLEARINGS ARE MADE.

At a few minutes before ten o'clock the clerks begin to arrive at the Clearing-house, and each settling clerk as he enters passes to the manager's desk, his credit ticket showing the amount of exchange with which his bank is to be credited. These amounts are entered as rapidly as possible in the credit column of another blank called the "Clearing-house Proof," which is given on a subsequent page. So rapidly is this work done by an expert, that within a very few minutes after the last credit ticket is received the entries in the credit column are completed and footed, showing the total exchange of the day if no error has been made. Just before ten o'clock a stroke of the manager's bell calls the clerks to order. They take their places at their respective desks, the settling clerks inside, and the messengers outside, the former with his statement so far as completed, the latter with the "Settling Clerk's Receipt," and the actual vouchers for the banks to which they are to be presented. Another stroke of the bell, at ten o'clock precisely, is the signal for the exchanges to commence. No variation from this time is allowed on any pretext whatever, and on this point the Clearing-house is no respecter of persons. A few years ago Mr. Windom, Secretary of the Treasury, desired to witness the exchanges, and was apprised of the inflexible punctuality required. He arrived some minutes late, only to find that the clearings had taken place just as if he had been an individual in a private station.

At the second stroke of the bell, each messenger advances one step, which brings him to the desk of the first bank at which he is to deliver vouchers. He hands over the exchange package designed for that bank, also the "Settling Clerk's Receipt," on which the settling clerk enters his initials against the amount, as a voucher to show that the exchange has been received. The receipt is then handed back to the messenger, who passes on and repeats the operation at the desk of every other bank for which he has any vouchers, finally, coming around to his own desk after having delivered all his packages. Supposing him to have a package for every bank except his own, each of the sixty-four messengers has delivered sixty-three packages. The number of accounts thus settled between the banks is, therefore, 64 × 63 = 4032. The time required for delivering the exchanges is ten minutes at New York, and five minutes at Boston. In the old way of exchanging it would have taken several hours. At Boston there is no "Settling Clerk's Receipt," and the messengers deliver at each desk the check ticket already mentioned, showing the amount of each package delivered.

The messenger having completed his circuit, takes back to his bank the return exchange left at the desk of his bank by the messengers of the other banks, with a statement showing in round numbers the result of the clearing. The return exchange, consisting of the vouchers payable at the bank to which they are delivered through the Clearing-house, is, when brought to the bank, delivered to the paying teller for examination, after which, if they are all right and the drawers have sufficient funds, the checks and other paper are delivered to the bookkeeper and charged to the proper accounts, thus closing the transaction. All checks, drafts, notes, or other items in the exchanges, returned as "not good," or missent, are to be returned on the same day to the bank from which they were received, and this bank must make good the amount received through the Clearing-house for them; but when returned for want of endorsement or informality, they may, after being certified by the returning bank, be passed through the exchanges of the following morning to the amount of $5,000. Errors in the exchanges are also adjusted between the banks, the Clearing-house not being responsible.

After the departure of the messengers from the Clearing-house, the settling clerks continue their work, none of them being allowed to leave until the settlements are completed, without the consent of the manager. Each clerk, as soon as he has footed the credit column of his statement and carefully revised the work, strikes a balance between the total debit and the total credit exchange, which shows how much his bank is to receive or pay. He then copies these footings into what is called the "balance ticket," as follows:

No. 61.		NEW YORK CLEARING-HOUSE, *January* 17, 1884.
	Debit FOURTH NATIONAL BANK amount received..$ 3,297,323 04	
	Credit * * * * brought.. 3,638,397 78	
	$...............Debit balance due Clearing-house.	
	Credit balance due THE FOURTH NATIONAL BANK. $ 341,074 74	

(Left margin: New York Clearing-house.)

This is passed to the manager's desk. The amount brought has been already, as before stated, entered in the credit column of the Clearing-house proof. The amount received is now entered in the debit column, and the balance in the column "Due Banks" against the name of the Fourth National Bank. The next bank may have a balance against it, which should be entered in the left-hand column under the heading "Due Clearing-house." When all the balance tickets have been delivered at the manager's desk, and the entries from them made in the proof, the debit and balance columns are footed, the credit column having been already added. As the total amount brought must be the same as the total taken away, the debit and credit columns of the proof will agree if the work is correct, as also the totals "Due Clearing-house" and "Due Banks." If the footings show this agreement, the proof is made, and the settling clerks are allowed to leave. It is a very rare occurrence that the footings agree on the first trial. An inspection of the Clearing-house proof will show that it contains about thirteen hundred figures. Each entry in the proof may represent the result of sixty-three entries in the settling clerk's statement, and these probably contain from 60,000 to 70,000 figures, made and footed with great rapidity, the entries being frequently made with pencil. The credit column of the settling clerk's statement, too, must be made up and footed within the short time allowed at the Clearing-house. Under these circumstances it is natural that mistakes should frequently occur, any one of which destroys the exact balance which should exist between the debit and credit sides of the proof. When the proof is footed, and the footings fail to agree, the manager or his assistant announces the fact: " The difference is $5,530.25," or whatever the amount may be. While the preparation of the proof has been in progress the clerks have been at work verifying their figures by means of the check tickets and otherwise, and the error or errors may have been discovered as soon as the discrepancy is announced. Usually all errors are discovered and corrected within an hour from the announcement of the clearing, but sometimes an error occurs which defies detection for a long time, and keeps the whole force of clerks at work for two hours or more. Forty-five minutes are allowed for the completion of the settlement. Any delay beyond this subjects the delinquent bank to a fine. At 11.15 A. M. the fines are doubled, and at 12 M. quadrupled, so that the fines accumulate rapidly on the delinquent bank after 11.15. The object is to offer an incentive to the banks to have at the Clearing-house clerks whose figures are distinct and legible, and who are rapid and accurate calculators. If the examination of the check tickets fails to disclose the error or errors, the settling clerks are ordered by turns to pass around to the different desks, each calling off the amount of his exchange to every other. This is usually the final method of revision, and seldom fails to disclose the error. The Settling Sheets are sometimes exchanged to facilitate the detection of errors in the footings. The corrections as fast as made are incorporated with the proof, and the figures appended to the footings, added or subtracted, as the case may be, preserve a permanent record of each correction. Finally, the manager, or his assistant, calls off from a balance sheet corresponding to the two main columns of the proof, the amount in thousands of dollars to the debit or credit of each bank in the exchanges of the day, also the time at which the proof was announced, and the fines and corrections, which the settling clerks transfer to corresponding blanks in their possession. These they take away for the information of their respective banks, which thus have a record of the Clearing-house dealings of all their associates.

The table on the next page is a specimen "Clearing-house Proof." The totals show the actual transactions on the day named, but the figures are transposed so that they do not show the actual transactions of any single bank, these not being published. Consequently, some of the banks appear as having much larger, and others as having much smaller transactions than they actually had.

It is the custom at some Clearing-houses to add together both the debtor and creditor sides of the proof, thus duplicating their figures, but the footing of one side evidently represents the total amount of the vouchers exchanged. The highest bank number represented above being eighty-two, the natural inference would be that this was the number of members in the Clearing-house. An inspection of the proof will, however, show that there are eighteen missing numbers, leaving but sixty-four members at the date given. The missing numbers represent banks which were once members, but are so no longer, most if not all of them having failed or discontinued business. The number eighty-two represents the total number of members that have ever belonged to the Clearing-house. The failure of the Marine National Bank makes another missing number, leaving only sixty-three members, of which sixty-two are National or State banks, and one the United States Assistant Treasurer at New York, who joined the Clearing-house in 1878. The Assistant Treasurer is almost uniformly debtor to the Clearing-house, and rarely receives a balance from the associated banks.

HOW CLEARINGS ARE MADE.

NEW YORK CLEARING-HOUSE PROOF, THURSDAY, JANUARY 17TH, 1884.

No.	Banks.	Due Clearing-house.	Banks. Dr.	Banks. Cr.	Due Banks.	No.
1	B'k of N.Y. Nat'l Bk'g. Ass'n.	—	555,426 59	640,226 05	84,799 46	1
2	Manhattan Company	—	145,288 58	212,612 44	67,323 86	2
3	Merchants' National Bank	—	4,992,040 48	5,019,117 85	27,077 37	3
4	Mechanics' National Bank	—	1,558,990 98	1,621,001 58	62,010 60	4
5	Union National Bank	—	391,230 71	442,737 91	51,507 20	5
6	Bank of America	240,166 60	3,953,478 88	3,713,312 28	—	6
7	Phenix National Bank	—	355,740 06	370,645 55	14,905 49	7
8	National City Bank	—	295,991 67	339,918 24	43,926 57	8
10	Tradesmen's National Bank	—	327,909 22	346,296 51	18,387 29	10
11	Fulton National Bank	72,773 87	3,172,963 98	3,100,190 11	—	11
12	Chemical National Bank	—	361,734 69	465,735 40	103,980 71	12
13	Merchants' Ex. National Bank.	—	2,238,239 44	2,243,398 34	5,158 90	13
14	Gallatin National Bank	—	5,312,533 22	5,615,593 10	303,059 88	14
15	Nat'l Butchers & Drovers' B'k.	100,768 39	205,107 29	104,138 90	—	15
16	Mechs. & Traders' Nat'l Bank.	363,755 14	976,559 38	612,804 24	—	16
17	Greenwich Bank	768,506 78	3,758,949 54	2,990,442 76	—	17
18	Leather Manufac. Nat'l Bank.	350,350 00	3,878,212 46	3,527,862 46	—	18
19	Seventh Ward National Bank.	—	5,967,092 97	5,995,624 06	28,531 09	19
20	Bank of the State of New York.	20,378 71	191,849 61	171,470 90	—	20
21	American Exch. Nat'l Bank	2,879 28	60,291 80	57,412 52	—	21
23	National Bank of Commerce	171,677 53	9,649,314 97	9,477,637 44	—	23
25	National Broadway Bank	302,353 98	1,257,022 39	954,668 41	—	25
27	Mercantile National Bank	118,407 94	387,803 45	269,395 51	—	27
28	Pacific Bank	—	960,685 27	996,475 44	35,790 17	28
29	National B'k of the Republic	—	4,307,775 00	4,423,944 75	116,169 75	29
30	Chatham National Bank	18,533 68	1,207,505 86	1,188,972 18	—	30
31	People's Bank	—	236,562 71	241,168 93	4,606 22	31
32	Bank of North America	49,085 42	229,831 48	180,746 06	—	32
33	Hanover National Bank	—	187,623 38	245,019 99	57,396 61	33
34	Irving National Bank	—	3,087,088 42	3,215,685 56	128,597 14	34
35	Metropolitan National Bank	57,569 69	529,928 31	472,358 62	—	35
36	National Citizens' Bank	982,829 90	1,157,771 97	174,942 07	—	36
40	Nassau Bank	7,773 16	174,925 37	167,152 21	—	40
42	Market National Bank	23,407 05	204,151 12	180,744 07	—	42
43	St. Nicholas Bank	73,039 08	191,562 14	118,523 06	—	43
44	Nat'l Shoe & Leather Bank	—	2,375,331 70	2,821,885 55	446,553 85	44
45	Corn Exchange Bank	—	175,124 66	206,311 33	31,186 67	45
47	Continental National Bank	3,055 80	50,190 04	47,134 24	—	47
49	Oriental Bank	—	96,509 06	157,119 62	60,610 56	49
50	Marine National Bank	—	8,041,705 30	9,106,865 27	1,065,159 97	50
53	Imp. & Traders' Nat'l Bank	—	2,500,726 63	2,857,928 13	357,201 50	53
54	National Park Bank	—	3,797,522 36	3,917,726 81	120,204 45	54
56	Wall Street National Bank	—	3,576,107 39	3,680,171 46	104,064 07	56
58	North River Bank	—	8,436,107 93	8,458,096 40	21,988 47	58
59	East River National Bank	79,083 87	2,815,333 78	2,736,249 91	—	59
61	Fourth National Bank	—	3,297,323 04	3,638,397 78	341,074 74	61
62	Central National Bank	495,589 87	5,040,416 87	4,544,827 00	—	62
63	Second National Bank	—	282,296 79	411,134 69	128,837 90	63
64	Ninth National Bank	26,098 22	516,945 63	490,847 41	—	64
65	First National Bank	232,579 90	1,838,598 47	1,606,018 57	—	65
66	Third National Bank	71,549 58	479,168 18	407,618 60	—	66
67	N. Y. National Exch. Bank	—	2,843,717 01	2,938,415 45	94,698 44	67
70	Bowery National Bank	70,604 13	144,180 40	73,576 27	—	70
71	New York Co. National Bank.	13,861 23	44,478 91	30,617 68	—	71
72	German-American Bank	—	99,738 66	121,461 32	21,722 66	72
74	Chase National Bank	—	1,406,323 07	1,829,143 74	422,820 67	74
75	Ass't Treas. U. S. at N. Y.	29,406 91	174,674 69	145,267 78	—	75
76	Fifth Avenue Bank	—	13,981,992 88	13,988,451 27	6,458 77	76
77	German Exchange Bank	—	4,371,989 88	4,520,951 88	148,962 00	77
78	Germania Bank	—	5,682,807 77	6,269,436 01	586,628 24	78
79	United States National Bank.	8,471 12	576,078 07	567,606 95	—	79
80	Lincoln National Bank	349,169 67	1,262,334 29	913,164 62	—	80
81	Garfield National Bank	—	185,452 43	208,589 21	23,136 78	81
82	Fifth National Bank	30,811 55	2,534,168 75	2,503,357 20	—	82
		5,134,538 05	139,096,548 03	139,096,548 03	5,134,538 05	

CHAPTER V.

HOW OUTSIDE BANKS MAKE CLEARINGS.

In addition to the banks which are members of the Association, most of the other New York City banks effect their exchanges through the Clearing-house by the agency of some bank that is a member. The bank for which the clearing is done is required to keep an adequate fund on deposit at the clearing bank, both as a compensation for the service rendered, and as a guarantee against loss. The vouchers to be cleared are sent every morning or oftener to the clearing bank, and are classified and distributed among the exchanges of the latter as if received by it on deposit. The return exchange is also received by the clearing bank with its own exchanges, as if payable by it, and after being charged to the bank for which the clearing is done, is transmitted to it as speedily as possible, usually by messengers dispatched by the latter directly after the clearing. In case of the return of checks for want of funds or other reasons, the matter would naturally be adjusted through the agency of the clearing bank. The regulations of the New York Clearing-house provide, that "whenever any member of the Association shall send through the Clearing-house the exchanges of any bank or banks in the city or vicinity, who are not members, such sending shall, *ipso facto*, and without other notice, constitute said member the agent for said bank or banks at the Clearing-house; and said member shall be liable in the premises the same as for its own transactions, and its liability in all such cases shall continue until after the completion of the exchanges of the morning next following the receipt of notice of discontinuance of such agency." A similar regulation is in force at New Orleans.

At Boston the Clearing-house embraced, in January, 1884, the operations of twenty-four banks in the vicinity which were not members; at Pittsburgh forty-six, and at St. Louis four. At Boston, banks outside availing themselves of the privileges of the Clearing-house must pay towards its expenses a sum to be annually determined by the Clearing-house committee. At some of the Clearing-houses, members are not allowed to make the exchanges of any bank outside. This is the case at Indianapolis, Lowell and Worcester.

A plan for clearing gold checks was adopted February 14, 1872, and the exchange of such checks commenced in March following and was continued until the resumption of specie payments, January 1, 1879. This exchange was kept distinct from the exchange of currency checks, but took place at the same time and place and was conducted in the same way. The total of gold clearings during this period of nearly seven years was $ 14,066,282,911.94, and the balances paid in gold or gold certificates amounted to $ 2,236,-317,602.24, or 15.9 per cent. of the clearings.

CHAPTER VI.

PAYMENT OF BALANCES.

The exchanges being completed, the next step is the payment of balances. At New York the balances must be paid by the debtor banks to the Clearing-house between 12½ and 1½ o'clock, P. M., either in actual coin, United States legal-tender notes, or in United States or Clearing-house certificates. At 1½ o'clock, or as soon thereafter as the accounts can be made up, the creditor banks receive the balances from the manager at the same place, provided all the balances due from the debtor banks have been paid. Should any bank make default in the payment of its balances at the proper hour, the amount of that balance must be immediately, on requisition from the manager, furnished to the Clearing-house by the several banks exchanging with the defaulting bank in proportion to their respective balances against that bank resulting from the exchanges of the day. The amounts so furnished constitute claims against the delinquent bank only, the Clearing-house being in no way responsible. The defaulting bank is immediately suspended from the Clearing-house. At several of our American Clearing-houses the regulations provide that until the settlement is completed and balances are paid the exchange shall be in trust only, that the vouchers delivered at the Clearing-house shall, until that time, remain the property of the bank presenting them, and that in case of default by any member in paying its balances, such vouchers shall be returned unmutilated to the banks from which they were received. Some recent complications at New York, arising from the failure of the Marine National Bank and of Grant and Ward, suggest the advisability of some similar regulation there. It may be stated here that the operations of the Clearing-house have received legal recognition, and a presentation of a demand through the Clearing-house is a legal presentation by virtue of custom among bankers and merchants.

Errors in the exchanges, and claims arising from the return of checks, or from any other cause, are adjusted directly between the banks who are parties to them, and not through the Clearing-house, the association being in no way responsible for them.

As the banks severally pay their balances the manager gives each a receipt in the following form:

No. 6.	NEW YORK CLEARING-HOUSE,
	January 17, 1884.
Received from the Bank of America Two hundred and forty thousand one hundred and sixty-six $\tfrac{60}{100}$ dollars in full for balance due the associated banks.	
$240,166.60.	............................*Manager*.

Each bank keeps a current ledger account with the Clearing-house, charging it with all money or vouchers sent, and crediting it with all that is returned; and this receipt is charged as a voucher on the books of the paying bank. The messengers also give to the manager, in a book with suitable forms prepared for that purpose, receipts for all balances delivered to them. It is only for a period of about one hour, while receiving and paying the balances, that the Clearing-house has the custody of any money, and during that time only as trustee, receiving from one to pay another.

Reclamations for errors and deficiencies, in specie or United States legal-tender notes, received at the Clearing-house, contained in bags or packages, sealed and marked in conformity with the rules of the Clearing-house, must be made by one o'clock on the following day by the receiving bank against the bank whose mark the sealed package bears. Notice of such error must be sent immediately upon discovery, the Clearing-house not being responsible for the contents of such bags or packages. Serious difficulties recently arose at New York in a matter of this kind, growing out of the failure of the Marine National Bank. On the sixth of May, 1884, this bank enclosed in the usual manner in a sealed envelope, marked with the aggregate amount, containing as items constituting its claims upon the First National Bank for exchange through the Clearing-house, three checks drawn by Ferdinand Ward upon the First National Bank, amounting together to $215,000. As Ward at that time had in the First National Bank only $2,213.98, the latter refused the checks. The Marine National Bank having in the meantime failed, after paying its balance of $550,000 at the Clearing-house, the First National Bank informed the Clearing-house that the checks were not good and claimed to be reimbursed by the associated banks or the Clearing-house.

A special committee of the Association, appointed to consider the subject, decided against this claim, but the affair resulted in the adoption, June 4, 1884, of two amendments to the Constitution of the Association. One of these authorizes the Clearing-house committee to examine any member of the Association, and to require security for the payment of its balances to the Clearing-house; the other provides that in case of refusal or inability of any bank to refund the amount of checks, drafts, or other items returned as not good, the bank holding them may, before one o'clock, report to the manager the amount of the same, and the manager, with the approval of the Clearing-house committee, is to take from the settling sheet of both banks the amount of such checks or other items so reported. This will, of course, increase any balance due from the presenting bank, for which all the banks having balances against it are responsible. The Clearing-house has also recently taken action on another matter which has been agitated for many years, namely, the payment of interest on deposits. On the recommendation of a committee appointed June 4, and subsequently increased, the associated banks on July 29, 1884, adopted, subject to the ratification of the banks individually, two amendments, one forbidding any member to pay interest on, or allow compensation for, deposits after January 1, 1885, the other providing that no checks shall pass through the Clearing-house except those drawn on members. Under this amendment, if it shall come in force, banks outside could still clear on one side through members—that is, the checks and other claims on the members—but the Clearing-house would be closed against checks drawn on banks outside, and these checks would be less current. The outside banks may thus be forced to become members, and bear a share of the expense from which they have hitherto, to the prejudice of the members, escaped.

CHAPTER VII.

CLEARING-HOUSE CERTIFICATES.

The labor, responsibility and risk attending the handling of the funds used in paying the balances have been greatly abridged by the use of certificates. These are of three kinds—Clearing-house gold certificates, United States gold certificates, and United States legal-tender certificates. Clearing-house gold certificates are issued in accordance with a plan adopted in September, 1853, against gold deposited with one of the associated banks, and are of the denominations of $1,000, $5,000 and $10,000. They are numbered, registered and countersigned by the proper officer, and are endorsed when paid into the Clearing-house by the paying bank, and when paid out are charged to the receiving bank, so that they can always be traced by the records. They are to be used only in settlements between the banks, and any member of the Clearing-house which shall pay or deliver to any party, not a member, any such certificates, is subject to a fine of one hundred dollars. The Bank of America was selected as the depository of the associated banks at the time the Clearing-house was established. The issue of legal-tender notes by the Government and the suspension of specie payments reduced all ordinary settlements to a paper basis, and the issue of Clearing-house certificates was discontinued. In 1879, after the resumption of specie payments and the discontinuance of further issues of gold certificates by the Government, the Clearing-house gold certificates were revived, the Bank of America being again selected as the depository. The first of the new certificates were issued October 14, 1879. The amount of these certificates outstanding June 30, 1881, was $41,858,000, but has since been reduced. United States gold certificates were authorized by Act of March 3, 1863, and were used for Clearing-house purposes soon after the passage of the National Bank Act. The first issue was made November 13, 1865. They are issued against deposits of gold coin and bullion made with the Secretary of the Treasury, in denominations of twenty dollars and upwards, corresponding with the denominations of United States notes. Further issues were discontinued December 1, 1878, but were resumed under Act of July 12, 1882, and they have, in part, superseded the gold Clearing-house certificates. The United States legal-tender certificates are issued under Act of June 8, 1872, against deposits of legal tenders made with the Secretary of the Treasury by any National banking association, in amounts of $10,000 and upwards, and are of denominations not less than $5,000. They are payable on demand in United States notes at the place where the deposits were made, and are counted as part of the lawful money reserve of the National banks. Before the resumption of specie payments they were much used in the Clearing-house settlements, being frequently called Clearing-house legal-tender certificates, and the amount outstanding June 30, 1875, was $59,045,000. The amount now in use is comparatively insignificant, and they appear only to a small extent in the Clearing-house settlements. The amounts and percentages paid in coin, currency and certificates in the Clearing-house settlements at New York, in 1883, were as follows:

Paid in gold coin	$ 197,000 00	.0
United States gold certificates	504,213,000 00	36.1
Clearing-house gold certificates	990,925,000 00	63.3
United States legal-tender certificates	1,575,000 00	.1
Legal tenders and change	7,768,096 49	.5
	$ 1,564,678,096 49	100.0

It will be noticed that only one-half of one per cent. of the balances was paid in actual cash, and this amounts to only one-fiftieth of one per cent. of the clearings.

The system of paying Clearing-house balances wholly or partially in certificates has been adopted at Boston, Philadelphia, Chicago, Baltimore, San Francisco, Milwaukee, and St. Paul. At Cincinnati, St. Louis, New Orleans, Louisville, Columbus, and Memphis, the manager of the Clearing-house issues checks or certificates on the debtor in favor of the creditor banks, which must be paid to the satisfaction of the latter. The form used at St. Louis, which will serve to illustrate, is as follows:

$5,000. ST. LOUIS CLEARING-HOUSE, July 18, 1884.

In the settlement of the balances of the Exchanges made between members of this Association to-day, there is due from (No. 6) the Commercial Bank, five thousand dollars, payable on demand to (No. 8) the Fifth National Bank.

Not transferable, and without recourse upon any other member of this Association after two o'clock P. M. of this day.

E. CHASE, *Manager*.

The forms are different at different Clearing-houses, but their purport is substantially the same in imposing upon some debtor bank the duty of paying a certain sum to some creditor bank in settlement of the balances. In this case the payment of balances, as well as the exchange of vouchers, is a matter settled exclusively between the banks, the Clearing-house handling no money and having nothing to do with the matter, except to apportion the payments.

At Providence, Hartford, New Haven, Worcester, Springfield, Lowell, Syracuse, and to some extent at Portland, Maine, balances are paid by checks on New York or Boston, except where they are for small amounts. This plan is similar in principle to that prevailing in the British and other European Clearing-houses. The handling of cash is entirely dispensed with, so far as checks drawn on some common depository are used. The check issued in these cases would be forwarded by the creditor bank to its New York or Boston correspondent, which might also be the depository of the debtor bank. If not, the check would be either collected directly, or through the New York or Boston Clearing-house.

CHAPTER VIII.

THE RECORDS KEPT AND THEIR USES.

The payment of the balances being completed there remains the duty of making up a record of the day's business for preservation and future reference. This is a matter the importance of which is sometimes overlooked. However small the transactions of a Clearing-house may be they are destined to be of value in the future as a means of measuring growth, if nothing else. There are, too, many problems of interest to bankers, on which light would be thrown by a study and comparison of Clearing-house data carefully and intelligently prepared. In the interests of philosophic inquiry it is worth while to preserve all facts relating to operations of so interesting a character as those of the Clearing-house. At New York, where the volume of business justifies it, very full and elaborate records are kept, showing every important fact connected with the business, and it is possible to learn there many particulars of which no record is preserved at other Clearing-houses. A ledger is kept in which are posted the daily footings of the proof, "exhibiting a continuous history of the aggregate dealings of the banks." The entire proof, also, is transferred into a book kept for that purpose. "In like manner, the daily debit and credit exchange of each bank is posted to its account, and shows not only the *extent* of its business, but measurably its *character* also. This is the most essential of all the records. It is that which brings the banks separately within the supervision and control of the Clearing-house —a necessary complement of the joint responsibility created by the organization."* If the daily records of its transactions show that its reserves are undergoing constant depletion without any known source of replenishment, its credit at the Clearing-house is affected, and it may be subjected to an examination by a committee consisting of the Clearing-house committee and a committee of five bank officers, which joint committee has power to suspend any bank from the privileges of the Clearing-house, "in case of extreme emergency," until the pleasure of the Association is ascertained. To effect a suspension a majority of each committee must

---

* Gibbons' *Banks of New York and the Panic of* 1857.

be present and the vote must be unanimous. The Association alone has the power of expelling a member.

A summary book is made up from the daily postings, showing the total receipts and payments by each bank for the week, and also for the month and year. The adverse balances of one period may be compensated by the favorable balances of a succeeding period, and thus the state of the reserve of each bank is followed up with unfailing precision. "If at the end of a month it appears that a bank has paid in to the House one million of dollars more than it has received, and if it has no foreign sources of replenishment, the conclusion is that it has supplied itself by purchase. If the same result should be shown at the end of another month, without signs of recuperation, and so on continuously, it becomes evident that the institution is carrying a forced average of loans, and it will receive a call from the committee. . . . But this extreme case is most unlikely to happen. The credit that every member derives from the Association is too valuable to be cast off or treated with lightness. The action of the Association is too impartial and just to give offence, or to admit excuse for disregarding its advice."

"A positive principle, or rule of financial government, has been demonstrated by this action of the Clearing-house on the city banks, that is, the restriction of loans by the necessity of maintaining a certain average of coin [or legal tenders] *from resources within the bank*. Borrowing from day to day will no longer do. It cannot be concealed. The records will show conclusively whether the average is kept up by a healthy business, or by a forcing process."*

"The limitation imposed does not stop at the bank loans, but passes through them into the commercial system. The loans rest on the coin (or legal tender) average, this rests on the deposits, and the deposits rest on the means of trade. The Clearing-house has not created any new dependence of this kind, but it has brought the facts into a manageable shape, and established something like an axiom in the banking business. It is not a mere arbitrary requirement that a specific average of coin (or legal tenders) must be maintained, but it is the constitution of that average as a *result*, and the control of it by an organization which permits no escape and works no injustice—and what that organization is for the City of New York, the city is for the country; a restrictive power over the general currency of trade must be exerted through this channel to its remotest sections."

Weekly publication of bank statements had been required by law even before the establishment of the Clearing-house, but many ways of doctoring such statements were devised, so that the objects of the law were only partially realized. Each bank in the Clearing-

* Gibbons' *Banks of New York and the Panic of 1857.*

house is required to furnish to the manager every Saturday, on or before 12 o'clock M., a statement showing the average amount of loans and discounts, of specie, of legal-tender notes, of deposits, and of circulation, for the preceding week. These statements are tabulated by the manager and given to the public. They have this advantage over the statements made under the law, that the daily operations of the Clearing-house furnish a means of testing their accuracy. Deception may still be practised, but it is likely sooner to come to light than it would but for the searching test afforded by the daily settlements.

"The improvement in the character of its loans is consequent upon the fact, that if a bank becomes embarrassed by their imprudent extension, it can get *a good class* of paper rediscounted, and thus obtain immediate relief; whereas if its discounted paper is of a low grade, or if the assistance required is to help the directors only, and not its dealers generally, it loses sympathy and reputation. The *character* of its discounted bills is, therefore, its sheet anchor in a storm. In fact, the credit of the Clearing-house Association would itself be impaired if it should allow one of its members to fail from inability to convert good assets into cash funds."* One of the ways by which relief is afforded in such cases is by the issue of Clearing-house certificates against a deposit of securities, such certificates to be available in the settlement of balances at the Clearing-house. In the late crisis at New York some $25,000,000 of such certificates were thus issued to different banks against accepted securities, certificates in no case being issued to an amount exceeding seventy-five per cent. of such securities. This measure afforded substantial relief, and the certificates were mostly withdrawn within sixty days. The same plan was tried with good results in 1861-2 and in 1873.

Other records of Clearing-house operations may be made possessing practical value. Says Col. W. M. Grosvenor, in a paper which was read at the Convention of the American Bankers' Association in 1882: "In the mere observation of the course of exchanges in different sections and at different localities, many business men affirm that they have gained important advantages. They have been warned in season, when the business of a distant city was being diverted to others, or depressed by social or political influences. They have been advised in season, by gradually expanding exchanges, that industry in a distant region was reviving, and prompt effort in that direction has been rewarded. Investors have been guided in the choice of securities by evidence of rapid growth in the business of cities. Lenders have been warned by unnatural expansion and violent fluctuation in the exchanges at a particular

* Gibbons.

city, that excessive speculation was approaching its climax there, so that loans were 'extra-hazardous.' Information of more general importance has repeatedly been obtained. The inquiry is yet in its infancy, and comparatively little is known of the meaning of records which, in due time, will enable men to note the coming of many financial storms as surely as the march of an area of low barometer across the country is traced by the signal service."

At the last meeting (1884) of the Bankers' Association, Mr. Comegys, President of the Philadelphia National Bank, suggested that the Clearing-house might keep another record, with a brief explanation of which we shall close this chapter. The risks and losses growing out of the purchase of one-name paper are well understood, especially among bankers. To lessen the risk thus incurred, he proposed that a credit-ledger should be opened in the Clearing-house of any city, in which should be kept a record of the names of payers and endorsers, and dates of maturity of all notes amounting to one thousand dollars, or more, held by the banks, purchased of brokers. The reports of such paper, he further proposed, should be made to the Clearing-house anonymously, and information concerning such names should be given only to members of the Clearing-house. Large sums of money, he declared, might be saved to banks by means of this information.

CHAPTER IX.

FINES.

The minor delinquencies of the banks in their relations with the Clearing-house are dealt with by means of fines. The following scale of fines at New York will serve as an illustration:

First.—All errors on the Credit side of the Settling Clerk's Statement (*i.e.* in the amount brought) whether of footing or entry, and all errors causing disagreement between the credit entries, the check tickets, and the exchange slips..each $3 00
Second.—Errors in making the Debit (*i.e.* the amount received) entries, each $2 00
Third.—Errors in the Tickets reported to the Clearing-house, causing disagreement between the balances and aggregates....................each $2 00
Fourth.—Errors in footing the amount received........................... $1 00
Fifth.—Disorderly conduct of Clerk or Porter, at the Clearing-house; or disregard of the Manager's instructions......................each offence $2 00
Sixth.—Clerk or porter failing to attend punctually with statements and tickets complete at the morning exchanges........................each $2 00
Seventh.—Debtor banks, failing to appear to pay their balances before 1½ o'clock P. M... $3 00
Eighth.—Errors in delivery or receipt of exchanges....................each $1 00

Forty-five minutes are allowed for the proof. For all errors remaining undiscovered at 11.15 A. M. the fines are doubled, and at 12 M. quadrupled. Once in each month the manager reports to each bank the amount of fines against it for the preceding calendar month, with the total amount of fines from all the banks and the number of banks fined. Clerks are required to conduct themselves in a quiet and orderly manner, to be attentive to their duties, and to remain at their desks while the proof is being made, and until it is announced. Loud conversation, or anything tending to create disturbance or confusion, is not permitted. The fines, though not large considering the amounts involved, are sufficient to make it an object for banks to employ clerks who are rapid and accurate in figures, though there are very marked differences of aptness in this particular.

CHAPTER X.

HISTORY OF THE NEW YORK CLEARING-HOUSE.

The first proposition for the establishment of a Clearing-house in New York was made by Albert Gallatin in 1841. To Mr. Geo. D. Lyman, the first manager of the New York Clearing-house belongs chiefly the credit of systematizing its details and planning its records in its earlier history. Mr. Lyman thus concisely sums up the economy of time and labor effected by the Clearing-house:

"On the day when the Clearing-house began business, about twenty-seven hundred open, active accounts on the ledgers of the associated banks were balanced—the most of them for the first time,[*] and all of them finally. The business which had rendered necessary this large number of accounts was thenceforth accomplished more quickly, with less annoyance to bank officers, and with greater safety to all concerned. The results may be briefly enumerated as follows:

"*First.*—The condensation for each bank of forty-eight balances into one, and the settlement of that balance without a movement of specie.

"*Secondly.*—The avoidance of numerous accounts, entries and postings.

"*Thirdly.*—Great saving of time to the porters and of risk in making exchanges and settlements from bank to bank.

"*Fourthly.*—Relief from a vast amount of labor and annoyance to which the great army of cashiers, tellers and bookkeepers were subjected under the old system.

"*Fifthly.*—The liberation of the associated banks from all injurious dependence on each other.

"*Sixthly.*—The absolute facility afforded by the books of the Clearing-house for knowing at all times the management and standing of every bank in the Association."

Mr. Lyman remained manager of the Clearing-house until 1864, a period of more than ten years. On the twenty-second of August in that year he was succeeded by the present manager, Mr. William A. Camp, who has brought the details of the business to a per-

---

[*] "The practice of the banks had been to draw settlement-checks on each other for even thousands of dollars near the balance due, and the account was never settled to a point."

fection not previously attained. Mr. Camp was born at Durham, Connecticut, Sept. 23, 1822, was appointed in 1855 discount clerk in the Importers and Traders' Bank of New York (his first banking experience), and was made first teller of the Artisans' Bank in 1856. In June 1857 he was made assistant-manager of the Clearing-house, so that he has now been connected with the establishment twenty-seven years, twenty years of that period as manager. To executive ability of a high order, he unites unusual accuracy and promptness in the despatch of business, as well as a wide acquaintance, both theoretical and practical, with financial subjects. It speaks volumes for the care and scrupulous accuracy with which the business has been conducted, that in the entire history of the Clearing-house, extending over nearly thirty-one years, its transactions have always balanced to a cent. The only instance on record of an error in any statement emanating from it occurred a few years ago in the weekly bank statement, and this was due to an error of one of the clerks in transcribing the figures. In making the entries, the officials at the Clearing-house and their subordinates use ink only. The clerks sent by the banks may at their option make their entries in pencil.

The first day's clearing at New York, October 11, 1853, was $23,-938,182.25. The total of its gold and currency clearings to December 31, 1883, was $695,304,252,496.30, and of the balances, $30,250,-800,308.61. The largest transactions (clearings and balances combined) in any one day were $295,821,422.37, February 28, 1881, when the clearings amounted to $288,555,981.58. The largest exchange ever brought to the Clearing-house by any bank was on the same day, $31,772,391.45, brought by the Bank of New York, its return exchange being $31,512,015.47. The largest balance paid by any bank was $10,585,471.31, November 17, 1868. The smallest balance ever paid by any bank was one cent, September 22, 1862. The smallest balance ever paid to a bank was ten cents, November 16, 1863. No bank ever came out exact without a balance either way. The largest amount ever cleared in one year was in 1881, $49,376,-882,882.54, and the smallest in any whole year was in 1858, $5,376,-151,036.92. Formerly bank notes were included in the clearings, though to a less extent after the establishment of the National banking system than before. The trouble of assorting the country bank notes gave general dissatisfaction. "The Park Bank then undertook, for a consideration of about five thousand dollars a year, to assort the country bank notes of all the other banks in the city, and this arrangement was prolonged for nearly two years, the plan of working meanwhile gradually improving in efficiency, when it was interrupted and superseded by the establishment of the Redemption Bureau in the office of the United States Treasurer at Washington, for the purpose of redeeming the notes of all National banks."* Bank notes may now be included in the exchanges, but, in practice, are not. The paper exchanged now consists of checks, drafts and certified notes.

Banks desiring to become members of the Clearing-house Association must apply to the committee on admissions, who make such examination of the bank as they deem necessary. The personal character and standing of its managers is also considered. The bank may be admitted to the Association by a three-fourths vote (by ballot) of the members present at any meeting, on such conditions as three-fourths of those present may deem expedient. The new member must assent to the Constitution and pay an admission fee, varying from $1,000, where the capital does not exceed $500,000, up to $7,500, where the capital exceeds $5,000,000. Any member increasing its capital must pay an additional sum corresponding with these rates. A bank may withdraw from the Association at pleasure, first paying due proportion of all expenses incurred, and signifying its intention to withdraw to the Clearing-house committee. The expense of printing for the several banks is apportioned equally among them. The other expenses are met by an assessment of $200 on each bank, and the balance necessary above that amount *pro rata* according to the average amount sent to the Clearing-house for the preceding year. A fine of three dollars is imposed on any bank not represented at roll call at any duly called meeting without reasonable excuse. Any member of the Association guilty of participation in any scheme for withdrawing legal tenders from use may be suspended from the Clearing-house.

* Kinahan Cornwallis in *International Review* for Sept.-Oct., 1876.

CHAPTER XI.

CLEARING-HOUSES OUTSIDE OF NEW YORK.

The Boston Clearing-house, like that of New York, has had but two managers, Mr. Henry B. Grove, from the organization of the Clearing-house in 1855 to his death in April, 1877, and Mr. Nathaniel G. Snelling, the present incumbent, from that date until the present time. Mr. Snelling was assistant manager from 1861 to 1877, and has therefore been connected officially with the Clearing-house for twenty-three years. The clerks and porters, as well as the manager, give bonds. The daily routine is substantially the same at Boston as at New York. The hour for clearing is ten o'clock, A. M. The debtor banks are required to pay their balances by 12.15 P. M., and the creditor banks receive them at 1½ o'clock P. M. Thirty minutes are allowed for the proof and for delivering check tickets, and for each fifteen minutes' detention beyond that time two dollars are added to the fine incurred. About half an hour is required to prepare the exchanges for the Clearing-house. The messengers complete the delivery of the packages at the Clearing-house in about five minutes. They receive the return clearings in about ten or fifteen minutes, and are generally back at their respective banks by fifteen or twenty minutes past ten. The paying teller completes the examination of the return exchange usually by eleven o'clock, and then delivers the checks and vouchers to the bookkeeper, who enters them on his books in ink of a different color from that used in charging those paid over the counter. Usually the bank sending paper to the Clearing-house marks its number on the back of each check or voucher in blue ink, but the practice is not uniform. Although the check tickets are usually prepared at the bank and delivered by the messengers, this is not obligatory. It is sufficient if the check tickets are all delivered before half-past ten o'clock, for failure to do which a fine of one dollar is imposed. No failure has ever occurred among the banks connected with the Boston Clearing-house, though the Mechanics' Bank (No. 30) never came in, and the Metropolis (No. 38), discontinued business many years ago. Provision is made in the Constitution for making one of the associated banks a depository of coin against which certificates may be issued. But this provision is at present dormant, United States gold certificates being used instead. In case of default by any bank in paying its balances at the Clearing-house, the Constitution, in addition to provisions similar to those of the New York Clearing-house, provides that any bank responding to the manager's requisition for the deficiency may have its exchanges with the defaulting bank canceled, and be restored to the position in which it stood before the exchange was made. Weekly statements are required from the banks, as in New York.

At Philadelphia there are two clearings daily. The first, and principal clearing is at half-past eight o'clock, A. M. The balances of this clearing are paid in legal tender notes or United States certificates, between the hours of eleven and twelve o'clock. A second, or "runners'" exchange, is held at half-past eleven, for the settlement of the items formerly taken to the different banks by the runners, namely, the notes and checks received by the morning mail. The balances of this exchange are paid by due bill, which goes through the next morning's exchanges. The clearing methods are similar to those at New York. Weekly bank statements are also published.

At Chicago the hour for clearing is eleven o'clock daily. Balances must be paid by the debtor banks between the hours of twelve and half-past twelve, and the creditor banks receive them between half-past twelve and a quarter of one o'clock. Balances are, by the rules of the Clearing-house, payable in gold coin, legal tenders, National bank notes, United States and Clearing-house certificates. It is customary, however, for the banks to save the handling of actual cash to a greater or less extent by the following expedient: A debtor bank sells to some creditor bank New York or Boston exchange, and receives from the latter a check or order on the Clearing-house, the form of which is printed on green paper, and is as follows:

No........ CHICAGO..................1884.
W. S. SMITH, *Manager*,
    Chicago Clearing-house.
Pay..or order
....Dollars,
and deduct from balance due us this day.
$........ ....*Cashier*.

The debtor bank delivers this voucher at the Clearing-house in settlement of the amount which it represents, and it is available to the Clearing-house in settling with the creditor bank without handling any cash. At St. Paul a similar usage prevails, the check or order on the Clearing-house being printed on light yellow paper.

At Chicago all checks and vouchers exchanged at the clearing are held in trust only by the member receiving the same until returned, or the amount thereof paid. In case of failure on the part of any bank to pay its balances at the proper hour, it is to return such checks or vouchers, without mutilation, to the Clearing-house before one o'clock P. M., and it is to receive back the vouchers it sent. Elaborate provisions are made for the protection of the associated banks in such cases. The work of clearing, in its various stages, occupies about two hours. Thirty minutes are allowed for the proof. The paper exchanged is stamped "Paid through the Chicago Clearing-house to" (name of member clearing same to be here inserted), with the date, in lieu of written endorsements, and the bank using such stamp thereby makes itself responsible for all items so stamped by it, and for all informalities of endorsements thereon. The business hours of the different members must be uniform, and are regulated by the Association. Each member of the Association is required to furnish to the manager, as often as five times yearly, and at such other times as may be required by the Clearing-house committee, a sworn statement of its condition, in the form and manner prescribed for the statements of National banks, such statements to be open to the inspection of the members, but to be otherwise confidential. The scale of fines shows some peculiarities, among which may be mentioned those for being late at the morning exchanges. For the first five minutes, or part thereof, late, the fine is $3; for the second five minutes, or part thereof, $10, and for being over ten minutes late, $25. Creditor banks are also fined $3 in case of failure to take away their balances by 12.45 P. M. All fines are collected by the manager at once. The manager may require from members the signatures of such persons as are authorized to receipt for balances. The expenses of the establishment are about $8,000 per annum, assessed upon the banks in a manner similar to that at New York.

At St. Louis the hour for making the exchanges is ten o'clock A. M. Each clerk must report the debits against his bank within twelve minutes after commencing; for failure to do which the bank is fined $2, with two dollars more for every five minutes' additional delay. The time required for completing the morning settlement varies from fifteen to thirty minutes. At eleven o'clock the manager issues his certificates of indebtedness by the debtor on the creditor members, the form of which has been already given, each creditor bank receiving, on an average, two certificates. The payment of balances, which are not handled at all by the Clearing-house, but are settled wholly between the banks, occupies from one to one and one-half hours. As at Chicago, the exchange and delivery of checks at the Clearing-house is in trust only until the debit balances are paid, and such checks must be returned unmutilated by any defaulting member. All checks sent to the Clearing-house must, in lieu of written endorsement, bear the impress of a uniform stamp, showing the name and number of the bank sending it, and the date, with the words, "St. Louis Clearing-house." The by-laws define proper clearing matter as follows:

1. All checks or drafts upon, or certificates of deposits, demand or matured, of any member of the Clearing-house or any bank clearing through any member.

2. Any other matter specially agreed to by any member, or bank clearing through it, until notice is given to the contrary.

3. Mercantile or other paper payable at any bank shall not be cleared against such bank unless authorized by the same.

4. All unstamped checks will be considered improper matter for clearing.

5. Any bank clearing paper not proper, as aforesaid, shall be fined for disregard of instructions.

Clerks duly authorized may return at the Clearing-house matter not authorized according to the foregoing to the clerk of the bank clearing it, who must receive and charge his bank with it in his debit list. The initiation fee is only $25, and the expenses, amounting to about $6,000, are paid by the members in proportion to their clearings. To be eligible as members, banks must have a paid-up capital of $150,000. Instead of a "settling clerk's statement" all on one blank, each clerk has two statements. One called a "Credit List," begins "St Louis Clearing-house...................1884, from..................Bank No....," and contains the exchange brought by the bank. It corresponds with the debit column in the "settling clerk's statement," as already given. The other statement is called the "Debit List," and begins "St. Louis Clearing-house, ...1884, on..................Bank No....." It corresponds with the credit column in the settling clerk's statement. The manager compiles periodical statements showing the condition of the banks from returns made by them. While the method of paying balances employed at St. Louis saves one handling of the funds so paid, it must usually happen that another great economy effected by the Clearing-house is lost, namely, the settlement of the whole debtor or creditor balance in one item. It would be a very remarkable circumstance if the balance due from any debtor bank should be exactly the same as the balance due to some creditor bank. Whenever it is otherwise, the demand due to the one, or from the other, must be divided into two or more payments. The relative advantage of one or the other method of paying balances must, however, be determined by the circumstances of each Clearing-house. What might be most convenient under certain conditions, might be quite inconvenient or impracticable under different conditions. The manager and a porter have charge of the Clearing-house.

The regulations of the San Francisco Clearing-house are very similar to those at New York. As at Philadelphia, there are two clearings daily, these being the only Clearing-houses in the country having more than one. The hours of clearing are for ordinary days ten o'clock, A. M., and two o'clock, P. M., precisely. At half-past two o'clock, P. M., the debtor banks pay their balances to the Clearing-house, and at three o'clock, P. M., the creditor banks receive their balances at the same place. On Saturdays the exchanges occur at eleven and half-past eleven o'clock, the settlements being made at twelve. About ten minutes are occupied in getting the proof, about thirty minutes in receiving debit balances, and about twenty minutes in paying credit balances. United States certificates began to be used in paying balances March 5, 1883, and Clearing-house certificates June 5, 1883. Formerly the gold balances were paid in gold coin, the silver in silver coin, and the currency in currency. This was the case before the resumption of specie payments. There are no fines or penalties other than suspension or expulsion. If a bank defaults in the payment of its balances, the amount of that balance is furnished to the manager in memorandum checks by the banks to which the defaulting bank is a debtor, in proportion to the amount due each, and the claims of the banks which have balances against the defaulting bank, and the claims of the defaulting bank against banks which may, in that exchange, have exchanged with it, shall be placed in precisely the same position as before the exchanges commenced. New members must pay an initiation fee of $500, as compared with $200 for the original members. To provide for the annual expenses, each bank also pays an annual subscription of $150, any balance required being made up by a *pro rata* assessment according to the amounts cleared by each bank. The work at the Clearing-house is in charge of the manager and one clerk.

At Baltimore the banks make their exchanges daily at the National Union Bank of Maryland, which is the depository of the associated banks. The hour for clearing is 8.45 o'clock, A. M. The balances are paid by the debtor banks at ten o'clock, either in legal-tender notes or certificates, and are received by the creditor banks at noon.

At New Orleans the hour for clearing is nine o'clock, A. M. At 11.30 o'clock, A. M., or as soon thereafter as the amounts can be made up and proved, the creditor banks receive from the manager at the Clearing-house in settlement of their balances checks on the debtor banks, which checks are not transferable, and are to be in no case sent through the exchanges. The liability of the associated banks on such checks ceases at two o'clock, P. M., on the day of their issue. Any bank unable to pay its balances is required to notify the manager and other members of the Association, and if any bank fails to respond to the manager's checks before one o'clock, P. M., such checks are to be returned to the Clearing-house. The manager at once notifies the other associated banks, and strikes from the lists the exchanges of the defaulting member, which is required to hold in trust for the other banks the checks received from them until called for by them. The manager then makes a supplemental adjustment between the other banks, without recalling the checks already issued by him upon the responding banks. He charges back to them the checks brought by them against the defaulting bank, and credits back to them, 1st, the checks brought against them by the defaulting bank, and, 2d, the amount of the manager's checks issued to them upon the defaulting bank. He then issues supplemental manager's checks for the settlement of the balances which result from these debits and credits. The defaulting bank ceases to be a member of the Association, and can only be readmitted by a three-fourths' vote of the Association as in the case of new members. Each member of the Association is required to keep on hand in coin, United States legal-tender and National bank notes and sight exchange on New York, twenty-five per cent. of its net liabilities subject to check as they appear each morning after the exchanges, and twenty per cent. of such liabilities in coin, legal tenders, and National bank notes. Every member of the Association is required to furnish to the Association every Saturday morning a report of its average condition for the week ending Friday morning, showing, 1st, specie (coin); 2d, United States legal tenders and National bank notes; 3d, cash items; 4th, sight exchange on New York; 5th, foreign exchange; 6th, due from distant banks and bankers; 7th, loans and discounts; 8th, other cash assets; 9th, circulation; 10th, deposits (net, after exchanges); 11th, due distant banks and bankers, subject to check; 12th, other liabilities to banks and bankers; 13th, other cash liabilities. Members are required to pay an admission fee, and the expenses (except printing, which is shared equally) are apportioned according to the average amount of the clearings. No exchanges are made with members before a-quarter to ten o'clock, A. M., except through the Clearing-house. The exchanges are delivered at the Clearing-house in sealed envelopes. The clerks, as well as the manager, must give bonds with sufficient sureties. Minute rules prescribe the manner in which bundles of currency must be assorted, wrapped up and sealed for greater security when designed to be used in paying balances.

At Cincinnati the routine is substantially the same as at St. Louis, the former having served as the model for the St. Louis, Louisville and Columbus Clearing-houses. At all of these, except St. Louis (as formerly at this, also), the official statements of clearings and balances represent (or lately did) the total of both sides of the Clearing-house proof, and must be divided by two to get the true clearings. The same was formerly the case at Kansas City, Milwaukee and St. Joseph. The hour for making the exchanges at Cincinnati is two o'clock P. M. At half-past two the manager, in settlement of balances, issues his checks or warrants upon the debtor members to the creditor members, which must be promptly paid to the satisfaction of the latter. If payment is not made before four o'clock on the same day the Clearing-house must be notified immediately, otherwise the other members are free from responsibility on such checks. In case of default the other members must make up the deficiency in proportion to the checks they have cleared on the defaulting member on that day, and the latter is required to return the checks it has received unmutilated, and in case it refuses or cancels such checks, the same are treated as if returned.

At Pittsburgh the hour for clearing is nine o'clock A. M., and the average time occupied is twelve minutes. The checks to be exchanged are put up in large, unsealed envelopes. The debtor banks pay their balances in cash, inclosed in sealed envelopes, between 10½ and 11 o'clock A. M., and the creditor banks receive them between 11 and 11½ o'clock A. M., a receipt being given in each case. All checks sent to the Clearing-house are marked with the stamp of the bank sending them. The manager compiles periodical statements showing the condition of the associated banks and of the banks which clear through them.

At Providence, where there is no regularly organized Clearing-house, nineteen banks clear through the Merchants' National Bank, and fifteen through the National Bank of North America. The routine, as stated by Mr. John W. Vernon, Cashier of the Merchants' National Bank, is as follows: Each bank, instead of assorting the checks and other clearing matter it holds, and depositing the packages made up against every other bank, deposits its exchange in bulk with its clearing bank, and the latter assorts the checks and notes, making up new packages against each bank. When the two clearing banks have finished assorting the checks and other items and making up the packages, they exchange with each other, settling the balance in New York or Boston funds. The time required for assorting and exchanging the checks and notes is such that, although the exchange is to be deposited at 10½ o'clock A. M., the clearing banks are not ready to settle balances until about one o'clock. Between one o'clock and three P. M. the clearing banks pay the creditor banks, and are paid by the debtor banks in cashiers' checks on New York or Boston banks, at the option of the payee. The banks clearing through the National Bank of North America stamp all the checks deposited by them with a circle containing the clearing number of the bank. Each bank clearing through the Merchants' National Bank stamps the checks it deposits with a triangle containing its clearing number. National bank notes as well as checks are included in the exchanges.

At Milwaukee the hour for clearing is 10½ o'clock A. M. The various stages of the work occupy about an hour. Debtor banks pay their balances to the Clearing-house at two o'clock P. M., either in lawful money, National bank notes, or such Clearing-house certificates as may be agreed on from time to time. At 2¼ o'clock P. M. the creditor banks receive their balances. In case a bank defaults in the payment of its balances the other banks are to make up the deficiency on the manager's requisition in proportion to their balances against the defaulting member, and until the settlement is completed the exchange is in trust only, and the vouchers remain the property of the members presenting them and are to be returned if required. Checks not good are to be returned before 12½ o'clock to the member sending the same, which is to reimburse the holder by one o'clock. The expenses (about $850) are borne by assessment to be fixed by the Clearing-house committee, and to be paid quarterly in advance. The members are required to keep uniform hours, and are not allowed to receive on deposit checks upon any banks or bankers in Milwaukee which are not members, unless such banks or bankers clear through some member. The banks stamp checks sent to the clearing-house. Any member may be subjected to examination, or required to furnish security, upon representation that its capital is seriously impaired.

At Kansas City the hour for clearing is 12.30 o'clock P. M., and the manager's certificates are issued in settlement of balances as soon as the proof is made. They are, in form, identical with that used at St. Louis, except that recourse may be had on the other members up to 2½ instead of 2 P. M. The Constitution is almost word for word identical with that of St. Louis, and checks cleared are stamped in the same manner. The hours of the members are to be uniform, as regulated by unanimous vote. Proper matter for clearing, according to the by-laws, consists of checks, drafts, certificates of deposit, demand or matured, and any other matter specially agreed upon, and any bank clearing paper not proper is subject to a fine. The manager makes monthly or quarterly statements, showing the clearings and balances of each member for the month or quarter, the amount of fines imposed upon each member, and the causes thereof. Only National and State banks having a capital of $50,000 or more are eligible as members.

The Louisville Clearing-house is modeled mainly after that of Cincinnati. Checks only are cleared; balances are settled by manager's check, which must be collected on the same day, or the holder loses recourse.

The Detroit Clearing-house is conducted on principles similar to those of the Chicago Association. The clerks, as well as the manager, furnish bonds with sufficient sureties. The hour for clearing is 12.15 o'clock P. M. A fine of one dollar per minute is imposed for tardiness, and the clearings are in no case delayed more than five minutes by the absence of a member. Fifteen minutes are allowed for the proof, but the average time occupied is only ten minutes. Fines are doubled in thirty minutes, and quadrupled in one hour. The debtor members pay their balances to the manager between 1 and 1.30 P. M. in coin, legal tenders, National bank notes, Clearing-house certificates provided for by the rules of the Association, or New York exchange. At last accounts the practice, since the Association was formed, has been to pay balances in New York exchange only. At 1.30 P. M. the creditor banks receive their balances. The exchange is in trust, and vouchers remain the property of the member presenting them until balances are paid, and in case of default must be returned to the Clearing-house unmutilated by 1.30 P. M. The defaulting bank is also entitled to receive back the vouchers it has presented, and the exchanges with it are cancelled. If the New York exchange given in settlement of balances is dishonored, the deficiency is assessed upon the banks having debit balances against the defaulting member in proportion to such balances. To provide for expenses the members each pay $50, and an equal share to the cost of printing. All beyond this is provided by an assessment on the banks in proportion to their exchanges sent to the Clearing-house. The paper cleared consists of checks, drafts and certified paper. Some of the members affix some distinguishing mark to paper cleared, but this is not required by the rules of the Association.

At Cleveland the clearings are made at one o'clock P. M. Balances of more than $1,000 are settled by New York exchange. When balances are under $1,000, a balance check is given which is put through the clearings of the next day. Consequently, no cash is handled in paying balances. Checks cleared are marked with a Clearing-house stamp.

At St. Paul the regulations are modeled after those at Chicago and Milwaukee. The clearings are made at 10.30 o'clock, A. M., and the average time occupied is seven minutes. Checks only are cleared. A clerk of the First National Bank of St Paul, where the clearings take place, acts as manager. The "paid" stamp of the sending bank is the only distinguishing mark affixed to checks passing through the Clearing-house. Balances are payable in coin, National bank notes, legal tenders, and gold or silver certificates. No silver dollars are ever offered by mutual understanding.

At Indianapolis the manager receives at the room of the Association from members, between 12 o'clock noon and 12¼ P. M., the checks, drafts and notes to be exchanged, and immediately afterwards collects from or pays to each bank at its place of business the balances resulting from such exchange. No member is allowed to receive in payment a check on any Indianapolis bank not a member, and no paper payable at any bank not a member is allowed to pass through the Clearing-house. All checks received by members after one o'clock must be certified. All paper cleared must bear the endorsement of the sending bank, either in writing or by stamp, as an acknowledgment of payment and not as a guarantee, except as to the genuineness of other endorsements. The maker of a check dishonored for want of funds is discredited, the members are all notified, and no uncertified check of such a person is allowed to pass through the Clearing-house until his credit is restored by vote of the Association. All notes and acceptances must be certified before passing through the Clearing-house. The manager takes up the checks delivered to and by any defaulting member, and returns them. Expenses, except as provided for by fines, are paid by the banks in proportion to their capital and deposits. The manager is to be a notary and has the privilege of protesting such paper as the members have for protest, his fees being his only compensation.

At Hartford the business of clearing is done by the members in turn, each for one month at a time, some officer of the clearing bank being manager. The hour for clearing is 10 o'clock and 5 minutes, and the time occupied averages fifteen minutes. The debtor banks pay their balances to the Clearing-house at or before 11½, A. M., in checks on New York, except balances of less than $100, which may be paid in currency. The creditor banks receive their balances at 12 M. The matter cleared includes notes, drafts and checks, also bank notes of the members to a very limited extent. All paper cleared must bear the written or stamped endorsement of the bank sending it. In case of default the other banks make up the deficiency as at New York and Boston. All checks not good must be returned to the sending bank by 12 o'clock noon.

At Minneapolis the clearings occur at eleven o'clock A. M. The constitution is not printed, but the routine appears to be in general similar to that at New York.

At New Haven, as at Hartford, the banks take turns, each bank acting as the Clearing-house for three months. The exchanges are made at 9.15 A. M., and include checks, acceptances, notes certified the day before, and in fact everything in the form of an order on any member. Balances are to be paid by noon in drafts on New York.

At Memphis the exchanges occur at nine o'clock A. M., and the time consumed by the manager in the adjustment of balances is about thirty minutes. In settlement of balances the manager draws his check on the debtor in favor of the creditor members in the following form :

MEMPHIS CLEARING-HOUSE,
MEMPHIS, TENN..............1884.
...................BANK.
Pay to G. in settlement of balances this morning Six thousand five hundred and fifty $\frac{25}{100}$ dollars.

$ 6,550$\frac{25}{100}$.   ....Adjuster.

Instead of writing the name of the payee in full, the initial letter or letters simply are used. The amount of checks brought by each bank is entered on a credit slip, and the amount taken away on a debit slip. This latter also contains additional rulings to show the balance due to or from the bank, and against the initials of each bank is written the amount of checks drawn upon it or in its favor to settle this balance. Balances must be settled in current funds. Checks only are cleared, and they are delivered in sealed envelopes designated on the outside as follows .

MEMPHIS CLEARING-HOUSE,
July 1, 1884.
U. $10,000 from Commerce.

That is Union and Planters' Bank $10,000, from the Bank of Commerce.

At Peoria the clearings are made at 11.30 o'clock A. M., and occupy about half an hour. The clearing matter consists of checks. Members are to report upon balances resulting from the exchanges before one o'clock, after which hour the balance becomes the debt of the bank. Balances must be paid by the debtor banks at the counters of the creditor banks before three o'clock, in currency, unless arrangements have been made before that hour for payment in exchange on other points. Checks not good must be returned before 1.30 P. M.

At Portland the six National banks, without being formally organized as a Clearing-house, settle daily at ten o'clock A. M. The time occupied is about fifteen minutes. Portland checks only are included in the clearing. Balances are paid in legal-tender notes, or checks on Boston or New York.

The Worcester and Lowell Clearing-houses are organized on the same plan. Each bank belonging to the Association is required to make a deposit fixed by vote of the Association with the Clearing-house Committee as its proportion of a clearing fund. This fund is deposited with one of the banks selected as the clearing bank, free of interest, as a compensation for services and expenses. The clearing bank is changed each year at Lowell. The cashier of the clearing bank is, *ex officio*, the manager of the Clearing-house. No bank is allowed to make the clearings of a bank that is not a member. At Worcester the hour for making the exchanges is 12 o'clock noon, and the time occupied is about fifteen minutes. At Lowell the hour of clearing is eleven o'clock, and the time occupied is from seven to ten minutes. The clearing matter of both consists of checks, drafts and notes. At Worcester paper cleared is marked as follows: "Pay only through Worcester Clearing-house to........." At Lowell no distinguishing mark is affixed. At the latter balances are paid by drafts on New York or Boston; at Worcester by checks on Boston.

At Springfield the exchanges occur at eleven o'clock at the Chicopee National Bank, and occupy about twenty minutes. One clerk for each bank performs the duties of messenger and settling clerk. All kinds of paper are cleared, each item being stamped with the stamp of the sending bank. Balances of less than $200 are paid in currency; if more than that by New York or Boston drafts.

At Columbus, Ohio, the representatives of the banks clear at the Board of Trade Rooms in City Hall at two o'clock P. M. The exchanges occupy ten minutes, the adjustments twenty. Clearing matter consists of checks to which no distinguishing mark is affixed. Balances are paid by manager's checks on the debtor banks.

At Norfolk the banks select one of their number to be the Clearing-bank for one year, and the cashier of that bank is *ex officio* manager of the Clearing-house. The hour for making the exchanges is eleven o'clock precisely. At 12½ o'clock the debtor banks pay their balances at the Clearing-house in currency, and the creditor banks receive their balances at one o'clock. Checks not good must be returned by 12 M. to the bank sending them, and must be satisfied by 2.30 P. M. All checks presented in payment of notes and drafts (except when presented by the runner) must be certified by the bank on which they are drawn. Although the rules require the payment of balances in currency they are, as a matter of accommodation between the banks when exchange is plentiful, often paid by checks on New York, Philadelphia, or Baltimore.

At Syracuse the exchanges take place at 10.20 A. M., and occupy five minutes, the paper cleared being checks, certified notes and accepted drafts. No distinguishing mark is affixed to paper cleared. Balances are paid as convenient within two hours following the clearing in drafts on New York.

Notwithstanding the space given to the foregoing particulars in relation to the various Clearing-houses in the United States, many matters of interest have been necessarily omitted, while others of importance, familiar to those connected with Clearing-house business, may have been overlooked. In the collection of such a variety of data from so many different sources, errors, both of omission and commission, are liable to occur. Enough has, however, been brought together to furnish material for suggestive comparisons as to the methods in use at the various Clearing-houses. When all the Clearing-houses, however unimportant their operations may seem, shall preserve full and accurate records of their business in its various details, such comparisons will shed increased light upon the movements of our internal commerce, and, still better, repay careful study.

CHAPTER XII.

FOREIGN CLEARING-HOUSES.

Of foreign Clearing-houses, by far the most important is that of London, embracing twenty-seven banks, including the Bank of England, which only became a member about twenty years ago, and clears only on one side, that is, its charges on other banks. These, being obliged as members of the Clearing-house to keep an account with the Bank of England, pay in their charges against it to the credit of their account. A considerable number of London banks in high credit have so far been refused the privilege of membership in the Clearing-house. Indeed so exclusive was it formerly that until 1854 the joint-stock banks were refused admission. The West End and Scotch banks and others not yet admitted, clear through members.

The number of daily clearings at London is three, as follows:

Ordinary Days.

"Morning clearing to open at 10.30. Drafts, &c., to be received not later than 11. Morning clearing must be closed by 12.

"Country clearing to open at 12. Drafts, including returns, to be received not later than 12.30. Country clearing must be closed by 2.15.

"Afternoon clearing to open at 2.30. Drafts, &c., to be received not later than 4. Returns to be received not later than 5, excepting on settling days, when the last delivery shall be at 4.15, and returns at 5.15."

Fourths of the Month.

"Morning clearing to open at 9. Drafts, &c., to be received not later than 10. Morning clearing must be closed by 12."

Country clearing takes place as on ordinary days, and afternoon clearing as on settling days, except when the fourth of the month occurs on Saturday, in which case the hours are as on ordinary days.

Saturdays (not being Fourths).

"Morning clearing to open at 9. Drafts, &c., to be received not later than 10. Morning clearing must be closed by 11.

"Country clearing to open at 11. Drafts, including returns to be received not later than 11.30. Country clearing must be closed by 1.15.

"Afternoon clearing to open at 1.30. Drafts, &c., to be received not later than 3. Returns to be received not later than 4."

In explanation of certain terms used at the London Clearing-house it may be stated that an "article" is a bill, "or check or dividend warrant, or banker's payment slip, or memorandum for country notes, or indeed any article that is paid into the clearing for settlement there."

"A 'charge' is a batch of *articles* (*i. e.*, bills, checks, bankers' payments, &c.) sent into the Clearing-house by one banker to be *charged* by him against another.

"'Returns' are any *articles* which may be returned into the Clearing-house unpaid, from want of funds, irregularity of endorsement, no advice, or from any other cause."

The officer having charge of the clearing is called an inspector, and not a manager, as in this country. The London Clearing-house has two inspectors. Instead of blanks, such as are used at American Clearing-houses, books are used. The checks and bills to be presented by any one clearing banker upon any other are entered at home in the "Out-clearing book." There is also the "In-clearing book," in which are entered the amounts of the checks received in the exchange; the Out returns, the In returns, the Clearing Balance Book, the Clearing Difference Book, &c.

The London Clearing-house is a plain oblong room with rows of desks in compartments round three sides and down the middle. A small office for the two inspectors stands at one end. Each bank sends as many clerks to the house as may be requisite for the rapid completion of the work, some of the banks having as many as six clerks. The mode of conducting the business, as described in the last edition of *Gilbart on Banking*, is substantially as follows:

The matter cleared at the morning clearing consists, as a rule, of bills and marked checks. These bills are bills which have been discounted by the bank or held for collection on account of customers. During the afternoon of the day before they fall due, they are passed from the bill department into the clearing department, so as to let the clearing clerks get an early start next morning. On the morning of the day on which they mature, the clearing clerks sort them into various packages, one for each of the other twenty-five (or if the Bank of England twenty-six) clearing banks. Thus those which fall due at the London and Westminster Bank are sorted into one parcel, and the same in other cases. The amounts only are then entered in the spaces left under the respective headings of the other banks in the Morning Bill Book. The clearing clerks then sum up the entries in this book, and check the aggregate of the various totals with the sum supplied to them on a memorandum by the bill department of the bank.

If right, their clearing work is checked so far, and they then transfer the various totals into the Out-clearing Book. Having done this they next proceed to deal with the "marked checks." These are checks which have been paid in by customers on the afternoon of the day before, too late for the day's clearing. Every afternoon each bank sends these checks out to the other banks upon which they are drawn to be marked for payment. This marking consists of the initials of one of the cashiers put upon the checks as an acknowledgment that they are all right and will be duly paid in the clearing next morning. The banks send out these checks to be marked chiefly for the convenience of their customers, but partly for their own protection in case a cashier might pay against an uncleared check which might afterwards prove to be bad. If a banker chose not to send out such checks for marking, no question could be raised by his customer as to want of due presentation, because it is distinctly stated on the pay-in slips with which each customer is supplied, or the customer is acquainted in some other form, that checks not paid in by half-past three may not be cleared the same day. These marked checks are sent to the Clearing-house the first thing in the morning along with the bills, and the two together form what is termed the "first charge." Some of the banks try, and some manage, to get the remittances received in their morning letters into their first charge; but as the morning clearing closes for delivery at eleven o'clock, none but those bankers who begin business very early can put through so large an amount of work with any degree of satisfaction in time for the morning clearing.

Although the afternoon town clearing nominally begins at 2.30 P. M., and closes for delivery at 4 P. M., the Clearing-house clock is always kept five minutes behind Greenwich time, so that the representatives of the various banks have always five minutes grace allowed them.

To the afternoon clearing, which is the heaviest in the day, the banks, as a rule, send in some six or seven "charges." But, in exceptional times, for instance, during the progress of dividend payments, or when, from any cause, business is particularly brisk, many more charges are sent in. But in ordinary times about half-a-dozen is the usual number. At the opening of the afternoon clearing the first charge delivered is usually composed of remittances received in the morning letters. Then about three o'clock the second charge is sent in, and is composed of the checks and other vouchers received over the counter during the morning by the cashiers for the credit of customers. Then, about every twenty minutes or so, from three o'clock till four, charges of the same description are sent in. At two or three minutes past four (by the bank clock) a final charge, consisting of a few articles of large amount, or articles which, for some reason, the banker may be particularly anxious to clear, may be sent in. There is thus a clerk running between each bank and the Clearing-house from time to time, delivering the charges he has upon the other banks.

The first charge sent to the Clearing-house during the day is marked on the back of the last check thereof, with the total amount which in our Clearing-houses is entered on the exchange slip attached to the checks.

Country notes are not exchanged at the Clearing-house, but are taken round to the bankers who are agents for the country bankers, and exchanged for tickets, which are passed through the afternoon clearing.

As the clerks reach the Clearing-house with their successive charges they distribute their packages around the room to the desks of the clerks representing the several paying banks. These clerks, corresponding to our settling clerks, immediately begin to enter these charges in the In-clearing Books, in columns bearing at the head the name of the presenting bank. As soon as this is done the vouchers are immediately sent away to the bank at which they are payable, where they are critically examined and, if correct, posted in the ledgers. In case there is cause for refusing payment, either for want of funds, irregular endorsement, or irregularity of any kind, they are sent back to the clearing and returned to the delivering banker with a distinct answer marked upon each check of the cause of the return. These returns must be sent back to the Clearing-house not later than 5 P. M. on ordinary days, and not later than 5.15 in any event, and are entered again as a reverse claim by the bank dishonoring them on the bank presenting them. The clearing clerks do not wait for the returns before they begin the balancing for the day. The moment the Clearing-house clock strikes four (five minutes past by Greenwich time) they begin the process of balancing, leaving the returns, if any, to be entered afterwards. Notwithstanding the vast daily transactions of the London Clearing-house, the aptitude of the clerks for their particular work renders errors of infrequent occurrence. The system of marking the first and largest charge on the back facilitates the balancing by the opportunity it gives to each clerk of checking the major part of his work early in the day.

The In-clearing Book of each clerk ought to agree, of course, with the portions relating to him of the Out-clearing Books of the other clerks. The Out-clearing Book, it will be remembered, is written up *inside* the bank, and carried to the Clearing-house at four o'clock for the purpose of checking. Each clerk compares his work with that of the other clerks, one by one. If he is right with all he then balances, and there is no further trouble; but if he is wrong with any, to any large amount, he is bound to discover his error before leaving the house. The total amount of the morning and country delivery must be agreed by each before leaving the Clearing-house. As to the other clearing, a difference of £1,500 over (the in-clearing clerk being always supposed right), or of less than £1,000 short, is allowed to stand over until the following day if it cannot be readily discovered. Considerable confusion sometimes arises from shouting corrections across the room from one clerk to another.

The country clearing was introduced by Sir John Lubbock in 1858. Every bank in London receives during the day a large number of checks upon country bankers. Upon these checks the name of the London agent is printed. Every clearing banker in London is the agent for one or more country banks. Thus the London and Westminster Bank is the London agent for the North and South Wales Bank, the Nottingham and Notts Bank, and Hall, Lloyd & Co. On the checks drawn on these country banks the name of the London & Westminster Bank is printed as their respective agents. So when the clearing clerks of each bank get such checks from the cashiers, correspondence department, and other sources, they proceed to arrange them for clearing as they do town checks, sorting them and putting them up in packages according to the London agents at which they are payable. No credit is given in the clearing for these country checks on the day on which they are delivered. The amounts are simply settled by the delivering clerks and the receiving clerks, and then the articles are taken to the respective banks, whence they are sent by post the same evening to the country bankers by whom they are payable. If these checks, on reaching their destination, are found to be in order, they are credited in account with the London agent, and advised; but if any of them are not in order, either from insufficient funds or irregular endorsement, or any other cause, such irregular checks are returned direct to the banker whose crossing they bear. All country checks not returned or advised by the morning of the third day are assumed to be paid, and credit is accordingly given for them in the clearing of that day and the amount is settled for, along with those advised paid, in the final balance. All country checks held by London bankers, returned unpaid, must be returned into the hands of the clerk representing the delivering bank by half-past twelve on the third day, and they are simply deducted from the total of the country checks on the day of settlement. The balance only of the country clearing is brought into the final settlement on each bank's town clearing balance sheet, as will be seen by reference to the form given below. "C. H." on the same form means Clearing-house, and is meant for the adjustment of differences, and " Bank " means Bank of England.

Specimen Form of a London Bankers' Clearing Balance Sheet.
The National Provincial Bank of England.

Debtors.   *Creditors.*

£	s.	d.		£	s.	d.
			Alliance................			
			Barclay.................			
			Barnett.................			
			Bosanquet..............			
			Brown..................			
			Central.................			
			City....................			
			Consolidated...........			
			County.................			
			Dimsdale...............			
			Fuller..................			
			Glyn....................			
			Imperial................			
			Joint...................			
			Bank....................			
			London & South Western			
			London & Westminster..			
			Martin..................			
			Metropolitan............			
			National................			
			Prescott................			
			Robarts.................			
			Southwark *............			
			Smith...................			
			Union...................			
			Williams................			
			Country Clearing........			
			C. H....................			

This sheet when filled up shows the account of the National Provincial Bank of England with all the other clearing banks, their names being abridged to save space. It nearly corresponds with the settling clerk's statement in the New York Clearing-house, the name of the bank whose accounts it represents being given at the head and omitted in the body of the statement.

Balances are settled at the close of each day by transfers on the books of the Bank of England, at which a special account is kept, called the "Clearing Bankers' Account," in addition to the separate account of each bank. When the result of the day's clearing is a balance against one of the banks, Barclay & Co., for example, the transfer is made in the following form:

Settlement at the Clearing-House.

LONDON, *July* 1, 1884.

To the CASHIERS OF THE BANK OF ENGLAND :

    Be pleased to transfer from our account the sum of Fifty-one thousand two hundred and one pounds 4s. 2d., and place it to the credit of the account of the Clearing Bankers, and allow it to be drawn for by any of them (with the knowledge of either of the Inspectors, signified by his countersigning the drafts).

£51,201 4s. 2d.   BARCLAY & CO.

---

* This is the Southwark branch of the London & Westminster Bank which clears separately.

For which the Bank signs the following certificate:

SETTLEMENT AT THE CLEARING-HOUSE.

BANK OF ENGLAND: *July* 1, 1884.
A transfer for the sum of Fifty-one thousand two hundred and one pounds 4s. 2d., has this evening been made at the Bank from the account of Messrs. Barclay & Co. to the account of the Clearing Bankers.

£ 51,201 4s. 2d.   FOR THE BANK OF ENGLAND.
This certificate has been seen by me,
                                                                        ....*Inspector.*

On the other hand, when the balance is in favor of the bank, the National Provincial, for instance, the following forms are used:

SETTLEMENT AT THE CLEARING-HOUSE.

                                                                LONDON, *July* 1, 1884.
To the CASHIERS OF THE BANK OF ENGLAND:
Be pleased to credit our account the sum of Two hundred and thirty-six thousand and forty-four pounds 2s. 2d. out of the money at the credit of the account of the Clearing Bankers.   FOR THE NATIONAL PROVINCIAL BANK OF ENGLAND.

£ 236,044 2s. 2d.   A. B.
     Seen by me, ...
            Inspector at the Clearing-house.

For which the bank gives the following certificate:

SETTLEMENT AT THE CLEARING-HOUSE.

BANK OF ENGLAND: LONDON, *July* 1, 1884.
The account of the National Provincial Bank of England has this evening been credited with the sum of Two hundred and thirty-six thousand and forty-four pounds 2s. 2d. out of the money at the credit of the account of the Clearing Bankers.   FOR THE BANK OF ENGLAND.

£ 236,044 2s. 2d.

As the balances paid and the balances received are the same (errors excepted), so the amount credited to the clearing bankers' account each day must be the same as the amount debited. It is only a means by which the debtor banks pay the creditor banks on each day by a simple transfer, without handling any cash. Previous to 1854 balances were paid in cash. The per cent. of balances to clearings is considerably greater at London than at New York, and has shown a marked increase. In 1810 the balances were 4.68 per cent. of the clearings; in 1839, 6.94 per cent., and in 1879–80, 12.16 per cent., as compared with 4.96 per cent. at New York in 1879. The balances are probably greater on account of the country clearings.

By having three clearings instead of one, and allowing banks to bring so many successive charges at intervals to each clearing, instead of one charge delivered precisely at a given hour, the Clearing-house work occupies very much more time than at New York, where the transactions are considerably larger. In fact, substantially, the whole day is spent by the clearing clerks at the Clearing-house, or in going to and from it, whereas at New York an hour, or less, for each clerk and messenger suffices for the whole work. On the other hand, by having so many clearings, and the heaviest at the close of the day, mercantile paper sent through the clearing is more promptly presented.

The Manchester Clearing-house was established in 1872, and has, since that date, been under charge of Mr. D. T. Brewer, as inspector. The work there is performed on loose forms, and not in account books, as at London. The work is done more nearly on the plan prevailing at New York, which is, in several respects, an improvement on that prevailing at London. There are two clearings daily at the Branch of the Bank of England, the first at 11.15 A. M. (a preliminary one), and the second at 2.15 P. M. The clearing is quickly accomplished, and "goes on with noiseless ease, strongly contrasting with the turmoil of the London house." This is, of course, owing in part to the immensely larger transactions effected at the latter. At Manchester each of the twelve clearing bankers is represented by a single clerk, who delivers and receives the vouchers and adjusts the accounts. The balances for the day are settled after the close of the second clearing by transfers on the books of the Bank of England, the forms being very similar to those used at London. The Clearing-house at Newcastle-on-Tyne was established January 2, 1872, and embraces seven members. On ordinary days there are three clearings daily, usually at 11.15 A. M., 2.15 and 3.15 P. M. On January 1st there is one at 10.30 A. M. On Saturdays and holidays there are two clearings, usually at 11.15 A. M. and 1.15 P. M. Articles dishonored are returned through the Clearing-house on the same day, not later than forty-five minutes after the commencement of the last clearing. The methods of doing the business and paying balances are similar to those in use at Manchester. The total of its transactions in twelve years has been £332,470,125, as compared with £1,043,360,000 at Manchester. The operations of the Newcastle Clearing-house are conducted at the Branch of the Bank of England, under charge of a committee, of which the agent of the bank—at present Mr. J. B. Fairley—is chairman.

There are also Clearing-houses at Liverpool, Edinburgh and Dublin. At Edinburgh there is one general clearing daily, opened at one and closed for delivery at fifteen minutes past one P. M., except on Saturday, when it opens at eleven and closes at fifteen minutes past. The Bank of Scotland and the Royal Bank of Scotland undertake the settlement each alternate month. There is also a note exchange daily at 10 A. M., except on Monday, and a second exchange at 1.30 P. M. on Saturday for large notes only. On Monday and Thursday the balances are included in the general settlement of the exchange and clearing. On other days the settling bank receives from the debtors and · gives to the creditors exchange vouchers for the respective balances within one hour after the closing of the Clearing-house, and these vouchers are brought into the next clearing, and bear interest, included in them, at two per cent. until that clearing. Each document cleared, except notes, is to bear a Clearing-house stamp, containing the name of the clearing bank and the date, also the stamp of any district branch at which it may have been cashed. Documents dishonored are settled between the banks, unless drawn on a branch, in which case they may be sent through the clearing the next day. These banks use clearing books having every alternate sheet perforated down the inside margin. The charges against the other banks are written up in pencil on the unperforated sheets, and by the aid of a sheet of carbonized paper placed underneath, an impression of the items is taken on the perforated sheets. These duplicates are then torn out and handed over with the corresponding articles to the clerks of the other banks, who simply compare the one with the other, so as to save the time and trouble of taking down afresh in their own books the amounts of the various articles. When the clerks return to their respective banks, these duplicates are gummed upon the margins from which their own delivering sheets had been detached, preserving a convenient record of the articles delivered to, and the articles received from, each bank following each other. All abstracts of totals, balances and the like, are kept in a permanent form, written in ink. The paid-up capital of the Edinburgh clearing banks is £8,250,000.

The Dublin Clearing-house comprises four banks—all the banks of issue in Ireland—and was established in 1845. The capital of the four banks is £5,040,000. There are two clearings—in the forenoon, for notes and checks at 10 o'clock; afternoon, final clearing for checks at two o'clock. On Saturdays the hours are 9.30 A. M. and 12 M. Banks are admitted to the exchange for fifteen minutes after these hours. Balances are paid in Exchequer bonds, except for fractional parts of £500, which may be paid in notes of the debtor bank, the Exchequer bonds to be used for no other purpose, and to be stamped "Dublin Exchanges." Each bank is required to maintain its quota of a total of £400,000 of these bonds. The exchanges are made at the Bank of Ireland. All orders payable on demand, whether in Dublin or in country towns, are to be passed through the Clearing-house. Documents returned dishonored are not allowed to pass through the Clearing-house. Those banks in Dublin which are not banks of issue are not members of the Association, but deposit the checks they hold on other banks with the Bank of Ireland, with which they keep an account.

In preparing the foregoing account of British Clearing-houses free use has been made of *Gilbart on Banking* and Jevons' *Money and* the *Mechanism of Exchange*, and of a series of articles recently published in the London *Banker's Magazine* on the Clearing-house system.

The Liverpool Clearing Association was formed, according to United States Consul S. B. Packard, about 1878, and embraced, in 1882, ten of the Liverpool banks, leaving six establishments, mostly private banks, outside. These banks keep clearing accounts with each other of all checks drawn on any of their number. Each bank every evening makes up in its own books the accounts with each of the other clearing banks, and settles the balances due from or to it by means of transfers through the Bank of England's Liverpool branch, with which all the clearing banks keep an account. The capital of the Liverpool clearing banks, exclusive of two private banks, was, in 1882, £3,815,110.

Clearing-houses were established at Paris and Vienna in 1872. At the latter, in fact, there are two Clearing-houses, the Bankers' Clearing-house, and the Arrangement Bureau, or Stock Exchange Clearing-house. The latter alone has transactions of any great magnitude. The volume of the check exchange is small, as most of the public find bank notes cheaper and more convenient than checks, which are subject to a tax of two kreutzers (about 1 cent) each, regardless of size. The Paris Clearing-house has been already noticed. In 1876 a system of check exchange was started in Berlin, and developed to such proportions that in 1883 Clearing-houses were established in Berlin (April 2d), Frankfort-on-the-Main (April 25), and Cologne, Stuttgart, Leipsic, Dresden, and lastly Hamburg, in the course of the summer. The President of the Imperial Bank Directorium states that these institutions are not widely different from the Clearing-houses of London and New York. The most important of the German Clearing-houses are those of Berlin, Hamburg, and Frankfort-on-the-Main, the others falling far behind these. Previous to last December the volume of transactions at these Clearing-houses was not published. For December the aggregate for all was 887,546,700 marks, and in January, 1884, 930,707,700 marks, or at the rate of 11,168,492,400 marks—or about $2,680,000,000—for the year. This is a little more than Chicago, and a little less than Philadelphia. There are fourteen Clearing-houses in Italy, located at Milan, Leghorn, Genoa, Catania, Rome, Bologna, and other places. The transactions of these six Clearing-houses amounted, in 1884, to 1,685,345,781 f., or about $325,000,000, those of Milan and Leghorn being the only ones of importance.

The Banks' Clearing-house of Melbourne, Australia, is analogous to the other British Clearing-houses. On ordinary days there are six clearings; on Saturdays four; on Mondays eight; on Tuesdays five. An exchange slip accompanies each charge delivered at the Clearing-house. There is a special clearing for checks returned dishonored for any cause. Balances are paid every Tuesday, all even sums of £500 and upwards in sovereigns or parchment vouchers. These vouchers are issued against a deposit of sovereigns at one of the banks under the care of trustees, and are of denominations of £500 and £1,000. The total issue is £500,000. All sums under £500 are settled by checks, which are paid into a Clearing-house account kept at one of the banks. Bank notes have been included in the clearing since 1876.

CHAPTER XIII.

COUNTRY CLEARINGS.

At London, as already stated, the country Clearing-house has been in operation since 1858. But in this country clearing methods have hitherto been applied only to transactions among banks situated in the same place or its immediate vicinity, though susceptible of extension to transactions between different monetary centers and possibly even to international settlements. The establishment of some system for the more speedy and economical collection of country checks is a matter of growing importance owing to changes in the methods of doing business. Mr. C. B. Patten, Cashier of the State National Bank of Boston, furnishes some interesting facts in this connection in reference to New England, which doubtless hold good elsewhere. Formerly under the State bank system it was the almost universal custom for merchants in the interior to pay their bills in Boston by sending the money or a check on a Boston bank which they obtained from their nearest country bank, paying for the same the usual charge for exchange. But in later years a different practice has been growing up. The country trader now sends his Boston creditor a check upon the country bank where he keeps his account. The country banks, of course, expect to pay these at par at their own counters, but they will not as a rule provide funds to meet them in Boston without a charge for exchange, varying from one-tenth of one per cent. on the larger checks to one-quarter or even one-half of one per cent. on the smaller ones. So keen is the competition among traders, however, that these checks are taken by them at par, and the banks driven also by competition usually do likewise. To avoid the charges made by the country banks, checks are frequently sent home by the most circuitous routes, travelling about from city to city and from bank to bank for several days. An instance is given where a check for $48 on a bank in Mt. Gilead, Ohio, deposited at Columbus, was sent successively to Cincinnati, Cleveland, Urichsville, Coshocton, Newark, back to Columbus, and then to Cardington, before reaching its destination, being out eight days and traveling 650 miles when sixty miles would have sufficed. As the check was not paid it had to be sent back through the same channels. Another case has been given of an item returned protested nineteen days after it started for presentation toward a paying bank twenty hours distant. It is easy to see how by these delays endorsers may be discharged to the serious loss of some holder of the check, not to mention other contingencies. It would be difficult to show that due diligence was used in presenting a check by such a circuitous route. It is said, too, that these cases are by no means unusual.

The growing importance of the subject led to the consideration of the remedies to be adopted at the annual meeting of the Boston Clearing-house Association, April 9, 1877. A committee was appointed consisting of Messrs. George Ripley, John Cummings, Edward Sands, Edward L. Tead and Geo. R. Chapman, representing respectively the Hide and Leather, Shawmut, Traders', Exchange and Merchants' National banks. This committee in August made a majority report signed by Messrs. Ripley, Cummings, Sands and Chapman, and minority report signed by Mr. Tead. From the majority report it appears that the daily outstanding balances due to fifty of the fifty-one associated banks on account of New England country collections then amounted to $2,187,329. This had increased in November, 1883, to $4,300,000. The number of checks daily sent out in 1877 was 4,080, probably increased in like proportion, and the number of letters sent daily was 1,670, although there were only 272 towns in New England which had National banks. The amount paid yearly for exchange and expenses was computed to be $119,647, and interest on the outstanding balances at five per cent. reached $109,366, making a total annual cost of $229,013, increased to $398,000 in 1883. The cost of collecting each check was found by the committee to be, for exchange, .045 of a dollar; other expenses, .048; interest, .085, giving a total of .178 of a dollar, or about nine times the United States stamp tax on a check, which was justly complained of by business men and banks alike. The cost for each letter was forty-four cents—eleven cents for exchange, twelve for expenses, and twenty-one for interest. Under the arrangements then and still existing, remittances from country banks vary in frequency from once a week to once a month, in exceptional cases perhaps oftener. It was believed that by a consolidation of the business the amount of the outstanding balances might be reduced one-half by more frequent remittances; that the item of exchange largely made up of charges upon small checks of less than $200 could be very much reduced by having the remittances made in larger sums; and that the sending of 272 letters daily, one for each town having a National bank, would suffice, thereby saving 1,400 of the 1,670 letters daily sent out, and largely reducing the clerical expenses. The danger of loss resulting from delay in presenting checks would also be reduced to a minimum by the introduction of a better system. The majority of the committee reached the following conclusions:

"1st. That the business of making collections throughout New England, as now conducted, is attended with great unnecessary labor, risk and expense.

"2d. That its extent, though now large, will inevitably increase with the growth of our city.

"3d. That the only way materially to reduce the labor, risk and expense connected with it is to consolidate the business."

To this end they recommended the establishment of a National bank to be used as an agency in making such collections, the stock of the bank to be subscribed by members of the Clearing-house Association.

The minority report combats the proposed plan as exposing too much the business of each bank, and as not reducing the expenses as much as the majority anticipated. It was shown that ten banks having the largest foreign bank accounts, made more than one half of all the New England collections at an expense of $5\frac{3}{8}$ cents each, exclusive of interest, and that the superior facilities acquired by these banks after years of experience, could not be transferred to the proposed collection bank, but would be irretrievably lost to themselves by the proposed change. The indirect advantages derived by the banks from their collection business, in enlarged acquaintance and the maintenance of a more lively interest between the Boston banks and those of the country, were deemed a full equivalent for the necessary labor and expense involved.

It was found, on inquiry, that as a National bank cannot subscribe to the stock of another National bank, the proposed plan was not feasible. The steady increase of the business, however, again forced the matter upon the attention of the Association. Another committee was chosen, consisting of Messrs. George Ripley, John Cummings, Charles A. Vialle, A. L. Newman, and Walter S. Blanchard, representing, respectively, the Hide & Leather, Shawmut, Republic, Commonwealth, and Metropolitan National banks. This committee, in November, 1883, reported unanimously in favor of establishing an agency similar to the Clearing-house, which should have no capital and make no charge for its services, but whose expenses should be borne by the banks in proportion to the business done. On account of the expense attending such an organization this plan was defeated. The whole matter remains, therefore, in its previously unsettled condition. Mr. C. B. Patten, Cashier of the State National Bank, has suggested that the banks contract with one of their number to undertake this business for all, as more economical than the proposed Clearing-house for country checks, since an established bank "is already in possession of the 'plant' necessary for the transaction of such business, and could make money out of it, with a charge for exchange which would not support an independent Clearing-house." The unwillingness of the banks to expose their business to one of their number, or to give the collecting bank the advantage it would thus enjoy for obtaining country deposits, is likely to interpose a serious obstacle to the adoption of this plan.

The matter of country collections has also been discussed by the bankers of Pittsburgh and vicinity, where Mr. E. B. Isett, President of the Altoona Bank, submitted a plan for the formation of a Clearing-house among the country banks themselves, at some central point, by which the daily settlements could, it is claimed, be effected with nearly as much celerity for a district reached by one day's mail as in the Clearing-house of a city. Such an institution could but be a source of union and strength to the banks themselves, as well as a great convenience to the business community. It would enable the banks to exert a coercive power over those that refused to take part in the movement by rejecting their checks. These Clearing-houses would furnish an easy means of communication between banks in different parts of the country, and establish on a permanent basis, the system of par redemption for country checks at certain central points. The great difficulty with this plan is to arouse the country banks to a sense of their duty in the matter. Under the present system they enjoy, at the expense of banks at the great centers, all the advantages of par redemption of their checks. It is not just that the city banks alone should bear this expense. The receipt of country checks at par by banks in the great cities is a matter of common interest, not to them alone, but to the country banks and to their customers alike, and all should be required to share the necessary cost.

The commercial unity of the country demands a recognition in all business arrangements. Isolated action on the part of individual banks cannot permanently cope with the problem now before us. Concerted action among the banks at the principal commercial centers is necessary. If all cannot be induced to unite at first, let enough join in some common movement to give it a strength and prestige that shall gradually bring all into the arrangement. Those who are familiar with the history of the Suffolk Bank system for the par redemption of New England bank notes know what bitter opposition that system at first encountered on the part of the country banks. The Suffolk Bank, with the six banks which first inaugurated the movement, was styled in derision the "Holy Alliance," and sometimes the "Six-tailed Bashaw." Yet the system finally triumphed over all opposition, and became firmly established, to the great benefit of the country banks themselves. For forty years this system gave a unique and peculiar character to New England banking, by virtue of which New England bank notes attained, even in remote parts of the Union, a credit which was frequently refused to the issues of the local banks. The country banks will, no doubt, now cling to the small benefits they derive from the delays in presenting checks, and the charges they impose for exchange, until they can be made to take a broader view, and measure at their true value the indirect advantages which they themselves will realize from a comprehensive and liberal policy in extending increased business facilities to their customers. The internal commerce of the country should not be subjected to a tax on transactions between city and country nine times as great as the stamp tax on checks. This is one of the very evils that existed in England before the establishment of the country clearing. The latter has proved a complete remedy there as it would no doubt here. The details of some working plan must be elaborated by the bankers themselves, but that business is fast outgrowing the present system, if it has not already outgrown it, is a proposition which will receive very general assent.

As some of the Clearing-houses have until within a few years made no returns, while others have only recently begun to make up their statements by calendar years, an entirely accurate comparative statement cannot be given. The following shows approximately the stupendous growth of the system in this country :—

	No. of Associations.	No. Reporting.	Aggregate Exchanges, United States. Millions.	Exchanges Outside New York. Millions.
1853	1	1	* $ 1,304,9	
1854	1	1	5,798,6	
1855	1	1	5,673,7	
1856	2	2	8,404,2	$ 1,057,4
1857	2	2	8,591,4	1,395,3
1858	5	3	7,215,7	1,839,5
1859	5	3	9,069,3	2,470,5
1860	5	3	10,022,1	2,628,2
1861	6	4	7,507,4	1,991,0
1862	6	4	10,120,1	1,885,3
1863	6	4	20,442,4	3,014,7
1864	6	4	30,053,5	4,413,4
1865	8	5	30,437,0	4,579,0
1866	11	7	36,235,9	4,769,4
1867	11	7	30,322,2	4,511,0
1868	12	7	36,079,7	4,920,0
1869	14	9	41,157,1	5,616,0
1870	14	9	32,849,7	5,763,4
1871	16	10	37,200,5	6,557,5
1872	20	12	43,581,5	7,212,0
1873	21	13	37,686,6	7,846,2
1874	23	14	31,822,1	7,372,0
1875	23	15	32,339,7	8,025,9
1876	26	18	29,579,8	8,103,2
1877	27	23	31,944,2	8,143,5
1878	27	24	30,133,1	7,732,0
1879	28	24	38,591,2	9,355,5
1880	29	26	50,113,9	11,499,5
1881	30	27	63,414,6	14,037,7
1882	30	29	60,877,4	13,960,5
1883	31	31	51,827,1	14,392,8
Total......	—		$ 870,396,6	$ 175,092,4

* Three months only.

PART IV.

LOAN AND TRUST COMPANIES.

CHAPTER I.

HISTORY AND SCOPE OF LOAN AND TRUST COMPANIES.

Loan and trust companies may, with propriety, be termed American institutions. They had their birth in this country. Charters under which some are working to-day date back sixty to seventy years. One corporation in Philadelphia, doing a loan and trust business, was organized in 1812, and another in 1832. In New York one was granted a charter in 1822, and another in 1830. But the great majority have come into existence within the past twenty years. Twenty-five years ago but few of the loan and trust companies now doing business were in existence; hence it may be said that they are a modern institution. In many of the larger cities one or more may now be found. In New York there are eleven, in Philadelphia nine, in Boston eight, and in Chicago four, while in many prominent commercial centers there are none.

The original design of the early corporations was that of insuring lives and granting annuities. The business of holding trusts and procuring capital for various enterprises was a secondary consideration. Life insurance with some of the older companies was looked upon as the chief source of revenue. But the tendency of business toward specialization has had its influence upon these great financial corporations, as it has upon almost every department of business and social life. The business of life insurance has become a gigantic enterprise of itself, far surpassing in financial importance the operations of loan and trust companies. It is one, however, which does not come for consideration within the limits of this treatise.

The usefulness in the financial world of loan and trust companies is well understood. In some respects they are similar to banks; in others they are widely different. They receive deposits and make loans, but they do not issue currency nor undertake the general collection of commercial paper. The purposes for which they are organized and the services they perform are numerous. The scope of their business has broadened to correspond with their growth of capital and to keep pace with the vast sums of money they have charge of. By the great breadth of their charters they accept and execute all kinds of trusts. They act as registrars and agents for the transfer of stocks and bonds, as trustees for corporations, and as executors, administrators, guardians, and receivers of money for courts in complicated litigations. They do a general financial business for bankers and others, make investments, collect interest, and perform many other financial services. They are organized under special charters granted by the legislatures of the respective States in which they are located.

CHAPTER II.

HOW BUSINESS IS CONDUCTED.

A number of persons desire to construct gas works. The city where the works are to be built promises a liberal support to the enterprise. The project has been fully discussed by the business men and property owners of the place, and a number of them decide to combine their efforts in carrying it through. To build the works and lay the pipes requires a large expenditure of money. It is learned that for a good part of the necessary capital outside assistance must be asked. There is nearly always plenty of money for all such enterprises, provided it can be shown that the security is ample. In the large financial centers, it is known, there may be secured the desired means at a fair rate of interest when the investment can be shown to be a safe one. What steps are best to be taken? The promoters of the scheme propose to organize a joint-stock company.

Estimates have been made, which show that fifty thousand dollars will make a reasonable start towards carrying the project along. A canvass shows that capital stock to this amount would be subscribed for. The company is formed, a charter granted, and permission given by the city authorities to lay and maintain the pipe lines. Further estimates are now made, and it is shown that to build the works and lay sufficient piping for present needs there will be required, besides the already paid-in capital of the company, about two hundred thousand dollars. This must be secured by a loan.

The company decide to issue first mortgage bonds for the amount of money needed. If they can find persons in their own city or among the stockholders who are in position and are willing to loan the money they need not call for outside assistance. But in this they do not succeed. They then must go to some financial metropolis where money is seeking investment. Here they are confronted with the inquiry: How do we know that our investment will be a safe one? What assurance have we that your company is properly organized, and that the proper authority has been given for it to make this loan? And each person who might be willing to purchase some of the bonds demands the right to have an agent examine into all the facts, and report upon the conditions, before the money could be paid over. In this case the company must pay the expenses and fees of the agents and lawyers. They see such a course is going to make it exceedingly expensive. But the money must be procured, and what shall be done?

A happy thought occurs to them. They will go to a loan and trust company. They visit one of these institutions, and learn that they will have no trouble about securing the required loan, if a clear title to the property to be mortgaged can be shown, and the other usual requirements of investors in such securities are found satisfactory. "We will transact your business for you," says an officer of the trust company. "In the first place we must put the matter in the hands of our attorneys, who will report upon the legal status of your company. We must know how much of your capital has been paid in. The amount of work you have done in the new enterprise. What your assets and liabilities are. The recording of the mortgage bond of your company may be left with us, or our attorneys will look to see that it has been properly attended to. We will issue the bonds from our institution, make all transfers, and pay the interest for you when it becomes due. In fact, we will transact the whole business, turning over the money from the sale of your bonds as it is paid in. How much money do you want to procure?"

"We wish to procure two hundred thousand dollars, or what will come from a two-hundred-thousand-dollar bond. We have invested about forty thousand dollars. The money procured is to be applied in completing our works and in extending the pipe lines."

"If you have invested only about forty thousand dollars and are free of debt, we would suggest that the loan be made in installments. We could not undertake to issue the whole amount of the bonds, excepting as the work progresses, and until we are assured that the money received for bonds issued had been properly applied in the construction of the works. We would issue, say, twenty-five thousand dollars as the first installment, then we could issue fifty thousand as the second installment, and so on, increasing the issue according to the increase in the value of the security offered."

"And on what terms would you undertake this business?"

"We would charge you by the year, according to the amount of business transacted, or liable to be transacted. You would pay for the fees necessarily incurred at the start, and thereafter probably two hundred to three hundred dollars a-year, according to circumstances and arrangements."

An agreement is entered into. The officers of the gas company are put to no further inconvenience or delay. When they inform the money-lender that the —— Loan and Trust Company have charge of their mortgage business, and are issuing the bonds, no inquiries are made as to the legal status of the company or the mortgage. The capital is secured, and the company pushes ahead with its work.

LOAN AND TRUST COMPANIES. 285

Loan and trust companies have often proven of great service in the construction of railroads. Of course railroads would be built and bonds disposed of without the mediation of such agencies, but the trust companies have greatly facilitated the work and reduced the expenses.

A party of gentlemen, for instance, organize a company to build a railroad which shall run through several States. They cannot among themselves raise the necessary capital. They are willing to risk a reasonable amount of money in the project, if the amount required to complete the road can be secured after their own investment shall have been expended. They find, among wealthy capitalists, persons who are willing to advance the funds, but they do not wish to assume any risks as stockholders. They prefer to loan the money at a fair rate of interest. If the scheme is successful the projectors can pay the money back and own the property, thus derive all the advantages accruing from their wisdom and risks.

The following is the form of a receipt and transfer voucher:

No..................................   New York, 18....

.... For value received........do hereby assign and trans-

Folio..................... fer unto...

....

Folio Certificates.   ....Shares of the *Capital Stock* of

Canceled No............... the *..............................Company now

Issued No................. standing in .... name on the books of said

                               company.

                                             ....

When the promoters of the project visit a loan and trust company, they lay the facts before the officers of the company. They are told that when they have constructed a certain amount of road the trust company will undertake to place their loan on the market. First, the mortgage securing the loan must be recorded in every county of each State through which the road is to run. Satisfactory evidences that the mortgage is so recorded must be in the possession of the trust company. Arrangements can then be made to the effect that, as certain sections of the road are constructed, a certain number of bonds will be issued. The amount to be issued will depend on the cost per mile of constructing the road. Purchasers of the bonds rely on the loan and trust company to see that there is never an over-issue of bonds.

* The title of the corporation printed in full.

Suppose the understanding between the purchasers of the bonds and the railroad officials provides that for the completion of each ten miles of road there are to be issued bonds to the amount of fifty thousand dollars. It becomes the duty of the trust company to know that this amount is not exceeded. Any excess in issue would depreciate the value of the security. It is seen in this how the

---

For explanation of Forms, see closing paragraph of this chapter.

Right hand page.

REGISTER OF CERTIFICATES OF STOCK. *Countersigned by the*					
Date of Surrendered Certificate Canceled.	No. of Ctf.	No. of Shares.	In Name of	Remarks.

trust company serves the interests of both borrowers and lenders. The trust company not only attends to the business of the railroad company in securing funds, but guarantees to purchasers of its securities that there is no wrongful or over-issue. The part taken by the trust company is one, then, not only to transact the business for the corporation, but to supplement this service by aiding in securing the faith and confidence of investors that the securities they take are in every case what they are represented to be.

Another important service is rendered by loan and trust companies to corporations. That is, issuing certificates of stock, and, in case of sale from one person to another, making transfers of same. Many corporations leave the business connected with stock operations almost entirely in the hands of some loan and trust company. The purchase and sale of stocks of corporations, especially those whose stocks are on the market, is made mostly in some of the important financial centers of the country. Here too, is where the loan and trust companies are located. It is a special advantage to

Left hand page.

....					
........................*Loan and Trust Company.*					
Date of New Ctf. Countersigned and Issued.	*No. of Ctf.*	*No. of Shares.*	*In Name of*		*Remarks.*

holders of stocks to be able to have the necessary record made on the books of the company, showing that they are the holders, without having to forward the certificates to some remote place for that purpose. By an arrangement between the loan and trust company and the corporation, the former becomes the custodian of the transfer books. When an election of officers of the corporation takes place the transfer and stock books must be in the hands of the inspectors of the election. To meet this requirement the books are forwarded or handed over to the officers of the corporation by the loan and trust company.

When the holder of shares of a corporation sells his stock, and the purchaser wishes the transfer recorded on the books of the company he must present to the transfer clerk at the office of the loan and trust company the stock of the seller. This stock becomes the voucher of the transfer clerk, showing his authority for making the transfer.

| RECORD OF MORTGAGE BONDS OF THE BEE LINE R. R. COMPANY. | | | | |
1884.		*Bonds Received.*		
Oct.	10	Rec'd from the Bee Line R.R. Company per Jacob Trusty, President, 150 First Mortgage Bonds, Nos. 1 to 150 inclusive. To be issued according to the terms of agreement, in installments of ten each, upon completion of ten-mile sections of said railroad. Par value, $1,000.	150	150,000

On pages 286 and 287 the formular arrangement of a register for recording transfers of stock certificates is given. The form on 286 represents the left-hand, and on page 287 the right-hand pages of such a register. The headings over the several columns serve to explain fully the nature of the entries to be made in the book. The blank line at the top of the right-hand page is left for writing the title of the corporation from which the certificates are issued. The register is kept by the trust clerk. A separate register is kept for each corporation.

Loan and trust companies' records of mortgage bonds of corporations are made in a book with the ordinary journal-rulings, a column being added for giving the number of bonds received and issued. The form on page 288 represents the left-hand, and the form on page 289 the right-hand page of such a register. These books are merely books of record and do not form any part of the general set of books kept by loan and trust companies.

Much of the bookkeeping of loan and trust companies is similar in character to that of banks and bankers generally. These corporations often do a large banking business, and have dealers who keep running accounts. They more generally, however, have

Held in Trust and Delivered by the				
Loan and Trust Co.				
1884.		Bonds Delivered.		
Oct.	25	Delivered To J. C. Smith 3 Bonds at market value of $900......	3	2,700
		To A. Goodfellow 2 Bonds at market value of $900...	2	1,800
		To John Topheavy 5 Bonds at market value of $900...	5	4,500

the accounts of a class who do not so frequently disturb their deposits. Depositors with such companies as a rule are paid interest on their credit balances. This requires a slight alteration in some of the usual banking books to make them available. The dealers' or depositors' ledgers, for instance, are ruled with special columns for crediting interest on deposits.

The other records are kept through the use of an ordinary set of double-entry books. Of the various trusts managed by such companies there are required to be entered in the books of account only such items as affect the revenues and conducting expenses. The "Trust Account" is a record of the revenues arising from this department of the companies services, etc.

APPENDIX.

BANKING AS A PROFESSION FOR YOUNG MEN.*

It is generally true in mercantile life and in the learned professions, and *always* true in banking, that in order to insure success, a young man must have some end in view towards which all his exertions shall tend. Every young man should have some well-defined plan of life marked out before him, and all his energies should be directed to the realization of it.

Many have some general object in view, such as getting rich, or getting beyond hard work at some time of their life; while but few have a specific, noble mark, towards which they are aiming. This is the reason why there are so many second-rate young men to be found in every profession, and why so many men of riper years are neither one thing nor another—strung up and dangling between something and nothing—breathing in the unsatisfying east wind of a glorious mediocrity, and hoping that an undefined something may turn up one of these days, which shall relieve them and place them in an undefined blissful somewhere. According as a young man aims, so will his arrow fly. According to the energy with which he strives, and the talents which he brings to bear, so will he rise. But what are the objects to be aimed at by a young banker? For what end should he strive, and what is there ahead to reward his toil? What are the advantages of the banker's profession? The advantages enjoyed by persons in this profession, for the attainment of everything desirable in life, are very great, and the inducements held out by the profession to ambitious, enterprising young men, are enough to satisfy any reasonable person. A high eminence and a name are as sure of attainment as in any other business.

It should be the object of every young man who enters the profession, to become thoroughly acquainted with every part of it. He should strive to become familiar with it all, from the great general principles down to the minutest detail. While in a subordinate situation, he should not be satisfied with merely doing the

* The excellent ideas contained in this chapter first appeared in the *Banker's Magazine* nearly thirty-five years ago. Time has not impaired their value. They were written by George P. Bissell, a banker in Hartford, Conn.

work which is laid upon him, but while in this situation, he should be fitting himself for the next place above him. His aim should be to rise as rapidly as is consistent with a healthy growth, till he has placed himself at the head of an institution; and then his ambition should be, to be first in his profession, to reach an eminence and carry his bank with him. To aim merely at a cashiership, or to be president, is a low aim; but to be known as the best cashier or president in the country, is an aim well worthy of any man, and is the only one which should satisfy a young man entering this profession. A young man can rise as rapidly and as surely in this, as in any other profession; he can also rise as *slowly* and as surely, and he can remain as immutably stationary, as in any other calling under heaven. There are plenty of stopping places adapted to all phases of mediocrity, and these stopping places are very tenacious of their prey. A man once fixed in any of them, is there for life.

No one should enter the business unless he is determined to reach the top of the ladder. If a man is not somewhat ambitious, and unless he can see through a pretty long transaction, he generally becomes a fixture. Any one can tell, in the course of his first year, whether he is adapted to the business, and whether he will succeed. If a young man begin to feel the trap-door of a second-rate station, or a subordinate clerkship, pressing him down as he is trying to ascend the ladder, let him make a desperate effort to raise it; but if he cannot succeed, let him at once betake himself to some other ladder, under some other opening.

Let no one enter this profession with the expectation of becoming suddenly, or even speedily, rich, for this expectation will be disappointed; neither let any entering the profession be afraid of ever becoming poor. Labor is generally liberally rewarded, and talent is generally appreciated. There are some, it is true, in banks, who receive but small pay, and who delve for years in subordinate situations, but such are generally men not largely endowed with talent, whose aim is nowhere, and who consequently are paid about as much as they are worth. A man of talents and energy is always sure of good pay; sufficient for all the expenses attendant upon a genteel style of living, besides a handsome margin for moderate investment for the satisfaction of that great maelstrom account generally known as "sundries." He is always sure of a competence.

A competence is all we can enjoy,
O be content where Heaven can give no more.

It is impossible to name exactly the amount of salary which a young may expect to receive. It depends a little upon the locality and size of the bank, and a great deal upon what the young man himself is. A moderate young man in a moderately-sized bank, generally has a salary very nicely fitted to him, while an energetic, talented young man, in a good institution, can be the recipient of almost any sum that he has the face to ask for. Some idea upon which to base expectations may be formed from a knowledge of the fact, that tellers' salaries range from $500 to $1,800 per annum; cashiers' from $800 to $5,000, and presidents' about the same.* In some banks the office of president is a mere sinecure; in such banks the president receives no salary, but takes it out in honor. Let a young man fix in his mind the salary that he thinks he ought to be worth, and then work for it, and he will generally receive it. A banker, from the nature of his position in the financial world, has often opportunities thrown in his way for making money besides his salary, but this should not be counted upon by a young man, for it is very uncertain. If a young banker is working for a name, a reputation, and,—which follows as a matter of course,—for a high salary, his best course is to keep himself free from anything like speculating, shaving or dabbling in stocks. He should engage in no other business but his bank, and he should keep himself as far as possible from any course in which there is the least possibility of becoming in any way involved or embarrassed.

There is less anxiety of mind in this profession than in most others. It is true that the banker has a great many cares, and his mind has about as much as it can well do, but there is none of that terrible anxiety of mind which waits upon the merchant who has his warehouses full of goods, prices falling, and money scarce. The merchant at times is elated by prosperity, and again he is weighed down by anxiety, and either extreme, or the transition from one to the other is very wearing; but the banker has at *all* times enough to think of. He is never troubled with the alternations of excitement and depression; his mind is constantly active, not overtasked, and consequently its action is always healthy. During business hours he works hard, but at night he can throw off all care, and devote himself, if he choose, to literary pursuits, and to self-improvement.

There are times in great commercial distress when confidence is destroyed, that banks are crowded and pressed very hard; but with ordinary management they can be carried safely through. No bank ever failed where there was good management and no speculation. All that is required is caution and prudence: but the most incessant exercise of caution and prudence will not amount to that anxiety which produces sleepless nights.

A banker can have a great deal of time to devote to mental culture, and to the acquisition of useful information. He generally has his evenings to himself free from care, and much can be done

---

* Since this was written these salaries have increased until they are now (1884) about doubled.

by the improvement of such hours. His business is of such a nature that this is not incompatible with being first in his profession. There are some, however, who work night and day, and make slaves of themselves, but such are generally men who care but little for mental improvement, and whose whole aim seems to be to remain in a bank, and yet realize a treadmill. Let them work. They have the satisfaction of knowing that they are not always the best bankers. The best in any profession are those who have room enough in their brains for more than one idea, and who take time for something besides dollars and cents. A banker can, if he will apply himself, so cultivate his mind that he will shine as brightly in social life, and appear as well, even in literary circles, as men of liberal education.

These are some of the advantages of the banker's profession, and these are some of the inducements which are held out to those who wish to enter it.

A young man in order to succeed should maintain a straightforward course, both in his own affairs, and in the affairs of the bank; he should be possessed of a clear head, a mind not easily carried away by tempting offers for speculation, a disposition to receive very fair stories with considerable allowance; he should have urbanity combined with firmness and decision, and above all, he should have a deep-seated, stubborn passion for *good security*.

These are the traits which are absolutely necessary to insure success in banking. Without them, no young man should enter a bank. Without them, a young man should rather take himself to some one of the other professions, where even a fool can sometimes make a happy hit. In banking there are no happy hits to be made; the life is one long, dead pull upon talent, energy, and perseverance.

ADVICE TO DEPOSITORS.

If you are a stranger to the officers, and wish to open an account, get some respectable person who is known to them to introduce you either to the President or Cashier. Do not ask him to vouch for anything beyond your integrity and fairness in dealing. Tell your own story about capital, business, property, and other matters which pertain to your commercial prospects—and exaggerate nothing. There is no humbug that will recoil upon yourself so surely as an attempt to palm off big tales on a bank officer. Your deposit-tickets, your checks, your bills receivable, your endorsements, and your ledger account, make together a history that dispels all shams, and leaves little to say. A man who begins with an exaggerated account of himself is measured by it afterwards, and appears relatively small.

Borrow no money of your neighbors to swell your first deposits. This is a common practice, with the idea that it will make a favorable impression on the officers. They see through it at once, and take it as a proof of weakness.

Never try to bargain for special indulgences, such as the certification of your checks before your deposit is made, or the discount of your paper by the officers without its submission to the Board of Directors. The character of your account will settle these matters much more satisfactorily to all parties.

Let your intercourse with the officers be candid and courteous, and be sparing in your personal solicitation for discounts. Choose the earlier hours of the day for your interviews, and especially avoid the last hour before three o'clock.

Write your signature with the same freedom that you do in your own office, and never vary the style of it.

Teach your clerks to use always the deposit-tickets furnished by the bank, to examine the date and endorsement of every check, and also to see that the writing of the amount corresponds with the figures. Instruct them to learn and to follow the rules of the bank with respect to getting checks certified before deposit.

Make your deposit as early in the day as possible. If you are accustomed to have many checks, or large packages of bank bills, it is better to make two deposits—one at an early hour—than to hand in all at once just at three o'clock. Never change checks with other people merely to make larger figures. It causes needless labor to the bank clerks, makes you responsible for the debts of others, and is a real prejudice to your credit.

Never try to put in your deposit before those in advance of you, but take your place in the line, and wait your turn patiently. Never make deposits without your bank-book, if you can help it. Avoid all unnecessary conversation with the clerks, especially with the tellers.

Never get angry if the paying teller examines your account before certifying your check; nor if he keeps you waiting a few seconds before he can pay it.

Make it an invariable rule to give checks only out of your own check-book, and at your own office. When you want the endorsement of the person to whom you give it, if he wishes to draw the money, let him endorse the check in your presence, and write your own name below his signature, to assure the teller that it is right.

Never give out checks dated ahead. When you have need to cut checks out of the end of your check-book, mark in the margin what they are for—to supply duplicates, or otherwise. Keep your check-books out of the sight and reach of strangers. Never give a stranger a check unless you have some evidence that he is not seeking it for fraudulent purposes. Never draw checks against your account, on the ground that you have sent some abroad that will not return immediately. Always consider a check paid when you give it out.

Never attempt to pay a note with an uncertified check, at a bank where you keep no account. If you make your promissory notes payable at a bank, give the paying teller a list of them on Monday morning for the current week, or send him your bank notices on the day of their maturity.

When you want notes discounted, offer them on the regular days, and in good season for the clerk's convenience. Never call on bank officers to discount notes between the board meetings, if you can wait until the following discount day. Do not put off the offering of notes for discount until the last day of your need. It is better to keep from ten days to a fortnight ahead, and to let your balances remain in the bank until you require them. The loss of interest is very trifling at best. You lose more by anxiety and unfitness for business.

When you want your bank-book balanced, or entries made in it, apply to the bookkeeper early in the day. Never ask a service of him later than one o'clock if you can wait till the next morning. Do not allow your book to run too long without being balanced, and when balanced, examine your canceled checks without delay.

If the bank ledger shows a larger balance in your favor at any time, than your own check-book, acquaint the bookkeeper with it immediately. As you value your credit with the bank, never take advantage of deposits wrongly entered to your account, but let your dealings be strictly honorable.

If you have any cause of complaint against the clerks, state it directly to the officers. The clerks act under their instructions, which they dare not disobey.

The bookkeeper is the proper person to apply to, to know if collection notes are passed to your credit.

The note clerk will inform you of the maturity of notes for a future time. In the case of discounted notes apply to the discount clerk. The discount clerk, or the note clerk, will commonly tell the exchange or charges for collecting foreign paper.

When you have notes to send abroad for collection, deposit them in ample time for deliberate record and transmission by the bank.

If the drawers of any notes lodged as collateral to loans or discounts should fail, do not wait for the bank officers to discover it, but substitute good notes for them without delay.

The observance of these rules, and such others as may be suggested by your own observation, will be a great economy of time to yourself as well as to the bank clerks, and promote your real credit with the institution.

SUGGESTIONS TO YOUNG CASHIERS ON THE DUTIES OF THEIR PROFESSION.*

Banking has become a part of the very framework of our system of business. Even Mr. Calhoun said, as long ago as 1816, when the whole banking capital in the United States was only eighty millions of dollars, that "the question whether banks are favorable to public liberty and prosperity was one purely speculative. The fact of the existence of banks, and their incorporation with the commercial concerns and industry of the nation, prove that inquiry to come too late. The only question was, on this hand, under what modifications were banks most useful," etc. Banks now exist, in some form or other, everywhere, and will continue, probably, as long as property shall be bought and sold on credit. In all coming time, therefore, we are to have a class of men to deal in money, in promissory notes, and foreign and domestic exchange. The avocation has ever been honorable, to the last degree responsible, and exposed to many and to peculiar temptations.

The world, seemingly more inexorable with our profession than with others, deals out its direct maledictions upon those of us who err, and will hardly forgive the managers of a broken bank, or the officer whose "cash is short," even when there is no other guilt than credulity, too easy good nature, or incapacity. To stand upon our defence against *unjust* accusations, and to do what we can to diminish the causes of corporate and of individual delinquency, are duties which we owe to ourselves and to those who are to succeed us. Dispersed, as we are, over a vast extent of country, we can best correct public sentiment, and afford counsel and admonition to one another, as well as render our knowledge of banking available as common stock, by means of the work established for, and devoted to, our benefit.

Banks, with us, both public and private, differ—as none need to be told—in many things from those of England and of Continental Europe. It is known, also, that our system is not perfect, and that essential improvements can be made in it. Hence, whatever the value of essays upon foreign banking, papers devoted to our own are far more useful to us, regarded as a class; and hence, too, the

---

* This essay, by Lorenzo Sabine, of Framingham, Mass., was originally published in the *Banker's Magazine* in January, 1852. A few changes have been made to adapt it to the present work.

necessity for a free interchange of thought by bankers in different parts of the Union.

I pass now to topics immediately connected with the duties of a Cashier. The limits of this essay do not admit of elaborate reasoning, but demand, indeed, that mere suggestions shall be made with the brevity of proverbs. I may be permitted, then, to address myself to the young officer, directly, and, as it were, personally.

You are to lead a life so confined, sedentary, and, in some respects, so mechanical, that, unless you observe great care, you will become, in the lapse of years, a sort of machine for computing discounts, counting money, writing letters, and keeping books.* You are to transact business, and to have a constant intercourse, with men of every shade of character, of every variety of disposition, and of every degree of intelligence. Your temper is to be tried by interruptions at the most unseasonable moments, to attend to the calls of the impatient, or to answer the inquiries of the ignorant or inquisitive. You are to be tempted to embark in speculations in stocks: to be solicited to allow overdrawings and other irregularities by the companions of your social hours, and it may be, by one or more of your own directors; and you are to have the same domestic cares and afflictions, the same personal aches and pains as other men; and yet you are expected to be ever at your post, to be ever courteous, to stand fast in your integrity, and to seem cheerful, and even happy. In a word, and as Girard said, at the decease of his old and faithful cashier, "*the bank must go on,*" whatever your private griefs or individual disabilities. Your position is thus one of much difficulty, responsibility and peril; and you need a knowledge of the laws of your physical being, the counsel of wise friends, strict and daily self-examination, and deep religious principle, to enable you to sustain it in health and honor. But be of good cheer; be a true man, and you will overcome every obstacle in the way of a long and of a useful life.

Your bank has secrets; and, that they be kept inviolable, adopt a rule to speak of its affairs only to persons connected with you in its management.

You should embrace every opportunity to acquire information as to the standing of your customers; and whatever is imparted to you on the subject, whether in confidence, or otherwise, should be communicated to your directors, and to them alone.

* Every person of observation will attest to the need of the caution in the text. Long and close application to one branch of business, and the habit of being at one place for a course of years, produce wonderful transformations in the character. The case of Mr. Rippon, the late chief Cashier of the Bank of England, furnishes an illustration well worth citing. He was connected with that institution for more than half a century, and asked but for a single leave of absence from his post during the entire period, and in this instance, even, he applied at the suggestion of his physician, on the ground of ill health. Permission was granted, and our bank officer departed from London to be absent two weeks. But the country was without charms, idleness preyed upon his spirits, and the habit of years was so strong that, at the end of three days, he returned to the bank, solely to become happy again.

You should become acquainted with the laws relative to banking, and especially with those of your own State; and should be familiar with some work which treats of notes and bills, of the liabilities of sureties, drawers and indorsers. I recommend, as the easiest way to obtain, and to retain, knowledge in these particulars, that you make a manual, or brief digest, with marginal references to the authorities which you consult. The best books are *Daniel on Negotiable Instruments, and Morse on the Law of Banks and Banking*. To master these works, or even to obtain common knowledge of the immense learning which they contain, will require time—much time. But the leading principles applicable to promissors and other parties to commercial paper, are easily fixed in the memory, and no time should be lost in consulting the latter treatise, at least. I recommend to the young cashier to devote a part of his leisure to professional reading of a more general nature. The history of the system of credit is not only curious, but interesting and instructive. Strangely enough, as he will find, banking owes its origin to the Crusades, for the earliest institutions of which there is any account was a mere bank of *deposit*, established at Venice, late in the twelfth century, for the purpose of aiding those who fought to win the Holy Land from its unholy possessors. Such was the first element, and the degree of security and facility of commercial transactions of the period may be seen in the fact that, in England, contracts between individuals were discharged by payments in cattle, horses, dogs, and even hawks; and that rents, fines, and taxes due the crown were paid in the same kinds of property, in products of the soil, and in merchandise generally. In a word, the idea of paper money based on the precious metals, or on personal estate and credit, or on lands, had not been conceived, we may fairly conclude, anywhere. Next, if the notes of my own reading be accurate, and equally strange, we hear of some sort of *paper credit*, early in the thirteenth century, not in any trading country of Europe, but in far-off, and, as we commonly say, in barbarous China. So, again, toward the close of the last-mentioned century, we are told that the hated and hunted Jews and Lombards invented the *bill of exchange*, which afforded means for the silent and secret transfer of funds from country to country, to the infinite discomfiture of robber kings and of robber outlaws. Next, probably, in chronological order, was the *promissory notes*, which strange device, grave and learned judges, in solemn wig and ermine, dared at length to pronounce to worn and weary litigants, might, if traffickers so willed, pass current from one person to another, and be lawfully collected by the final owner.* Still, again,

---

* As late down as the reign of William and Mary, the courts of England refused to consider an inland bill of exchange a legal instrument; nor was it until the time of Anne, that a promissory note, in the hands of an indorsee, could be collected by law, of the maker.

about the middle of the fourteenth century, we meet with the origin of *public scrip* in the governmental certificates of Florence, which, I suppose, were the first ever issued in Europe. Thus, we have five elements in modern banking. Two others, namely, those of *discount* and *circulation*, were yet wanting. Neither power was conferred upon the Bank of Amsterdam, which, founded near the opening of the seventeenth century, was designed merely, as it would seem, to check the evils of a clipped and worn metallic currency. Nor was the Bank of Hamburg, which was established immediately after, hardly more than an institution for deposit and transfer. In the progress, however, of civilization, or commercial dealing and necessity, we come at last, and toward the close of the seventeenth century, to the Bank of England, which was invested with authority to receive deposits, to buy and sell exchange, to aid in the management of public securities, to discount promissory notes, and to issue a paper currency. And so it appears from this rapid view, that more than five hundred years elapsed before *all* the elements of modern banking are combined, arranged, and reduced to a system in which statesmen and merchants reposed confidence.

The young cashier having, by his researches, convicted me of inaccuracy, or having established the truth of the foregoing outlines of bank history, may, as opportunity occurs, pursue the subject still further. The first charter of the Bank of England is accessible, and he may study it with profit, and to ascertain the immense progress which has been made in the principles of banking, whether as relates to rights of stockholders or to public convenience and safety. He will find valuable lessons in the legislation of his own country; in the issue of paper money prior to the revolution, which at times flooded the colonies, and which in spite of the clamors of our fathers, was suppressed by Parliament; the marvelous tales and traditions which have come down to us of the never-to-be-forgotten "continental money," without which the bonds of colonial vassalage would not have been broken when and as they were; in the earlier charters of the different State Governments, and in the two charters of Congress of the great National institution which has now ceased to exist.

This general inquiry concluded, he will have improved his own mind, and be ready to meet and to reason with those who, because the system has not been perfected in a century and a-half (dating from the establishment of the Bank of England), demand its entire abolition, or at least such changes as would render it powerless for good, alike to individuals and to communities. He can say and prove that CREDIT, wide, liberal, beneficent credit, belongs to the era of liberty, and that it was unknown even in free England until after the expulsion of the Stuarts, and until the revolution there had secured personal freedom. He may stand upon the emphatic declaration of a great statesman,* that the system of credit, as it now prevails, is the vital air of commerce, and that "it has done more, a thousand times, to enrich nations than all the mines in all the world." He should, indeed, admit that its fluctuations, its ebbs and flows, sometimes cause desolation and ruin; yet he should not fail to insist that good and wise men steadily strive to improve it—that, as sweeping conflagrations allow of the straightening and widening of streets, and as disasters in traveling by steam suggest more careful management and better machinery, so do bank failures and the delinquencies of bank officers, however appalling the circumstances at the moment, serve to discover and to apply new checks and new remedies.

If your bank is old enough to have been through "a crisis," and if you have not served in it as an inferior officer, you have much to learn of its past business. Such an institution, for example, has a "suspended debt" account, or at best overdue paper secured by mortgage or other collateral; and assets of this description *always have a history*, and sometimes a very intricate, a very perplexing one. But you must become master of that history. Directors change every year; and in a little time, all who were at the "Board" when this class of paper was taken will have vacated their seats; while, then, some are still in the direction, make written memoranda of the principal facts.

Let it be manifest to your associates and stockholders, that you feel an interest in everything which relates to their welfare. To work the whole of your capital and of your deposits, to keep both actively employed at all times, and yet to be always able to meet the demands on you, require great wisdom; and the most skillful and experienced financiers sometimes find themselves at fault for the moment. Your duty requires continual experiments to effect this great object.

Need I suggest the benefits of a fixed system, and of method, even in matters seemingly of little consequence? Everybody finds —as seamen have it—that "a stern chase is a long chase." The business of to-day should never be deferred till to-morrow. Answer letters, and file papers, at the instant. Remember everything, if possible; but trusting to memory in nothing: let your books contain a record of all transactions. Allow no outstanding bills against the bank; and have a voucher for the smallest item charged to "Expense Account."

You can be, and you ought to be, ready for an "examination" by the "Commissioners," or other functionaries of the Government, and of your own "Board," without previous notice, and without the slightest special preparation. In fine, close your vault daily with

---

* Mr. Webster.

the reflection that no act has been neglected, and that, if sickness or death should occur "the bank can go on" with no loss to your family, sureties, or stockholders. Do not smile, if I add, that your banking-rooms should be swept, and your desks and counters be dusted daily; that *one* "slut-hole" is ample for all the twine and waste-paper; and that the accumulation of official papers and memorandums in your *private* drawer will cause both you and your associates serious delays and much inconvenience.

Panics and pressures are as certain in banking as storms in winter. When either exist, firmness and courage, if not really possessed, must be assumed. You are presumed to know the nature and extent of your resources under *all* circumstances, and at periods of general distrust especially; and if the amount of those *immediately* available are insufficient for every possible call upon you, thus advise your directors without delay.

A knowledge of human character is indispensable. Study it. The "actions, looks, words, and steps" of your customers "form an alphabet:" and your "eyes are spectacles to read others' hearts with." Careful, close, and continued observations will enable you to detect a counterfeit man as readily as you now do a counterfeit banknote. My own experience is, that those who change countenance, or the weight of the body from one foot to the other, when meeting a full, searching and fixed gaze, are not truthful; that those who ask for additional accommodations, prefacing the request with a story divided into acts like a drama, are already bankrupt; and that those who petition in whispers, in an unnatural tone of voice, in a cant, or a whine, are hypocrites. Some years hence, I shall be glad to ascertain how nearly *your* experience accords with mine.

You should be courteous and respectful to all. Self-command is a great virtue; indulgence of passion is a great fault. Impertinence and stupid ignorance might sometimes be rebuked, were it not for the danger of contracting a morose and irritable habit of speaking. There is no loss of dignity, or of self-respect, in perfect silence under the greatest provocation, and that, accordingly, is your safest course. The cashier's popularity or unpopularity gives character to a bank. The directors are seldom visible, and sometimes unknown to occasional customers; but their executive officer is an ever-present and a known man, and should bear in mind the Latin proverb, namely, to "be cautious *what* he says, *when*, and to *whom*."*

Should you acquire a reputation, you may be solicited to change your place; or, becoming discontented, may seek to do so on your

---

* A "bill-broker," says Mr. Windham Beaves, "should avoid babbling, and be prudent in his office, which consists in one sole point, that is, *to hear all and say nothing*."

own motion. In the former case you are to consider your directors as your friends, and, stating *all* the facts fairly, obtain *their* views before taking a single step to meet the overture made to you. This is an imperative duty; and performing it in honor, and acting under the advice of wise counselors, you can hardly come to a wrong conclusion. I assume here that your bank is sound, and that it is under the direction of competent and safe men. If unfortunately otherwise, if your reputation be at stake, and your directors, or a governing part of them, are ignorant or regardless of the principles of banking, or are "speculators," who seek their own accommodation, you should retire at once. But upon this point I will not dwell, since it is to be hoped that such institutions and such men have nearly passed away.

It is related that the eminence of the five brothers Rothschild, as bankers, is to be attributed in a great measure to their strict observance of their father's dying injunction, to "remain united." Well may it be so. Unanimity in the direction of a bank is always an element of success; and the result of my observation in this regard is, that more losses occur from divisions, than from any other single cause. Accommodation notes, large and standing loans to particular parties, and similar departures from legitimate banking are only to be tolerated in cases which receive the assent of the entire direction. Yet I have known one and all of these departures to be consummated, time and again, by directors who owned the smallest possible amount of stock, in opposition to the remonstrances of older and abler associates who were large stockholders; and years afterward, when legal remedies had been exhausted, and levies and set-offs had failed to restore more than costs of suit, have personally made wearisome journeys and devoted weeks to the service of closing up, as I best could, these unfortunate illustrations of the rule that "a majority should govern" in the directors' room, as in politics. In short, such, in my view, are the evils of the majority principle in this connection, that I would counsel a cashier, whether young or old, to insist upon a reasonable change, and a change refused, to seek an institution more wisely, more safely conducted.

You may be discontented without cause. I remember to have read a story, in which one of the characters was in possession of everything that heart could ask, but was miserable from this very circumstance, or because he *wanted—a want*. Such persons exist in real life. Be not of that unhappy class. Accommodate yourself to your condition. Do not seek for happiness in change of place, but in change of disposition. "The lazy ox wishes for the trappings of the horse, and the steed sighs for the yoke," is an old saw that has not yet lost its meaning. Nor should the topic be dismissed without recalling the pithy epitaph composed for the hypochondriac, who quacked himself into his grave: "I was *well*; but by endeavoring *to be better*—am here." Let the young cashier heed the moral contained in these several apt sayings, and remember that care and perplexity exist everywhere. To smoothe and fashion the rough stone of life is a religious duty. The change of one's home involves a change of society, of privileges of worship, of schools, of facilities in traveling, of household expenses, of access to books, and various other essentials; and should be carefully considered in every aspect before it is actually undertaken. And I bestow the more attention upon the point, because the propensity to remove from one place to another is so common, and because within the circle of my acquaintance, many have been ruined, and but few have improved their condition or increased their happiness, by seeking a new abode. In middle age, the experiment is doubly hazardous. Take up a full-grown tree, and will it live unless some of the old earth go with it? Sunder the ties of sympathy and affection; exchange old faces and associates for new ones, and what is the condition of a man?

To resume my personal address to the young cashier, you should not possess an overweening desire of praise, nor invite commendation. Nor should you be intoxicated with your own merits.

You should never speak of your official acts, except in explanation and in self-defence. In all pleasantry, I will add, that, in old age, you may tell the son who succeeds you what you were in your youth; but, now, be content with the quiet appreciation of others. Delicate attentions and marks of respect are the surest and best manifestations of regard, and if you have these, do not pine in discontent or discouragement.

In your *official* intercourse with the president and directors, observe great deference; and at the "Board" it may be proper to address the former by his title.

Never speak of the real or supposed faults of character of a director in the social circle, nor bear tales or remarks from one director to another. Whatever your preferences, likes, and dislikes—and you will probably have both—your *conduct* should be uniformly respectful to all. Whenever your opinion is asked, or given, without solicitation, state your views modestly, and in a conversational tone of voice. Should the "Board" differ from you in judgment, and decide contrary to your convictions, betray no feeling, but promptly and cheerfully execute their vote.

Frequent communications with the directors, relative to the general concerns of the bank and to your own particular duties, will be of essential service: since *they* will thus obtain a knowledge of details, and *you* will have the benefit of their reflections and suggestions. "Conference," says the wise Lord Bacon, "maketh a ready man."

Your style of living is a matter of momentous consequence; and, possibly, the hinge on which your final destiny will turn. Not only live within your income, but so regulate your expenses that, unavoidable misfortunes or sickness excepted, you shall be sure to save at least a quarter part of your salary, as a fund for old age, unless, indeed, your patrimonial estate be ample for such a purpose.* But, whatever be your receipts or expectations from other sources, do not allow your expenditures to exceed your personal earnings. Be this the great economic maxim of your life.

Economy is the parent of honesty, of freedom, and of mental ease and quiet. Poverty can never enter your abode, if content with satisfying your real wants; while you will never enjoy independence, if you live in accordance with the world's caprice.† If you possess an inordinate craving for great wealth, or a desire to indulge in luxuries and amusements such as men of fortune alone can afford, you have mistaken your profession, and should abandon it. For your life, if you remain in it, will be a perpetual struggle against your natural inclinations; and the danger is, that, finally yielding to them, you will involve yourself in irretrievable woe.

The road to disgrace is short. Persons who have traced the footsteps of more than one unhappy bank officer that has trodden it, have found that extravagance and defalcation were but a few

---

* I designed to say a word in the text on the subject of salaries. As a general rule, the compensation to bank officers is too small. According to a return to Parliament, in 1832, the number of persons employed in the Bank of England and its branches, was nine hundred and forty, who (to average the salaries) received only £225, or about eleven hundred dollars each, per annum. Since several who filled the higher posts were paid very much larger sums, it is evident that a considerable part of this numerous corps could not have received more than a moiety of the above average. Yet, as at the same time there were one hundred and ninety-three on the pension list who enjoyed annually (on the average) £161, or about eight hundred dollars each, the faithful officers of that institution who were then in actual service, could hope for relief in their declining years. In the United States, the system of pensions is not, perhaps, practicable or desirable. But since marriage, a flock of little ones, *the owning of a house unincumbered with mortgage*, and a choice collection of books, are all Virtue's sentinels, directors ought always to have reference to the support of a family in fixing the compensation of their executive officers. Indeed, such officers, like capable and faithful men in other pursuits, should be allowed to provide something for old age. It is fair, I suppose, to assume that the expense of the executive department, as a common thing, is not far from one per cent. on the capital stock, or, in the proportion of one thousand dollars salary to one hundred thousand dollars capital. If this be so, it is manifest, at a glance, that a large part of the bank officers in the United States (as gentlemen are now *compelled* to live both in city and country) are required to consult the maxims of "Poor Richard" every day in order to secure a moderate competence. The interests of stockholders are not promoted in the long run, by low salaries, for low salaries not infrequently, as experience shows, induce speculations in stocks, and other irregularities, which terminate in defalcation. As a class, bank officers are not so well paid as officers of railroads and manufacturing establishments, while their duties are quite as responsible.

† The great English banker, Thellusson, who, at one time, was partner with Mr. Neckar, the celebrated French financier, left three sons, and a fortune of three and a half millions of dollars, which estate, he said, he acquired by "industry and honesty." In his will he remarks: "*It is my earnest wish and desire that my sons avoid ostentation, vanity, and pompous show,*" etc. The three, it may be added, became members of the House of Commons, and the eldest, a peer of the realm.

strides apart.* A sensual man is disqualified, by his very physical organization, for *any* office in the executive department of a bank, and ought no more to be there than in a pulpit. I make the remark considerately—for good reasons—and not to round out a period. And should this essay meet the eye of the father of a son ready, by age and education, to enter upon some employment, I venture to counsel that, if banking be thought of, the moral qualities and the strength of the appetites, as developed in early life, are the first things to be considered. The youth who, in childhood, stole slyly to the closet for his mother's sweetmeats, who was never content at table with the share of niceties allotted to him, who shirked his known tasks, and imposed their performance upon a younger and more dutiful brother, and who, as years wore on, evinced a disposition to rely upon others, and to earn nothing for himself, but yet who showed a determined purpose to feed on the best, and to dress in the finest—such a youth, though as quick at figures as Colburn himself, should never be placed in a bank.

"Speculation in stocks" is another fruitful source of ruin, and I cannot forbear a word of admonition. The careful investment of your earnings or patrimony, and a similar service for friends and customers, define, in my judgment, the general limits of your operations in the stock market. To say nothing of their hopes and fears consequent upon the adventures of a dealer, and nothing of their influence upon your mind and temper—already sufficiently tasked—I may ask, in all seriousness, what assurance have you, what assurance can you have, that your virtue will resist the temptations sure to beset you? Once embarked and afloat on the stock exchange, either alone or with partners, you cannot move without means: and who shall answer for the money intrusted to your care? Who shall answer that you will not "borrow" from your vault—as others have done—feeling sure that you can "return" the sum you need "in a few days with interest?" At the outset you will not "risk much;" you desire only "to gain something to add to a moderate salary." But encouraged, at length, by your own success in small operations, or excited by the real or reported good

---

* "The London banker of the old school," says Mr. Lawson, "had little resemblance to the modern gentleman who is known by the same title. He was a man of serious manners, plain apparel, the steadiest conduct, and a rigid observer of formalities. As you looked in his face, you could read in intelligible characters that the ruling maxim of life, the one to which he turned all his thoughts and by which he shaped all his actions, was: '*That he who would be trusted with the money of other men should look as if he deserved the trust, and be an ostensible pattern to society of probity, exactness, frugality, and decorum.*'" And further, says the same writer: "The fashionable society at the West End of the town, and the amusements of high life, he never dreamed of enjoying, and would have deemed it nothing short of insanity to imagine that such an act was within the compass of human daring, as that of a banker lounging for an evening in Fop's Alley at the opera, or turning out for the Derby with four grays to his chariot, and a goodly hamper swung behind, well stuffed with perigord pies, spring chickens, and iced champagne."

fortune of those around you, the resolution *may* be formed to win a competence at a single cast of the die: you lose, and are ruined! Be warned, I entreat, in time. No bank officer—in charity, we may believe—ever meant to be a defaulter; no one, at the beginning of an irregular course, thought defalcation and disgrace possible. Yet, alas for the many victims of self-deception! alas for the self-confident, and for those who neglected the great duty of self-examination! Most affectionately and earnestly do I charge you, as you value your peace, as you would save your integrity, as you would not be driven forth, a broken and shunned man, to resist every seduction of avarice from within, and every solicitation of companions from without. No matter what pretence or excuse a stifled conscience may allow you to frame, *the cash in your vault is not your cash, and you touch it for your private benefit, or relief even, as a robber, and at the peril of your soul!* Think, ere you yield, of the long roll of sad-faced men who once were honored and trusted, but who, when tempted, fell! Think of those who, wrecked in character, in fortune, and in hope, have become bloated, ragged wanderers! Think of those of whom fathers and mothers, and even wives and children, dare not speak save in whispers, and at the family fireside! Think of those who have been hurried to the prisons and to the tribunals! Think of the graves of the suicides!

A single warning more, and I pass to less painful topics of discourse. Allow no customer to overdraw his account upon your own responsibility or without the express sanction and authority of directors.* The habit is a bad one, every way, under *any* circumstances; and I wish it could come to an end at once, everywhere and forever. But if it be permitted in particular cases in your bank, have neither part nor lot in the matter, save to execute a positive order. Discourage the practice in every possible manner, and if fortunate enough to put an end to it, you will deserve the praise of every correct banker in the country. At your post, and in bank hours, you are to have no friends to indulge with favors, no enemies to punish with refusals. Then and there all men should be alike to you. The motto of the *Banker's Magazine* should be yours, without reservation or condition.† In fine, perform no act that you would omit in the presence of the full "Board," or in that of the sureties on your official bond. This rule will carry you safely through every difficulty and every temptation.

Pardon me if I now suggest the importance of maintaining a reputation for strict, exact veracity. An aged judge is said to have

---

* I believe that no customer of the Bank of England, whatever his rank, is allowed to overdraw.

† "No expectation of forbearance or indulgence should be encouraged. Favor and benevolence are not the attributes of good banking. Strict justice and the rigid performance of contracts are its proper foundation."

remarked, ironically, that "half the cases he had tried on the bench arose from *good understanding* between the parties;" and by this he meant, that half-made bargains and agreements lead to disagreement and litigation. Avoid misunderstandings from this source. Many, indeed most, of your transactions will be upon verbal contracts. But you may use words so terse, so precise, that misconception will be hardly possible.

The honor of a cashier and the honor of a woman are alike. Suspicion of either in the public mind is as fatal to reputation as convicted guilt. Stand by, stand for *your* honor, then, against all comers, and to the last. Preserve your own respect, though you be fed by the hand of public or of private charity. Napoleon, at the hour of his downfall, deposited the remains* of his fortune with Laffitte, and refused an offered and customary certificate, saying: "I know you—I hold you to be an honest man." The Paris banker, in the course of events, became a cabinet minister; but such a testimonial to his probity from a man whose estimate of human virtue was too low to be just, and who, at the moment he uttered it, was, as he imagined, the victim of faithlessness and treachery, will be remembered when the records of his political honors are torn and scattered. But yet, any man, in his own circle, may, if he will, have it said of him: "I know you—I hold you to be an honest man." My young friend—now starting upon a banker's career—burn these words deep into your memory!

As in some things there are marked distinctions between banks in different sections of the country, and between country and city banks in the same State, and corresponding differences in the duties of a cashier, it is obvious that no series of "suggestions" can be alike applicable to all. But I may still hope that the *young and inexperienced* officer will not fail to find *some* useful hints in the preceding remarks, whatever his particular position or special charge.

And while this may be so, the country cashier may yet need cautions and recommendations adapted to his peculiar official and social relations. Such, then, as I deem the most important, I shall briefly and respectfully offer. First, as it sometimes happens that the person selected for the executive department has had little or no experience in banking, and is to be connected with directors whose knowledge is as limited as his own, the duty of consulting well-informed officers of city banks is manifest. The country cashier is often alone. Without paying or receiving tellers, bookkeeper, or discount or collection clerks, but invested with the functions of all, skill, system, and an economical use of time, are indispensable to success. I have known gentlemen who, though possessing quick

* Five millions of francs.

and clear perceptions, and almost every other natural endowment, were still, at the time of their election, incapable of opening or of properly keeping a single bank-book. Some of these, remarkably cautious in their habits of business, and profiting by mishaps, escaped serious losses, and, in the end, became accomplished officers; while others, more sanguine in temperament, and more self-confident, and unwilling to *seem* novices, involved themselves in difficulties which caused them much mental disquietude and pecuniary embarrassment. Now, it is apparent at a glance, that both classes, had they started right, might have avoided a great deal of painful experience.

I commend to you, therefore, if not bred to banking, the sources of information, which are open to you, and to all who desire to increase their knowledge. Accuracy in the count of money is the first, accuracy in the keeping of accounts is the second, qualification in a country cashier; and, while you may acquire the first by practice, you may go wrong with your records all your life.

A small bank should be conducted on a plan as systematic and as regular as a large one. Experience has shown, I think, that bank accounts should be kept in "double entry," and that each department of bank business requires a separate book. Thus in an institution with a capital of only fifty thousand dollars, I consider that a general and deposit ledger, that books for cash, deposits, discounts, credits, collections and trial-balances, are as essential as in one of a million of dollars. And the same remark is true of stockholders' and directors' records, of a book to show the state of the bank, and of another to exhibit the paper to mature in any given week.

The general and the deposit ledger may be one; the former occupying some seventy-five or one hundred pages, and embracing accounts with *things*, the latter with *persons*. The cash should be settled daily at the close of business, when, also, a trial balance should be taken of the general ledger postings. On the last business day of the month, the depositors' accounts should be adjusted, and the balance of each be transferred to the trial-balance book to ascertain whether the deposit ledger has been correctly posted. The daily settlement of the cash—neglected in *some* country banks, unless the reform has been very recent—need occupy but a few minutes, since a vault-book accurately kept, leaves for actual count the cash in drawer only. "Memorandum checks," and similar vouchers—to say nothing of the grave consequences which sometimes result from their use—are great pests in a cashier's drawer, and should not be allowed there, except in the most urgent cases. Some cashiers keep "ragged bills," never intended to be reissued, in vault for months, and even years; but the practice is attended with obvious risk and inconvenience, and should not exist.

As already intimated in another connection, your directors, however worthy and respectable as citizens and gentlemen, may be poorly versed in the science of banking, and may not, at first, appreciate the force and the reason of the rules which you deem necessary to adopt in transactions with them and with others. But evince no impatience. I assume that a majority of any and of every "Board" are men of honor, and mean to do right; and that, in explanations and conversations with yours, you have but to calmly point out the evils likely to arise from a course opposite to that which you insist upon, to obtain their approbation. Yet you yourself should be well assured that these rules are consonant to law, or are such as are imposed in well-regulated banks, or such as, in your peculiar position and relations, are imperatively demanded.

It is possible that your predecessor allowed improper indulgences to a particular director, or had favorites among your customers, and that you will feel constrained to put an end to these and to similar irregularities. To accomplish this, in harmony, will require all the wisdom and good-nature that you can command. It is possible, too, that overtures may be made to you to grant favors inconsistent with your duty; but, as such cases will arise from thoughtlessness or ignorance, as often as from unworthy motives, you should be silent, except when corrupt intentions are too apparent to be mistaken, or the importunities of the same person become so frequent as to be troublesome.

The customers of a country bank, unlike the merchants of large and busy cities, expect of the cashier some inquiries about their families, and remarks upon the news of the day, upon the crops, the weather, and other matters of personal or local interest. To a reasonable extent this expectation should be gratified. But discussions across your counter on topics of sectarian theology and party politics are to be avoided—entirely avoided. Nor, if you hear, should you reply to, or take part in, tales of scandal and neighborhood gossip. Polite to all, sociable to a degree not to interfere with your duties, inviting and giving friendly greetings, your deportment is yet to be dignified, and such as becomes a well-bred gentleman.

You will transact business with persons who cannot even write a note of hand in proper form; with those who cannot be made to acknowledge the necessity of a notice to an indorser; and with those who will pertinaciously insist upon having their own way, whatever your reasoning or objections to the contrary. Teach the ignorant, without giving them pain; be firm with the self-willed, without evincing impatience or anger; for the smart of a sharp word, or of a proud toss of the head, is sometimes felt for years. "Contempt," says an Eastern proverb, "will penetrate the shell of a tortoise;" be sure to remember it will pierce deeper into the epidermis of a fellow-man.

To require, and to insist upon, regular bank hours will occasion *some* difficulty in *some* places. People whose business at banks is rare, seem to forget that a cashier, like other men, has a love of fresh air, or that he needs exercise and relaxation; and thus cannot or will not understand why he is not ready to accommodate them early in the morning, and late in the evening. These persons seek him in his moments of rest and recreation, ask him to receive money at his house, or in the village stores, and complain if he refuses such *reasonable* requests. You will be unjust to yourself if you submit to these, or to similar demands. The intervals between bank hours are yours by positive contract, and by the very necessities of your physical and mental being. Do not permit inroads upon them, save in extraordinary exigencies; in these, leave your bed even, to serve a customer. Still, as loose and unsafe habits may have been encouraged by your predecessors, or countenanced by directors, measures of reform will be odious, unless gradual. Under kind and considerate treatment your laggards may become punctual, and untimely requests to open your vault entirely cease.

A single "suggestion" more. The private and social relations of a country cashier are of consequence, and ought not to be overlooked. And, first, a salary officer, under ordinary circumstances, needs not to be in debt for his personal or family expenses; and, as cash payments are sure to show whether he is "living beyond his means," may I not commend the safe rule of "paying as you go?"

Again, may I not be allowed to suggest the duty of constant attendance at church, even though you cannot worship with persons of your own faith; and also of manifesting an interest in schools, public lectures, lyceums, and other means employed to promote the welfare of society? The community in which you live have a claim upon you, not only for an exemplary life, but for contributions of money in proportion to your ability, to aid in the maintenance of the religious, literary and benevolent associations established among them.

To conclude. Should it be thought that I might have omitted the discussion of some topics, and have treated others with greater brevity, I submit, with deference, that I have endeavored to be a careful observer. More than twenty-five years have elapsed since the commencement of my connection with banks and banking; and, as I now look back and recall the facts elicited by judicious inquiry, and the facts embraced in other well-authenticated accounts which relate to bank officers who have fallen, never again to rise, or whose lives have been saddened and embarrassed by want of firmness in resisting the allurements of pleasure, or the solicitations of the companions of their social hours—by an overweening self-confidence—by too great faith in others; as, too, I remember the complaints against another class, who, though without a moral stain, have still injured themselves and the institutions with which they are concerned by churlishness and irritability; I find no cautions and admonitions to omit, no recommendations that may not, I think, assist in forming the character of the officer for whom these suggestions are intended.

A single word more. Many of the cashiers whose private virtues and professional ability adorn the annals of banking in the United States, receive salaries nearly equal to the emoluments of cabinet ministers, or military officers of the highest rank, and are intrusted with powers so ample, that they seem to be private bankers, wielding their own capital. These gentlemen have attained the crowning honors of their profession. Let the "young cashier" aim to reach the same eminence among men and among bankers. Let him remember that, whatever the influence of friends at the outset of his career, his position in the maturity of his years must, in the very nature of things, depend upon himself, upon his capacity, his courage, and his probity.

I have here spoken to him as to my only son, and take my leave, in the earnest hope that, in the labors of some one of his seniors, communicated to the "Magazine" upon the invitation which, perhaps, I have unwisely accepted, he will be sure to find a path marked out for him which will lead him to the rewards of a well-spent life.

Depositors' Balance Ledger, July, 18....

Depositors.	18		19		20	21
H. M. Lutz........	270 50 18 42 5 10	585 10	107 10 46 60 3 27	585 10 346 10	774 23 910 53	
Theo. Kitchen........		1,624 75	8 75 75 80 327 40 8 25	1,330 73		
G. A. Lewis........		1,210 40	13 15 27 50 105 86 10 10	1,210 40 516 80	1,570 60	
E. P. Graham........		482 50		482 50	482 50	
W. H. Webb........	250 50 13 25	1,540 82	75 80 37 50 42 60	1,277 07 275 10	1,306 27	
G. A. Linton........			36 40 27 85	1,255	1,190 75	
John Rapson........				1,842 70	1,842 70	
J. D. Brown........			8 40 10 75 41 85	540 15	479 15	
J. W. Torrey........				178 40	178 40	
	557 77	5,443 57	1,014 92	4,883 80 4,954 25	8,825 13	

www.ingramcontent.com/pod-product-compliance
Lightning Source LLC
Chambersburg PA
CBHW030009240426
43672CB00007B/888